Better than Best Practice

Better than Best Practice offers a new way of thinking about classroom practice, professional development and improving teaching and learning. This book and companion website together offer a selection of rich and realistic video-based case studies, context and narrative, step-by-step guidance through key issues and commentary and debate from a range of expert contributors.

Carefully chosen video clips from primary school literacy lessons show real teachers in a variety of often knotty situations: classroom conversations that take unexpected turns; grappling with assessment; managing disagreements, to name a few. The book explores the educational potential of classroom talk and, in particular, the promise and problems of dialogic pedagogy.

With an emphasis on the complexity and 'messiness' of teaching, *Better than Best Practice* considers how to learn from observing and discussing practice in order to develop professional judgment. It offers practical advice on how to organize and facilitate video-based professional development in which teachers share their practice with colleagues in order to learn from one another's challenges, problems, dilemmas and breakthroughs.

This exciting new resource argues that critical discussions of practice, which highlight dilemmas instead of prescribing solutions, help to develop and support thoughtful, flexible and insightful practitioners: an approach that is better than best practice.

Adam Lefstein is Senior Lecturer in Education at the Ben-Gurion University of the Negev. His research and teaching focus on the intersection of pedagogy, classroom interaction and teacher development. Previously he worked as Senior Lecturer at the Institute of Education, University of London, and directed a comprehensive school reform programme at the Branco Weiss Institute in Jerusalem.

Julia Snell is Lecturer in Sociolinguistics at King's College London. Originally trained as a linguist, her research and teaching currently focus on the intersection between sociolinguistics and education. She has recently used findings from her study of working-class children's language in the north-east of England to challenge the discourses of linguistic deficit that have re-emerged in debates about language, class and educational failure.

'This unusual report of classroom research is especially valuable on three counts. First, it offers a vision of teaching as the sensitive and flexible expression of professional judgment – what others are calling for as "adaptive professionalism," which is "better than best practices" that teachers in the US and elsewhere are being forced to adopt. Second, empirical chapters on "dialogic conversation" in a London primary school include commentary from 17 international educators, further enriching our understanding. Finally, there's a how-to chapter on video-based professional development so we can do it too. A Best Buy and Must Read.'

Professor Courtney Cazden, Harvard Graduate School of Education

'This really is the book we've been waiting for. *Better than Best Practice* is not just another evangelizing text about the need to move classroom talk beyond the default of closed questioning, recall answers and minimal feedback but an offering that is richer, more subtle and much more useful. Alongside a rigorous but accessible examination of the thinking and evidence behind dialogic pedagogy, the book provides videographic and transcript case material of dialogue as it happens, together with contextual information and commentaries. This makes enthralling reading and viewing in its own right as well as superb material for professional discussion and development. But perhaps the book's central virtue is that it lives as well as commends the dialogic principle. For this is a book of many voices – children, teachers, authors, researchers and invited commentators; and they do not necessarily agree, which is precisely the dialogic point. So it's impossible to evade the message that dialogue is indivisible. If it's good for young learners then it's essential for their teachers – and for all of us.'

Professor Robin Alexander, Cambridge University,
University of York and Chair of the Cambridge Primary Review Trust

Better than Best Practice

Developing teaching and
learning through dialogue

Adam Lefstein and Julia Snell

LONDON AND NEW YORK

First published 2014
by Routledge
2 Park Square, Milton Park, Abingdon, Oxon OX14 4RN

and by Routledge
711 Third Avenue, New York, NY 10017

Routledge is an imprint of the Taylor & Francis Group, an informa business

British Library Cataloguing in Publication Data
A catalogue record for this book is available from the British Library

Library of Congress Cataloging in Publication Data
A catalog record for this title has been requested.

ISBN: 978–0–415–61843–4 (hbk)
ISBN: 978–0–415–61844–1 (pbk)
ISBN: 978–1–315–88451–6 (ebk)

Typeset in Galliard
by Cenveo Publisher Services

MIX
Paper from
responsible sources
FSC
www.fsc.org   FSC® C013056

Printed and bound in Great Britain by
TJ International Ltd, Padstow, Cornwall

Contents

Figures

Tables

Contributing commentators

Robin Alexander is Fellow of Wolfson College at Cambridge University, Professor of Education at the University of York, and Chair of the Cambridge Primary Review Trust. He has produced over 260 publications, including *Culture and Pedagogy* (2001 – winner of the AERA Outstanding Book Award), *Essays on Pedagogy* (2008), *Towards Dialogic Teaching* (2008) and *Children, their World, their Education: final report and ecommendations of the Cambridge Primary Review* (2010).

Jeff Barrett worked in five schools during 31 years in primary education, 14 of them as head teacher. He served as Head Teacher of Abbeyford Primary School while the lessons appearing in this book were recorded, and participated in all the workshops in which the teachers and researchers analysed video-recorded episodes.

Melanie Cooke has worked as a teacher in adult and further education in the field of English for Speakers of Other Languages (ESOL) and is now a researcher and lecturer in the Centre for Language Discourse and Communication, King's College London. She is currently working on a PhD on ESOL and citizenship and is co-author (with James Simpson) of *ESOL: A Critical Guide*.

Pie Corbett, educator and author, has written extensively on teaching creative writing, worked as a teacher, head teacher and inspector. Currently, Pie continues to develop 'talk for writing' through teacher-research and development projects across the country. He is also a poet and storyteller. His poem, *The Owl*, is the focus of class discussion in Episode 6 (Chapter 8).

James Cresswell is Assistant Professor of Psychology at Booth University College, Winnipeg, Canada. He is interested in cultural psychology and how philosophers focusing on dialogue (e.g. Mikhail Bakhtin) can contribute to this field.

Roxy Harris is a senior lecturer in Language in Education at King's College London. He is the author of *New Ethnicities and Language Use* (2006) and co-author of *Urban Classroom Culture* (2011).

Lucy Henning has been a primary national strategies literacy consultant for two West London LEAs. She taught across the primary age range for fourteen years and is currently a lecturer in Primary English at St. Mary's University College, Twickenham. She is currently conducting PhD research on young children's early encounters with formal literacy teaching at King's College London.

Laura Hughes graduated as a teacher from University of Lancaster in 1998. She was the Assistant Head Teacher of the large Inner London school described in this book, and later moved on to become the Deputy Head Teacher there. She is a Certified Teacher of PSHE (Personal, Social and Health Education) and is currently studying for a Masters in Education.

Dennis Kwek is a senior research associate at the Centre for Research in Pedagogy and Practice, National Institute of Education, Singapore. He is investigating the practice of 'weaving' in Singapore classrooms, a pedagogical model of connected learning across different types and forms of knowledge.

Janet Maybin is a senior lecturer in Language and Communication at the Open University. Originally trained as a social anthropologist, she has written extensively for Open University courses in language and education and also researches and writes on children and adults' informal language and literacy practices.

Gemma Moss is Professor of Education at the Institute of Education University of London. She has extensive experience of researching classroom literacy practices using ethnographic tools, and is the author of *Literacy and Gender: Texts, readers and contexts* (2007).

Glenda Moss is Professor and chair of the Department of Teacher Education and Administration at the University of North Texas at Dallas. She worked for 13 years as a middle school teacher. Her areas of expertise include middle school teaching, portfolio assessment, multicultural education and teacher professional development through critical, narrative action research. She is author of *Crossing Boundaries and Building Learning Communities*.

Louai Rahal is a doctoral student in Human Development, Learning and Culture at the University of British Columbia. His earlier research focused on using critical discourse analysis to examine the erasure of difference in young women's magazines. His current qualitative research explores the experiences of children with autism from the vantage point of sociocultural theory.

David Reedy is Principal Adviser for primary schools in the London Borough of Barking and Dagenham and current General Secretary of the United Kingdom Literacy Association (UKLA). He is a former Visiting Fellow at the Institute of Education, University of London.

Greg Thompson is a visiting assistant professor in the Department of Anthropology at Brigham Young University and is an Affiliated Researcher with the Laboratory of Comparative Human Cognition at University of California, San Diego.

Jennifer A. Vadeboncoeur is Associate Professor in Human Development Learning and Culture at the University of British Columbia. The focus of her research includes the creation of informal learning contexts with and for young people, as well as rethinking learning and teaching relationships from a Vygotskian perspective. Her work includes *Re/Constructing "the adolescent": Sign, symbol, and body*, co-edited with Lisa Patel Stevens in 2005, and a forthcoming Yearbook for the National Society for the Study of Education on *Alternative and flexible contexts for learning*.

Jayne White is Senior Lecturer in the Faculty of Education at University of Waikato, New Zealand. Her recent co-edited books include *Bakhtinian Pedagogy: Opportunities and challenges for research, policy and practice in education across the globe* (2011) and *Educational research with our youngest: Voices of infants and toddlers* (2011).

Acknowledgements

We owe a considerable debt to many people who have contributed to this book, directly and indirectly, over the course of its long gestation. We would like to acknowledge and thank the following individuals and organizations:

David Reedy from the London Borough of Barking and Dagenham assisted in finding an appropriate research site, and in understanding the educational history of the borough. Both he and Nikki Gamble of *Write Away* were critical friends throughout the research process.

Chris Husbands and Sue Rogers at the University of London Institute of Education freed up our time for conducting the research at a time of severe budget constraints.

Robin Alexander, Leah Meyer Austin, Joshua Glazer, Ray McDermott, Toni Mittleman, Yael Ofarim, Yael Pulvermacher, and Ben Rampton read and commented on select chapters.

Adi Mendler did outstanding work on the illustrations and cover art.

The 18 commentators contributed sensitive and sometimes surprising interpretations of the episodes.

Rhiannon Findlay, Claire Westwood, and Helen Pritt at Routledge wisely guided and patiently prodded us through the publication process.

Our analysis has benefited from presentation and discussion of data and interpretations at over 35 events, including in Auckland, Be'er Sheva, Birmingham, Brighton, Brno, Copenhagen, Denver, Exeter, Glasgow, Göttingen, Greenwich, Jerusalem, Kingston, Lancaster, London, Ormskirk, Pittsburgh, Southampton, Tel-Aviv, and Vancouver.

We have been most fortunate to learn from a number of generous mentors and advisors, official and unofficial. We would like to thank Robin Alexander, Richard Andrews, Jan Blommaert, Anthea Fraser Gupta, Roxy Harris, Janet Maybin, Gemma Moss, Ben Rampton, Celia Roberts and Brian Street. We are particularly indebted to Ben Rampton for forcing us to look harder and more slowly.

Work on the study was generously funded by the Economic and Social Research Council (RES 061–25–0363) and the Centre for Excellence in Work-Based Learning for Education Professionals. We are also grateful to the Economic and Social Research Council for funding a post-doctoral fellowship (ES/I036605/1), which allowed generous time to work on the book.

This work has drawn upon material from within Adam Lefstein and Julia Snell, 'Classroom discourse: the promise and complexity of dialogic practice', in Sue Ellis and Elspeth McCartney (eds), *Applied Linguistics and Primary School Teaching* (2011) © Cambridge University Press, reproduced with permission; from within Lefstein, A. (2010) 'More helpful as problem than solution: some implications of situating dialogue in classrooms', in Littleton, K. and C. Howe (Eds.), *Educational dialogues: Understanding and promoting productive interaction*, Taylor and Francis; and from within Lefstein, A. and Snell, J. (2011) 'Promises and problems of teaching with popular culture: A linguistic ethnographic analysis of discourse genre mixing', *Reading Research Quarterly* 46(1): 40–69.

Finally, we are extraordinarily grateful to the pupils, teachers and Headteachers of Abbeyford Primary School for their time, generosity, hospitality and openness. Sadly, one of the teachers, Ms Lightfoot, passed away in December 2012. We dedicate this book to her memory.

Joe, Sharon and Ella: It's finally over. Thanks for understanding.

Key transcription conventions

(text)	Transcription uncertainty
(xxxxxxx)	Indistinguishable speech
(.)	Brief pause (under one second)
(1)	Longer pause (number indicates length to nearest whole second)
(( ))	Description of prosody or non-verbal activity
[[	Overlapping talk or action
text	Emphasized relative to surrounding talk (underlined words)
te:xt	Stretched sounds
sh-	Word cut off
>text<	Speech delivered more rapidly than surrounding speech
TEXT	Shouting
(.hhh)	Audible inhalation

Part I

Where we're coming from

Chapter 1

Better than best practice

Video is hot in educational improvement. It seems to promise an easy technological fix for a long-standing problem in teacher professional development, namely that teachers work largely alone, behind closed doors, and rarely have opportunities to learn from one another. With the advent of relatively inexpensive digital video technology, classroom practice can be easily captured, edited and made public. And, indeed, a number of teachers and researchers have begun to experiment with various models of video-based teacher professional development, in which participants view and discuss recordings of their own or others' practice. When done well, such activities are indeed promising. However, they are surprisingly difficult to do well, especially in settings in which classroom observation is associated with inspection and performance management, and a pervasive 'best practice' mentality shuts down possibilities for critical discussion of the complexities of teaching.

This book offers a vision of teaching as the sensitive and flexible exercise of professional judgment and repertoire, and a set of video-based practices for teacher professional development. It is based upon our experiences researching dialogic pedagogy in a London primary school, and facilitating a series of workshops in which the teachers at that school reflected on recordings of their literacy lessons and discussed how to improve their teaching. The book's primary goals are:

- to challenge current orthodoxies regarding 'best practice' in classroom teaching, advancing instead an approach to pedagogy and professional development that is sensitive to and appreciative of the tensions and dilemmas inherent to teaching and learning in classrooms;
- to develop a multidimensional approach to dialogic pedagogy that is informed by actual practice, is grounded in existing classroom conditions and acknowledges the complexities and problems inherent in dialogue;
- to offer a set of rich and realistic cases for reflection and discussion;
- to model the sorts of professional vision and analysis that we believe are particularly conducive to learning from video recordings of practice; and
- to offer practical guidance for organizing and facilitating video-based professional development.

In this first chapter we briefly outline our view of teaching practice and the implications of that view for teacher learning from video.

Problematizing 'best practice'

The idea of 'best practice' has become part of international educational common sense. In England, for example, it sits at the heart of ambitious and wide-reaching governmental reforms of teaching. The 1998 *National Literacy Strategy* (NLS) sought to radically transform curriculum content, lesson structure and teaching method in all primary classrooms across England, all at once. Michael Barber, then Chief Adviser to the Secretary of State for Education on School Standards and the architect of the NLS, explained the policy's rationale:

> For years and years primary teachers have been criticised for the way they teach reading. But then nobody ever said to them: 'Here's the best practice, based on solid international research and experience. If you use it your children will make progress.[1]

Barber's confident prognosis nicely captures both the tone and the content of the prevalent 'best practice' approach to educational improvement, which involves identifying, capturing and disseminating proven teaching methods.[2] In such a way, it is assumed, the vast majority of teachers are able to learn from and emulate the innovations and secrets of the gifted few. While such an approach has its merits, which we discuss below, we argue that it can only advance teacher professional practice so far. We offer here a complementary way of thinking about and conducting teacher professional development and educational improvement. This approach involves teachers sharing their practice with colleagues in order to learn from one another's challenges, problems, dilemmas and breakthroughs. Gifted teachers, in this model, appreciate the complexity of teaching, have the courage to expose their practice – 'warts and all' – to their peers and are adept at making sense of and learning from their own and others' experience. This approach is *better than best practice*, because it helps to develop and support thoughtful, flexible and insightful practitioners, who exercise a large degree of leadership in directing their own professional development.

Echoes of the 'best practice' idea resonate throughout the education system: Teachers ask, 'What is best practice for grouping children in mathematics lessons?' Scholars systematically review the research literature to ascertain 'what works' in teaching higher-order thinking skills. Policymakers wonder, 'What is the evidence that one early reading intervention is better than another?' The schools inspectorate publishes reports on 'learning from the best' education providers and schools. And government, education publishers, school improvement consultants and even the entertainment industry, produce and market videos of 'outstanding lessons', 'evidence-based methods' and 'best teaching practices'.[3]

We want to clarify from the outset that we see a role for research into which pedagogical practices are more or less effective (for which purposes and under what circumstances), and for demonstrations of productive practices and the principles underlying them, including through video recordings. Teaching involves structures, tools, techniques and routines that can be demonstrated and imitated, and it would be foolish to expect teachers to devise all their methods on their own.[4] Our concern is with teacher professional development that is focused *exclusively* on the inculcation of best practice through demonstration and imitation, and specifically with the dominance of this approach in the production and consumption of video recordings of practice.

So what is wrong with over-reliance on best practice? Our primary concern is that the best practice strategy is founded upon an unrealistic – and distorting – vision of teaching.

Teaching is complicated and difficult, but 'best practice' tends to iron out or overlook complexities, and thereby makes teaching practice appear relatively straightforward and even simple. Teaching is complex first and foremost because multiple factors interact to shape the success of teaching encounters:

- the *pupils* – their relationships with the teacher, their relationships with one another and social dynamics as a group, their differential levels of knowledge, understanding and interest;
- the *content*, its demands on teacher and students;
- *institutional requirements and supports*, such as assessment, performance management and professional development;
- the *physical setting*; and
- the *teacher*, their skills, manner and values; and more.[5]

Such complexity poses formidable challenges for designers of best practice methods: How can they ensure effectiveness across multiple, unpredictable situations? A method that works in one context – in the particular constellation of teacher, pupils, relationships, culture and setting – will likely unfold differently, and with different effects, in a different set of circumstances. Transferring good practices between teaching contexts is possible, but requires sensitivity, flexibility and judgement.

A further source of complexity in teaching is the overwhelming demands practice places on practitioners' attention. There is a lot going on in the classroom, all at once, and from every possible direction. Walter Doyle describes this phenomenon:

> During a discussion, a teacher must listen to student answers, watch other students for signs of comprehension or confusion, formulate the next question, and scan the class for possible misbehavior. At the same time, the teacher must attend to the pace of the discussion, the sequence of selecting students to answer, the relevance and quality of answers, and the logical development of the content.[6]

Teachers must interpret and act upon a great deal of information rapidly. There is insufficient time to process consciously the multiple signals, the issues they raise, the options available, their relative advantages and the overall lesson strategy. Instead, teachers rely heavily upon intuition and habit, and their knowledge about such habitual activity is primarily tacit, that is, knowledge that teachers don't know they possess or find difficult to articulate. Here then is a second challenge for the design of 'best practices': How to recognize, formulate and transfer such tacit knowledge? How can it be acquired except through direct experience?

Another cause of complexity in teaching, which undermines attempts to achieve agreement about which practices are best, are the many and contested goals of education. Teachers are supposed to impart academic knowledge and skills; and also to care for their pupils' emotional and spiritual well-being; and to promote their moral development; and to make sure that everyone is engaged and interested; and that no one is excluded (socially or academically); and to promote civic values such as tolerance and integrity; and to foster safe and caring learning environments; and to instil respect for authority while cultivating critical and independent thinking; and more. Goals conflict, sometimes deeply, such as the tension between maintenance of teachers' authority and cultivation of pupils' critical thinking, and at other times superficially, inasmuch as attending to pupils' emotional needs demands time that might otherwise have been devoted to academic content. Which goals should be given priority, and when? At any given moment goals shift as new opportunities and/or crises present themselves. So, teaching is not merely complex because teachers must simultaneously attend to multiple signals, but also because those signals beckon them to move the lesson in different directions, all legitimate and desirable.

In summary, many facets of teaching – its complexity and unpredictability; its dependence on the particularities of changing contexts; the centrality of tacit knowledge and the multiple and contested nature of educational goals – all resist reduction to a single, 'best practice' method. On account of them, teachers and pupils often enact 'best practices' in ways that significantly deviate from designers' intentions. For example, in a study of teachers' use of *National Literacy Strategy* lesson plans and related guidance, we found teachers often adhering rigidly to surface features of the guidelines (for example, using the activities provided, or posing the recommended questions) in ways that actually undermined the lesson objectives (for example, by closing down open questions in the subsequent interaction).[7] In these gaps we find another limitation of an over-reliance on 'best practice', or more precisely of the guidance and related materials produced as demonstrations of best practice teaching methods: while these materials may show us what good practice looks like, they are much less informative about the processes through which teachers and pupils can achieve that practice. Learning how to enact a teaching method involves much more than observation and imitation of expert performance.

'Best practice' is particularly problematic when video is employed as a central means of representing recommended teaching methods. In order to focus viewers' gaze on the specific technique being demonstrated, producers of best practice videos typically wash the dynamic complexity out of teaching. Filming techniques simplify the scene, for example, through tight focus on the teacher and/or an individual pupil, with all the other pupils and issues held off camera. Likewise, clip selection and editing can distort, for example by using that one moment in hundreds of hours of filming in which the method worked effortlessly, exactly as planned, or by removing less productive pupil contributions to produce a seamless and elegant 'discussion'. And of course staging, direction and rehearsals can create idealistic images of classrooms as orderly and teaching as easy. Such films raise expectations about what practice should look like, inadvertently causing teachers to feel inadequate about their own practice, which rarely measures up to the unrealistic ideals presented.

David Labaree notes that one obstacle to improving education is that 'teaching is an enormously difficult job that looks easy'.[8] It is hard to persuade teachers, school administrators, teacher educators, education policymakers and the general public to commit the appropriate resources to and have the patience for lengthy processes of teacher professional development if a distorted and simplistic view of teaching is popular. In this regard, realistic representations of the complexities and difficulties of practice are better than best practice.

Professional practice: sensitivity, interpretation, repertoire and judgement

We have argued that an approach to teaching and its improvement that focuses exclusively on the implementation of best practices is problematic and in some cases even counterproductive. We offer a more balanced approach, according to which good teaching requires sensitivity, interpretation, repertoire and judgement.[9] To explicate these four capacities, we find it helpful to ground our discussion in an actual example of practice. Below we briefly introduce a critical moment in Ms Leigh's Year 5 classroom (the full episode is presented and discussed in Chapter 5).

Classroom episode: responding to a pupil challenge

Ms Leigh is teaching the second of two consecutive lessons on story openers. She has just demonstrated to the class the lesson's key idea and objective – to open their stories by dropping the reader right into the action – and begins to set them the task of working in pairs to act out the opening to their own story in order to get ideas about how to improve it. Before she finishes her instructions, however, she is interrupted by an interjection from William: 'Miss, I don't really like that'.

This interjection was both exceptional and mundane. Exceptional inasmuch as Year 5 pupils don't typically challenge their teachers so explicitly. Nor was there anything in the rather emphatic way in which Ms Leigh introduced the main idea of the lesson to suggest that she wished to open the issue to discussion. William also spoke without raising his hand or being called upon (although this was not all that unusual in this classroom). While the particularities of this event may make it seem rare, there is nothing more mundane than a lesson not going exactly as planned. Every lesson is composed of dozens of such moments, in which a teacher must decide – in less time than it takes to read this sentence – how to proceed.

Experienced teachers have developed routine ways of dealing with disturbances to the flow of the lesson. After all, we cannot stop at every moment to reassess what we are doing and where the lesson is going. Such constant 'reflection-in-action' would lead to paralysis.[10] Indeed, Ms Leigh immediately responded with a statement that sounds like the first step in the polite dismissal of William's objections: 'Well it depends on how you want to start your story, doesn't it?' William assented, and she continued, 'So you could have –'. But she stopped mid-sentence. Caught short, perhaps she realized she didn't know what William meant, or recognized an opportunity to explore the issue further. She then proceeded to question William, '[Do] you mean talk as the narrator or talk as the actors?' We see in Ms Leigh's hesitation and shifting course the marks of her *sensitivity*, her attentiveness and openness to recognize the critical moments, problems and/or opportunities.[11]

Having noticed that something demands attention, Ms Leigh must also *interpret* the situation, and the problems and concerns it raises. So, what is happening here? For example, why is William challenging her? Is he genuinely concerned about story openers, or looking for an opportunity to assert his individuality by undermining the teacher's authority? And where is William's question leading, and how might it fit into the curriculum? Can addressing it advance the lesson objectives, or perhaps it offers an opportunity to explore other, even more important issues? What's happening with the other pupils – what's their state of mind? Will pursuing this issue engage them and be productive for them, or might it confuse them? And what might the pursuit or shutting down of William's question say to William and the rest of the class about what sorts of pupil contributions are and are not legitimate and even valued, and what are the implications of this for developing critical and independent thinking? What will it say to William and to the class about what sort of pupil William is?

We are not going to address these questions yet. For now we hope that posing them illuminates the complexity of the moment and the sort of issues that must be considered in order to respond adequately.

In terms of response, what were Ms Leigh's options at this point? What would you have done were you in her place? Most teachers to whom we've shown the video recording of this incident – stopping right after William's challenge – have suggested that Ms Leigh should dismiss this issue and get on with the lesson, perhaps by postponing the discussion of his reservations, or by accepting his views as legitimate, but noting that today the class is going to learn how to do it *her* way. But let's assume for a moment that Ms Leigh has recognized William's challenge as a good opportunity to explore alternative methods of opening a story – How might she achieve that goal? One possibility might be to probe William's views by looking at the opening of his story, and perhaps opening the issue to discussion with the rest of the class: What do they think about William's strategy?

Or Ms Leigh might collect from the class a range of different ways of opening stories and discuss their relative advantages and disadvantages. Or change the task: require each pupil to compose and contrast two openings to their story, one with description and one dropping the reader right into the action.

Ms Leigh might implement a tool or technique that she picked up in a best practice professional development session. For example, she might use the think–pair–share technique, in which students first think individually about the topic (here, for example, what is the best way to open a story), then discuss their ideas with their partner, and finally share with the rest of the class.[12]

Alternatively, she might inject some new texts into the discussion – to enrich the dispute by looking at how accomplished authors choose to open their stories.

We could continue this list of possibilities for many more pages, but it should be sufficient to impress upon the reader that there's more than one path forward. We call the flexibility and depth that allow a teacher to call upon a wide range of possible courses of action, and to successfully implement them, *repertoire*.[13]

Which course of action is the best one, right now? Deciding how to act requires *judgement* about how each possibility will likely unfold, and about their relative merits. Each of the possibilities is good for addressing some of the many issues posed by the situation, but less helpful – or even problematic – *vis-à-vis* other issues. The question isn't one of finding the one best, right solution to the problem, but of balancing conflicting concerns. For example, elaborating and exploring William's ideas versus bringing other pupils into the conversation; addressing the question raised by a pupil vs covering the predetermined lesson topics; protecting William's identity as a committed learner versus refuting a bad idea that also threatens to undermine the lesson objective. Classroom practice is experienced by sensitive teachers as problems and dilemmas, which require judgement.[14]

The premise of this book is that sensitivity can be deepened, interpretation enriched, repertoire expanded and judgement sharpened through facilitated reflection and discussion about video recordings of practice.

A balanced approach to the problem of practice

Two entrenched dogmas currently divide thinking about teaching and teacher professional development. Neither provides a good basis for confronting the complexities of classroom practice or the challenges of educational improvement. The first, which we have characterized as 'best practice', views teaching primarily as technique or method, and educational improvement as a problem of identifying, disseminating and mandating the most effective methods. The second, opposing dogma views teaching as fundamentally personal and particular, and teachers' professional autonomy as a key condition for educational improvement.[15] In England, where we have been working, the former 'best practice' view has gained ascendance, and hence this chapter and book have focused on the shortcomings of that view, and have sought to counterbalance it by emphasizing the critical roles of professional sensitivity and judgement. We want to caution, however, against embracing the opposite extreme, and viewing all externally devised methods as undermining teacher professional judgement.

Our perspective seeks to avoid the extremes of both dogmas. Professional teaching practice involves sensitivity, interpretation, judgement *and* a flexible repertoire of methods. Sensitivity, interpretation and judgement are fundamental for knowing when and how to use techniques; and, conversely, judgement is only useful in practice inasmuch as it is informed by a broad repertoire of techniques and strategies. Moreover, methods and routines can free teachers' attention so that they can focus on critical issues necessitating interpretation and the exercise of judgement. Ultimately, a comprehensive programme for improving practice will involve multiple forms of professional development: one cannot learn how to implement a technique by merely hearing about it in a reflective discussion, nor are best practice demonstrations a good means of honing judgement.

What's in the book?

This book is designed as a casebook to support the development of teachers' sensitivity and judgement about the problems and possibilities of dialogic pedagogy. At its heart (Part 2) are a series of eight classroom episodes intended as material for teacher reflection and discussion. These episodes were recorded in literacy lessons in Years 5–6 classrooms in one East London school during the 2008–9 academic year. Each episode is presented to the reader through a video recording and a detailed transcript on the companion website, www.routledge.com/ cw/lefstein. There are narrative accounts of main events and key contextual information along with discussion of key pedagogical and interactional issues raised. Two to four guest contributors comment on each episode and on our interpretations of it. Readers can of course engage with these materials on their own, but we envisage them ideally being used as the basis for study groups in school-based learning communities, professional development workshops or higher education courses.

Preceding these case studies, in Part 1, we introduce our views of teaching, dialogic pedagogy and the research project upon which the book is based. Following the case studies, in Part 3, we conclude the book with a discussion of video-based professional development, including advice for collecting and preparing materials for investigation of practice in your own school or related setting. For those more interested in research methodology and theory, we've included an appendix with information about our linguistic ethnographic approach to analysing classroom discourse and interaction, and endnotes with suggestions for further reading and/or references to support our claims are included throughout the book.

Finally, we offer a few words about the different voices that inhabit the book. The main voices are ours, the authors, and we should say a few words about ourselves and our perspectives. Adam Lefstein is a lecturer and researcher in the Department of Education at the Ben-Gurion University of the Negev. He was a lecturer at the University of London Institute of Education when the research reported in this book was undertaken. He earned his doctorate in educational studies, examining literacy teaching from anthropological, philosophical, and sociolinguistic perspectives. In a previous career he worked as a teacher and facilitator of teacher professional development (in Israel). To this day he wrestles with reconciling anthropological and pedagogical perspectives on classroom practice. Julia Snell worked with Adam as a researcher at the Institute of Education between 2008 and 2010 and is currently a lecturer and researcher in the Department of Education and Professional Studies at King's College London. Her background is in linguistics, but her research has always focused on educational settings, investigating, for example, the relationship between language, identity and learning.

We recognize that our perspectives on the episodes and related questions explored in the book are partial, reflecting our unique backgrounds and experiences. In order to open up the discussion, we have invited a broad range of educational practitioners and researchers to comment on the episodes and on our interpretations. The commentators include one of the teachers appearing in the episodes, the head teacher at the school in which we recorded the lessons, a local authority advisor, literacy consultant, a poet whose poem was analysed in one lesson, and leading researchers from the United Kingdom, the United States of America, Singapore, New Zealand, and Canada. We have also endeavoured, to the best of our ability, to bring the teachers' and pupils' own voices into the discussion. We thank them for their openness and generosity. The book would not exist without them.

Notes

1 Ghouri (1998).
2 Barber's confidence has not been vindicated by the NLS results. For an assessment of test scores, see Tymms and Merrell (2010). On evidence regarding changes in classroom discourse and interaction, see Smith *et al.* (2004). And for an exploration of the policy's enactment, and why it so frequently deviated from designers' intentions, see Lefstein (2008a).
3 Here are some examples that jump to mind: the Teachers' TV programme 'From Good to Outstanding' (http://www.teachersmedia.co.uk/series/from-good-to-outstanding); MediaMerge's 'Evidence-based Teaching DVD' (http://www.evidencebasedteaching.co.uk); Lemov's (2010) *Teach Like a Champion* (http://www.uncommonschools.org/our-approach/teach-like-a-champion); Ofsted's 'good practice' surveys and 'learning from the best' reports (Ofsted 2010, 2011); and even BBC Newsnight's 2005 reports on synthetic phonics teaching, which were essentially a hybrid current affairs–makeover programme (for description and analysis, see Lefstein, 2008b).
4 The question of how we should think about teaching – for example, as science, craft or art; or as primarily involving technique, habit or judgement – is an old debate, and we do not intend to rehash the arguments here. For a concise programmatic statement advocating scientifically-based, best practices in teaching (and education more generally), see Slavin (2002). For a critique, see Elliott (2001). For an overview of both sides, which shows how each depends on the other – no teaching method without teacher subjectivity and *vice versa*, see Lefstein (2005).
5 For a concise discussion of the complexity of teaching (and related difficulties), see Labaree (2000). For a more extended exploration of the issue, see Cohen (2011). The classic statement of these ideas is Lortie (1975).
6 Doyle (1986).
7 For examples, see Lefstein (2008a, 2009). For an example of a teacher tacking new methods onto traditional teaching practices, see Cohen (1990).
8 Labaree (2000).
9 A similar approach to professional practice can be found in Alexander (1997: 267–87), which also includes a fascinating analysis of then-current thinking about 'good practice'. Alexander argues that good practice 'resides in the teacher having a clear sense of educational purpose, reflected in his or her planning and the context in which teaching and learning are to take place; a well-developed range of pedagogical skills, firmly grounded in appropriate knowledge of children, curriculum and pedagogy; and the capacity to judge how and when this repertoire should be exploited' (pp. 277–8).

10 Reflection-in-action, the way that professionals think about what they're doing while doing it, is developed in Schön (1983). For a discussion of the way the frenetic pace of teaching limits opportunities for reflection-in-action, see Roth, Lawless and Masciotra (2001).

11 It's not always so obvious that something is happening that requires our attention as teachers. In this case, William's direct challenge was difficult to miss, but imagine if he'd spoken under his breath, to the boy sitting next to him, or had made a disapproving face. A key element of good teaching is being attentive to these and other cues about pupils' thinking and social dynamics.

12 We mention this possibility in order to drive home a key point about the limitations of best practices. Think–pair–share is a useful method to have in one's repertoire, but there's no reason to assume automatically that it is best practice in any given situation. Imagine a teacher who used the method for each and every question that arose in class discussion. Think–pair–share would quickly lose its appeal. The key questions that must be asked before using this or some other practice is 'What is happening?' 'What problems do I need to address?' 'What are my options?' 'What are their relative advantages?' And only afterwards to decide on the best course of action.

13 The idea of repertoire is key to Robin Alexander's (2008a, 2008b) thinking about dialogic pedagogy.

14 For analyses of problems and dilemmas in teaching we recommend Alexander (1995), Berlak and Berlak (1981), and Lampert (2001). For an application of this view to teacher professional learning, see also Loughran (2010).

15 See Lefstein (2005) for elaboration and critique of this dogma.

Chapter 2

Towards dialogic pedagogy[1]

Do we really need another book about dialogue in education? Dozens of books about dialogic pedagogy or similar constructs have been published in the past decade, among them Robin Alexander's *Towards Dialogic Teaching*, Karen Littleton and Christine Howe's *Educational Dialogues*, Eugene Matusov's *Journey into Dialogic Pedagogy*, Neil Mercer and Karen Littleton's *Dialogue and the Development of Children's Thinking*, Debra Myhill and colleagues' *Talking, Listening, Learning: Effective Talk in the Primary Classroom* and Rupert Wegerif's *Dialogic Education and Technology*.[2] The UK government has similarly championed 'dialogic' practice, and a community of international scholars have recently established a *Dialogic Pedagogy Journal*.[3] So do we really need another volume about dialogic pedagogy? What more could possibly be said in such a crowded field?

We recommend the journal and those books as well as this one; each offers an important and useful perspective. Our unique contribution in this book is an approach to dialogic pedagogy that:

(a) is informed by actual practice and grounded in existing classroom conditions. Rather than starting with an ideal image of what we believe dialogue should look like and then criticizing teachers and pupils for not living up to that lofty standard, we start with the actual activities and communicative practices that we have encountered in English classrooms, and endeavour to understand them on their own terms. That is, we first seek to understand the rules of the classroom game and the conditions constraining teaching practice, and work out from them to the development of dialogic possibilities;

(b) is multidimensional, that is we examine a range of different aspects of classroom communication and interaction. These include communicative forms, interpersonal relations, the exchange and development of ideas, power, pupil and teacher identities and aesthetics. This multidimensional analysis locates classroom communication within broader contexts of pedagogic activity and educational and social structures. As such, our approach to dialogic pedagogy looks beyond classroom *talk* to consider additional factors such as the use of space, organization of the curriculum, design of learning tasks and assessment;

(c) views dialogue as a problem rather than a solution. We argue that dialogic pedagogy is most helpful as a set of dilemmas to consider, concepts to think with, commitments to pursue and balance and practices to add to our repertoires. It is less helpful as a narrow best practice solution to each and every classroom situation.

These three contributions probably seem rather abstract at this point. The rest of the chapter and indeed, book, is devoted to bringing them to life. First, we review key approaches to dialogue relating to multiple dimensions of communication. Second, we explore why educators are attracted to dialogue, as a form of pedagogy, at the current time. Third, we look at various translations of dialogic philosophies into models for teaching and learning in classrooms. Fourth, we critically examine 'best practice' dialogic teaching and justify the approach to dialogic pedagogy developed in this book. Readers who are put off by this slightly philosophical discussion may wish to skip over to the next part or even the next chapter, revisiting the theoretical background later, if at all. An understanding of our approach to dialogic pedagogy is not vital for understanding the episodes in Part 2 or the approach to professional development in Part 3.

What is dialogue?

Before discussing the concept of 'dialogue' in detail, it is useful to look at the situations in which it is commonly employed. We follow sociologist Zygmunt Bauman, who notes that while all words have meanings, some also have a 'feel'.[4] Like 'community', which is the focus of Bauman's study, 'dialogue' feels good. Even prior to agreeing about what it means – or perhaps *because* agreement has not yet been attempted – there is general consensus that 'dialogue' is beneficial, an ideal worth striving towards, and that it does not happen as often as it ought.

So what is dialogue? What does it look like? At a most basic level, dialogue is the process of talking or reasoning through an issue (this definition is a literal translation of the Greek: *dia* means 'across' or 'through' and *logos* 'speech', 'word' or 'reason'). Advocates of dialogue load the term with additional meaning: not every activity of 'talking through' counts as dialogue; rather, dialogue is a particular form of talking through an issue that serves particular purposes. In what follows we briefly review six approaches to dialogue, each emphasizing different dimensions of communication and aimed towards the realization of different purposes. This review is necessarily selective and partial.[5] It is designed, first and foremost, to introduce readers to the main ideas that have shaped our own and others' thinking about dialogic pedagogy. Appreciating the different layers and multiple meanings of dialogue is crucial for understanding the ways in which the concept is employed. Second, each approach addresses important educational goals, draws attention to key dimensions of human communication and raises important questions for analysing activity such as classroom pedagogy (summarized in Table 2.1).

Dialogue as interactional form[6]

At face value, and in its most common sense uses, 'dialogue' is a *form* of interaction, which typically involves two or more interlocutors freely exchanging ideas, listening to one another, affording one another equal opportunities to participate, addressing one another's concerns and building upon one another's contributions. Such a structure is often contrasted with 'monologic' situations in which only one person speaks, or highly adversarial situations in which participants talk over or past one another. In education, dialogue is often held up as an alternative to prevalent forms of pedagogic discourse, in which the teacher speaks most of the time, controls the topic and allocation of the floor, mediates all pupil–pupil communication, and primarily recognizes those pupil ideas that advance the teacher's own agenda.

Table 2.1 Six approaches to dialogue, with key questions, values and goals

Dialogue as...	Key questions	Dialogic values	Educational goals	Indicative thinker
Interactional form	Who speaks, how often, about what, to whom, and for how long? What discourse norms are established?	Interactivity Participation Reciprocity	Ensuring equitable opportunity to participate	–
Interplay of voices	Which voices are heard and allowed? How are they interacting?	Voice	Developing and realizing voice	Mikhail Bakhtin
Critique	What stances toward knowledge are being taken? Which ideas are and are not subjected to critical examination?	Questioning Doubt Humility	Questioning commonly accepted doctrines Getting closer to the truth	Socrates
Thinking together	What is the quality of the thinking being articulated?	Reason Inquiry	Development of higher mental functions	Lev Vygotsky
Relationship	How are participants relating to one another? What identities and concerns do they make relevant?	Care Respect Inclusion Community	Realizing humanity Fostering an inclusive, caring community	Martin Buber
Empowerment	How are power relations realized? Is everyone free to say what they please? Who benefits? How are differences managed?	Autonomy Freedom Equality Democracy	Empowerment Emancipation	Paulo Freire

The main advantage of treating dialogue as an interactional form is that dialogic structures can be easily translated into indicators, measures, norms and rules. We can ask of any discourse event who speaks to whom, about what, how often and for how long, and on the basis of the answers to those questions make judgements about how dialogic the event is and in what ways. So, for example, we might count and/or time the durations of turns at talk and see how equitably distributed they are. Or, we might look at whether and how participants address one another's ideas: Are exchanges 'chained into coherent lines of enquiry' or 'left stranded and disconnected'?[7] And what happens when participants act non-dialogically – for example, by dominating the conversation, or by excluding, ignoring or actively silencing others? Investigating how other members respond to such violations of dialogic expectations can tell us a lot about the implicit norms operating within a group. Finally, dialogic structures can be translated into explicit rules. For example, one classroom's 'Talking Rules' documented by Neil Mercer include: 'We share our ideas and listen to each other', 'We talk one at a time', 'We give reasons to explain our ideas' and 'We try to agree in the end'.[8]

The main disadvantage of focusing on dialogue's structural dimension is that dialogic form is not always a good indicator of dialogic content, function or spirit.[9] For example, interlocutors may exchange views on a matter of common concern but, owing to social pressure, all express the view they think the others want to hear; only one perspective is voiced. Or an equal distribution of time and turns can result in the majority view drowning out minority voices. Similarly, a question can be motivated by curiosity – by a desire to learn from the person to whom it is addressed, or by one-upmanship and an attempt to shame or silence them. These limitations lead us to consider other dimensions of dialogue: the content of the conversation, interpersonal relations and management of power imbalances.

Dialogue as interplay of voices

This approach to dialogue is rooted in the work of Mikhail Bakhtin (1895–1975), a Russian intellectual whose work spanned literary criticism, linguistics and philosophy.[10] Bakhtin argued that language is essentially dialogic: every utterance, every voice, every thought is related dialogically to the utterances, voices and thoughts to which they respond and to which they are addressed. 'Our speech is filled to overflowing with other people's words,' he writes.[11] Every time we speak or write we evoke those people and the ways in which they've used those words: 'each word tastes of the context and contexts in which it has lived its socially charged life'[12].

Human consciousness is likewise dialogic. Bakhtin describes the development of the individual mind as a site of 'intense struggle' between others' voices and our own, between 'authoritative discourse' (such as that of the Church, the State or the school) that is imposed upon us from without, and 'internally persuasive discourse' that we freely accept and load with our own unique intentions, meanings and contexts. The process of distinguishing one's own voice from those of others – the process of developing an individual voice – is not at all straightforward.[13]

Bakhtin's thinking raises critical questions for education: Which voices are heard and allowed in classroom discourse? Not who is actually speaking, but whose *voice* is being expressed, since a pupil who attempts to provide the teacher what she wants to hear is reproducing authoritative discourse rather than sharing his own thinking.

Dialogue as critique

The most famous practitioner of educational dialogue is undoubtedly the ancient Greek philosopher Socrates or, more precisely, the 'Socrates' character that appears in the dialogues written by Plato, his student.[14] And what does Socrates do? He seeks out conversational partners and inquires into their ideas. He questions them at length, subjecting their ideas and commonly held doctrines to intense critical scrutiny. He is driven to dialogue by passion for knowledge coupled with awareness of his own ignorance. He does not always infect his interlocutors with that passion, but he invariably provokes thinking.

Socrates reflects on the purposes and nature of dialogue in a key passage from Plato's *Gorgias*. Prior to this passage Socrates has been questioning Gorgias, a visiting teacher of rhetoric, about the nature of his art. Socrates takes a break in his examination in order to check with Gorgias whether to continue the conversation. Socrates explains that he hesitates to contradict Gorgias because often such moves lead to quarrels in which passions are inflamed, each side abuses the other, and even bystanders regret having been privy to such an ugly discussion. Socrates continues:

> Why do I mention this? Because what you are saying now appears inconsistent with what you said at first about rhetoric, and I am afraid to examine you further in case you

think that I am competing with you, not in order to clarify the issue but to defeat you. And so, if you are the same sort of person as myself, I will willingly go on questioning you; otherwise I will stop. And what sort of person am I? I am one of those people who are glad to have their own mistakes pointed out and glad to point out the mistakes of others, but who would just as soon be corrected as correct another; in fact I consider being refuted a greater good, inasmuch as it is better to be relieved of a very bad evil oneself than to relieve another. In my opinion no worse evil can befall a person than to have a false belief about the subjects which we are now discussing.

So if you are of the same mind, let us continue the conversation; but if you would rather stop, let us drop it at once and bring the argument to an end.[15]

Socrates clarifies here his purpose in dialogue: to critique ideas – that is, to attempt to refute them – in order to move beyond false belief to ascertain truth. This critique is accomplished through conversation: through the to and fro of question and answer, which helps to clarify positions and test claims, and through the challenge of argument and counterargument. However, not all conversations are productive or enjoyable; often they end in acrimony as each side lashes out at the other in an attempt to defend their own position. Critical to the success of dialogue are commitments to truth as more important than being right, to reason as the arbiter of truth, to putting ideas before people's feelings, including one's own, and – perhaps most importantly – to doubt and to the open-mindedness that comes from doubting one's own beliefs.

Viewing dialogue as critique raises questions about the status of knowledge and conventional wisdom: What stances towards knowledge do participants adopt? Which ideas are and are not open to critical examination?

Dialogue as thinking together

This approach to dialogue grows out of the work of Lev Vygotsky (1896–1934), a Russian psychologist who studied, among other topics, the relationship between language, interaction, thinking and development. In a famous passage, Vygotsky proclaimed the primacy of social interaction in human development:

Every function in the child's cultural development appears twice: first, on the social level, and later, on the individual level; first, *between* people (*interpsychological*) and then inside the child (*intrapsychological*) … All the higher mental functions originate as actual relations between people.[16]

Vygotsky argues that thinking originates in social interaction – that discourse between people is internalized as individual cognition. We can see this process occurring when we watch young children interacting with their parents. For example, James Wertsch gave children and their mothers the task of solving puzzles together. At first, the mothers guided their children with questions, 'What colour do you think we need here? Can you find a yellow piece that might fit?' Later the children began to ask themselves the same questions as they solved the problems without parental assistance. They had internalized their mothers' voices and with them their mothers' problem-solving thinking processes.[17]

By being exposed to and participating in certain ways of using language, one becomes a 'fluent speaker' of that language, able to use and understand its key concepts and expressions.

Similarly, habitual interactional patterns – for example, providing all participants opportunity to voice their views, demanding and providing justification for arguments, questioning assumptions, clarifying concepts and so on – are internalized as habitual ways of thinking.[18] Indeed, Anna Sfard argued that the similarities between interpersonal communication and individual cognition are such that they can usefully be thought of as different manifestations of the same processes.[19] In short, the ways of talking into which we are socialized shape both the cognitive tools at our disposal and the habits of mind whereby we put those tools to use.

This view of dialogue as thinking together raises important questions about classroom discourse: What is the quality of the thinking articulated by participants? For example, how valid, clear and relevant are the arguments? To what extent do inquiry and evidence conform to disciplinary standards?

Dialogue as relation

Dialogue can be threatening. Contrary to Socrates' view, few of us are happy to have our ideas refuted, and most prefer winning to losing an argument. Partly for this reason, discourse is rarely the cooperative, orderly and attentive affair commonly evoked by the word 'dialogue'. Indeed, attention to emotional and relational factors is important specifically because dialogue is also implicated with competition, argument, struggle to be heard, persuasion, 'ego' and power relations. Hence, Nicholas Burbules pointed out that the 'cognitive interest is not all that attracts us to the dialogical encounter, or keeps us in it when it becomes difficult or contentious'. This is one of the reasons that, for Burbules, dialogue is chiefly a relation, which thrives on emotions such as 'concern, trust, respect, appreciation, affection, and hope – [which] are crucial to the bond that sustains a dialogical relation over time'.[20]

The thinker perhaps most closely associated with the view of dialogue as a relation is Martin Buber (1878–1965), an Austrian-born philosopher and theologian who lived and worked in Germany until, fleeing from the Nazis in 1938, he emigrated to what was then Palestine (now Israel). Buber argued that people have two basic orientations toward others and the world: instrumental or dialogic.[21] To approach another instrumentally means to treat that person as an object, as a means to advance one's own interests. To approach another dialogically is to enter into a relationship of respect, mutual concern and solidarity. When we adopt an instrumental attitude, we relate to others partially – involving only those parts of our and their selves that are relevant to the transaction (for example, institutional roles and/or economic interests). The mutual concern in a dialogic relation is all-encompassing, and relates to both our and the other's whole beings. Dialogue, according to Buber, is unplanned and indeed unplannable, a matter of grace rather than calculation. Finally, Buber argues that we cannot live without instrumental relations, but we are not fully human without entering into dialogue.[22]

Viewing dialogue as a relation opens up questions about the quality of relations between the participants. For example, which part (or all) of their selves do they bring to the encounter? What are their motivations? To what extent are they accepting and caring of one another?

Dialogue as empowerment

Underlying the approaches to dialogue reviewed above is a basic assumption that participants freely enter into dialogue and enjoy equal rights and opportunities within the dialogic encounter. Yet, we live in an unequal society, which often constrains our participation and expression. Dialogue cannot be entirely isolated from the broader social and institutional contexts from which participants emerge and to which they return. Hence, power relations are a critical and indeed unavoidable dimension of dialogue.

One central thinker who wrestled with the political dimensions of dialogue was Brazilian revolutionary activist and educator Paulo Freire (1921–97).[23] Freire's educational thinking and work was committed to the emancipation of oppressed social classes and the creation of a more just society. Freire identified three sources of oppression: (a) *economic* – the lack of land or control of other means of production make the poor vulnerable to economic exploitation; (b) *civic* – lack of education – resulting, in particular, in the inability to read and write – precluded civic participation, since literacy was a prerequisite for voting in Brazil (until 1985); and (c) *subjective* – the oppressed are subjugated by their internalization of a dominant, capitalist ideology that casts their social condition as natural, inevitable and even just.

The emancipator–educator, according to Freire, must address all aspects of oppression. Literacy acquisition was key to democratic participation and thereby transformation of the social and economic order. Subjectively, educators must facilitate the development of a critical consciousness that recognizes the situation of oppression. Hence, Freire's adult literacy work involved political discussions alongside development of literacy skills: both 'reading the world' (reflecting on one's own experience, on society and oppression) and 'reading the word' (literacy learning). Dialogue, in which teacher and students jointly inquire into the object of study, is critical to this process of developing critical consciousness. While the teacher is typically more (formally) educated than the students, the latter bring to the dialogic encounter their own knowledge and experience of their social situation. This knowledge is fundamental – it is part of the truth of the matter – and also key to the students' empowerment. If an educator attempts to speak *for* the oppressed, she 'robs [them] of their words'.[24]

However, the Freirean recourse to dialogue can also be experienced as repressive. 'Why doesn't this feel empowering?' asks Elisabeth Ellsworth in an essay that shows how the call to dialogue can also be an exercise of power, in that it legitimizes certain ways of speaking and censures others.[25] Our own view is that 'dialogue' cannot resolve the issue of power relations by somehow creating a power-free space, but attention to the political dimension of dialogue can make us more alert to the ways in which participants can become empowered or oppressed, included or excluded. It raises key questions about the realization and conduct of power relations: Who participates in directing the interaction? How is that direction accomplished? Who benefits from interactional norms? How free are participants to express themselves? How are disagreements managed?

Interim conclusion: What to do with these six approaches to dialogue?

We hope that this whirlwind tour of six different ways of thinking about and justifying dialogue has not left you dizzy. What can we learn from them? Do we really need all six? And why bother with all this philosophy? After all, we promised a grounded approach, which works bottom-up from current classroom conditions and practices, rather than top-down from a 'who's who' list of early to mid twentieth century philosophers.

All six ideas about dialogue are important and necessary. Each highlights a critical dimension of dialogue – and communication more generally – which is in play in all social interactions. In every turn at talk we simultaneously address multiple dimensions, communicating about ourselves, our interlocutors, the relationships among us, our ideas and the conversation itself.

Consider for example Socrates' speech recounted above. He communicated about interactional form – whether and how to continue the conversation. He spoke about his and Gorgias' identities – what sort of person each is: one who argues for the sake of winning or one who strives for truth. He commented on Gorgias' ideas, specifically about an inconsistency that he had detected. He commented on the emerging relationship between them, questioning whether it could survive public disagreement. And finally, though he did not directly comment on power relations, we can see his entire speech as a power play, an attempt to shame Gorgias into continuing the conversation.[26] Since most or all of these dimensions are relevant in every social encounter, our thinking about dialogue will be incomplete if we do not take them all into account.

Second, the different dialogic goals, values and concerns often conflict with one another and make competing demands on teachers and other participants in dialogue. For example, care for participants is often in tension with critique of their ideas; reaching mutual agreement can conflict with developing independent voice; and holding thinking to disciplinary standards can be in tension with individual autonomy and equitable participation.[27] Hence, rather than choosing one approach to dialogue and ignoring or wishing away the other communicative dimensions and dialogic concerns, we advocate keeping all or most of the six approaches in mind as we attempt to navigate the tensions among them.

Regarding the final question, about the role of philosophical ideals in a grounded approach to dialogic pedagogy, our response is twofold: First, the bulk of the book proceeds bottom-up, from the classroom episodes to consideration of dialogue, only in this chapter do we explore non-grounded theories of dialogue. Second, we treat the six approaches, and especially the questions they raise, as tools for thinking about the episodes, rather than as criteria for evaluating the extent to which they might count as dialogic.

Why dialogue, as pedagogy, now?

Why has interest in dialogic pedagogy grown so strong in the past few decades? Education theorists and practitioners are attracted to dialogue for a variety of reasons, some of which were highlighted in the preceding section (see Table 2.1). Here we summarize the main justifications that emerge in current educational debates, especially in the United Kingdom:

- *Speaking and listening skills.* The 1998 UK *National Literacy Strategy* put a strong emphasis on reading and writing, according to critics at the expense of pupil 'oracy' or 'speaking and listening skills'. Dialogic teaching and learning is seen as a useful tool for redressing this imbalance and helping pupils develop their oral language skills.[28]
- *Children's rights and voice.* Educators, the public and children themselves increasingly advocate for children's rights, and at the very least for affording young people opportunity to make their voices heard. Dialogue is seen as an appropriately respectful and empowering way of treating pupils.[29]
- *Education for democracy.* In a healthy democracy citizens actively participate in public discussions of the common good and how it can best be achieved. Dialogic pedagogy can help initiate pupil-citizens into democratic participation by cultivating norms and rational deliberation and by facilitating pupils' acquisition of argumentation and public speaking skills.[30]
- *Unease with teacher authority.* A host of cultural changes – regarding family structure, social institutions, the mass media and the status of official knowledge – have made

many teachers (and parents) uneasy about imposing their authority. Dialogic pedagogy is seen by many as a more culturally appropriate and sensitive way for teachers to manage classroom life through negotiation with pupils.[31]

- *Effective means of learning and development.* A growing body of research – largely based on Vygotsky's ideas about the relationship between dialogue and thinking summarized above – demonstrates that participation in well-structured academic talk is an effective means of advancing pupil learning and cognitive development.[32]

- *Dissatisfaction with current classroom discourse practices.* Countless studies have found that discourse in most primary classrooms adheres to a three-part Initiation–Response– Evaluation (IRE) framework: teachers *initiate* discourse by asking predominately predictable, closed questions, usually designed to test pupils' recall of previously trans- mitted knowledge and/or to discipline inattention; pupils *respond* with one- or two-word answers; and teachers *evaluate* student responses, praising correct answers and censuring error. Teachers dominate talk by controlling the topic and allocation of turns, by speaking more often than pupils and for longer periods of time and, indirectly, by praising pupil contributions that are essentially a re-voicing of previous teacher utter- ances. This IRE pattern has been widely criticized as detrimental to pupils' independent thinking and learning. The structure positions teachers (and textbooks) as the sole legitimate sources of knowledge: pupils' main task is to recall and recite for evaluation what they have previously read or been told. The structure tends to produce rather disjointed lessons overall, with teachers moving from topic to topic without always making their line of reasoning explicit to pupils. Finally, to the extent that participants do engage in more demanding cognitive activities (e.g. explaining concepts, relating ideas to one another, challenging and/or justifying positions), the bulk of the work is performed by the teacher. Dialogue is seen as a promising alternative to this pattern.[33]

We are drawn to dialogic pedagogy for many of the reasons reviewed here: in particular, we see dialogue as an important means of educating pupils for democratic participation, and as an effective way of learning content matter and developing pupils' thinking. But for us dialogic pedagogy is important not only as a means; it is also an end in itself – a good way to live. We engage in dialogue because we are interested in what our interlocutors – includ- ing children and pupils – have to say. We engage in dialogue because we want everyone to have opportunity to develop and express their unique voice. We engage in dialogue because we do not know everything. And we engage in dialogue because we are social animals, who cherish and take pleasure in the company of others.

How are dialogic philosophies translated into classroom practice?

Moving from general philosophies of dialogue – as interactional form, as interplay of voices, as critique, as relation, as thinking together and as empowerment – to specific models of class- room practice is far from straightforward. First, the structural conditions of current classrooms militate against many critical features of dialogue. Lessons typically take place in small rooms occupied by large groups. In crowded classrooms, making space for everyone often necessitates pupils' sitting in rows or clumps, thereby constraining opportunities for all to communicate directly with one another in whole class discussion. Moreover, the size of the group – between 24–30 pupils in the classrooms studied in this book – makes broad participation in every discussion near impossible. Second, the institution of schooling assigns teachers and pupils clearly defined roles and responsibilities, and sets up inherently unequal power relations. Teachers are authorized to limit pupils' movement and speech, assign pupils tasks and evaluate the quality of pupils' work. Pupils are required by law to attend school and by school to comply with the teacher. Third, curricula and testing narrow the scope of legitimate topics and lines of inquiry, and very often impose clear end-points of authorized knowledge all must acknowledge.

One response to these constraints is to call for radical changes in school structures, conditions and goals as a prerequisite for developing dialogic pedagogy.[34] Though there are many aspects of the educational system that we would like to change, and not only because that would make classrooms more conducive to dialogue, predicating our model of dialogic pedagogy on such changes would for all intents and purposes postpone dialogue indefinitely. Instead, our approach is pragmatic: We favour models of dialogic pedagogy that are adapted to contemporary school contexts. In what follows we briefly review four such models. As above, our review is partial and selective; in each case we highlight features and strategies that we find particularly interesting and helpful.

Dialogically organized instruction

Martin Nystrand and his colleagues investigated literature teaching in over 100 US secondary school classrooms. They characterized the overwhelming majority of lessons they observed as 'monologically organized instruction', defined as teacher transmission to pupils of given knowledge through IRE-style recitation exchanges.[35] On a few occasions, they also found instances of more 'dialogically organized instruction', in which lessons proceeded as discussions of teacher and pupil literary interpretations and relevant personal experience in an effort to develop shared understanding. Nystrand and his colleagues found that dialogically organized instruction was associated with better learning outcomes, and also that it was much more prevalent in high rather than low ability tracks. Nystrand highlights three key teacher discourse moves that contribute to dialogic learning:

- posing *authentic questions*: 'questions for which the asker has not pre-specified an answer';
- *uptake*: 'incorporation of previous answers into subsequent questions';
- *high level evaluation*: teacher evaluation that both validates and elaborates a pupil's response.

Though Nystrand presents these moves as methods whereby teachers can shape classroom discourse, he emphasizes that teacher questions and evaluations are not in and of themselves the core of dialogically organized instruction. Rather, these and other practices cultivate a dialogic classroom culture, which in turn shapes how pupils perceive teacher questions, knowledge and the purpose of the discussion.

Exploratory talk

Neil Mercer and colleagues identified three forms of talk in pupils' small group interactions:

- *Disputational talk*: 'characterized by disagreement and individualized decision making … short exchanges consisting of assertions and challenges or counter-assertions ('Yes, it is.' 'No it's not!').'
- *Cumulative talk*: 'speakers build positively but uncritically on what the others have said.'

- *Exploratory talk*: 'partners engage critically but constructively with each other's ideas … Compared with the other two types, in exploratory talk knowledge is made more publicly accountable and reasoning is more visible in the talk.'[36]

In a series of ingenious experiments, Mercer and colleagues have shown that exploratory talk is associated with improved learning outcomes and cognitive development, and that pupils can be taught to use exploratory talk. The primary strategies used in the development of exploratory talk include teacher modelling, setting conversational ground rules and designing appropriately challenging joint tasks.

Accountable talk

'Accountable talk' is a term used by Sarah Michaels, Catherine O'Connor and Lauren Resnick to describe rigorous, academically productive classroom talk. Accountable talk is teacher and pupil discourse that is accountable to:

- *The learning community*: 'talk that attends seriously to and builds on the ideas of others; participants listen carefully to one another, build on each other's ideas, and ask each other questions aimed at clarifying or expanding a proposition.'
- *Standards of reasoning*: 'talk that emphasizes logical connections and the drawing of reasonable conclusions. It is talk that involves explanation and self-correction. It often involves searching for premises, rather than simply supporting or attacking conclusions.'
- *Knowledge*: talk that is 'based explicitly on facts, written texts or other publicly accessible information that all individuals can access. Speakers make an effort to get their facts right and make explicit the evidence behind their claims or explanations. They challenge each other when evidence is lacking or unavailable.'[37]

Teachers make these criteria explicit to pupils, and use them to build norms of rigorous and accountable academic discourse in their classrooms. *Accountable Talk* teachers further use a variety of moves to help pupils articulate and deepen their thinking, orient and listen to one another, and respond to one another's reasoning. Examples of these 'talk moves' include re-voicing pupil contributions and checking one's understanding, asking pupils to restate someone else's reasoning, asking pupils to apply their own reasoning to someone else's reasoning, prompting pupils for further participation, asking pupils to explicate their reasoning and giving pupils time to think ('wait time').[38]

Dialogic teaching

The model of classroom dialogue perhaps best known in the UK is Robin Alexander's 'dialogic teaching'. Dialogic teaching is:

- *Collective*: teachers and children address learning tasks together, whether as a group or as a class;
- *Reciprocal*: teachers and children listen to each other, share ideas and consider alternative viewpoints;
- *Supportive*: children articulate their ideas freely, without fear of embarrassment over 'wrong' answers; and they help each other to reach common understandings;

- *Cumulative*: teachers and children build on their own and each others' ideas and chain them into coherent lines of thinking and enquiry;
- *Purposeful*: teachers plan and steer classroom talk with specific educational goals in view.[39]

In addition to these principles, Alexander develops a list of 'repertoires' of learning talk (for example, analysing, speculating, explaining, arguing, etc.), teaching talk (rote, recitation, discussion, instruction, exposition, discussion and scaffolded dialogue), and organizational contexts (whole class, teacher-led or pupil-led group work, teacher–pupil and pupil–pupil pairs). He also explicates over 60 indicators of dialogic teaching, which draw attention to how all aspects of classroom pedagogy – organization of space and time, curriculum, tasks, assessment, and activity in addition to learning and teaching talk – are implicated in dialogic teaching. Teachers and local authority advisers use the repertoires, principles and indicators as tools for reflecting on their practice and how to improve it. We build directly upon a number of Alexander's ideas: the importance of a broad teaching repertoire (rather than one best method for all contexts), viewing dialogic talk as part of a larger system of pedagogy and culture and thinking about problems in enacting dialogic teaching as 'dilemmas, not deficits'.[40]

Interim conclusion: What to do with these practical models of classroom dialogue?

Readers will have noted connections between these models and the philosophies of dialogue reviewed in the previous section. In particular, Bakhtinian ideas about enabling and bringing together voices inform *dialogic teaching* and *dialogically organised instruction*, and Vygotskyan ideas about dialogue as thinking together underpin *accountable talk* and *exploratory talk*. Alexander's principles of *dialogic teaching* address concerns central to a number of philosophical approaches: collectivity and reciprocity are about interactional form; the cumulative principle is a way of (partially) describing dialogue as the interplay of voices; and the supportive principle addresses issues salient in dialogue as relationship.[41] In such a way, the abstract philosophies of dialogue are made concrete, relevant to classroom practice and accessible to all. Readers may wish to use these models alongside (or instead of) the goals, values and questions posed in the preceding section – as tools for interrogating the episodes in this book and/or their own practice.

The four models' designers employ a number of productive strategies for developing dialogic pedagogy in classrooms, including the following:

- *Explicit teacher education about dialogue*, what it looks like, why it is important, and how to conduct it;
- *Teachers' reflection on practice*, typically guided by principles or indicators of dialogic pedagogy;
- *Descriptions and models of teacher talk moves*, such as authentic questions or re-voicing;
- *Ground rules for classroom communication*; and
- *Attention to design* of curriculum, tasks and other aspects of pedagogy that shape dialogue.

We see each of these strategies as useful and important. The current book is devoted to developing dialogic pedagogy through critical reflection on practice, but – as we discuss in

Chapter 12 – we do not recommend that teachers and other would-be school reformers rely on such reflection alone. Reflection on problems of practice is important, but reflection cannot transform classroom practice in and of itself. A comprehensive programme for improving teaching would likely involve some or all of the other strategies listed above. In particular, since pedagogy is a complex system that integrates curriculum, assessment, learning tasks, timetable, spatial organization, textbooks, teachers' work conditions and more, changing pedagogy requires attention to most if not all these dimensions.

One difference between our approach and that of the four models presented here is that we do not offer a list of criteria or principles for judging practice as more or less dialogic. We can certainly see the advantages of such a framework for focusing teachers' gaze and for creating a common language. And we admire the elegant simplicity and plain language of, for example, 'accountable talk'. We hesitate to create such a checklist, in part, because we have not settled on a definitive conception of dialogic pedagogy that we think is appropriate to or desirable in every situation and for every pedagogical goal. We also hesitate on account of concern about how the prevalent 'best practice' teaching culture discussed in the preceding chapter affects the way such a framework might be used. We turn to this issue in the next section.

What's wrong with best practice dialogic teaching?

The growing popularity of 'dialogue' has led to its promotion by government as *best practice*. Alexander has severely criticized this official appropriation of dialogue, warning of the danger 'that a powerful idea will be jargonised before it is even understood, let alone implemented, and that practice claiming to be "dialogic" will be little more than re-branded chalk and talk or ill-focused discussion'.[42] We share Alexander's concerns, and note in particular how dialogic teaching is narrowed and distorted in official prescriptions of it as a best practice technique. Below we outline some of the main issues we've encountered – both in official guidance and demonstrations of dialogic practice,[43] and in the ways in which best-practice-oriented teachers have interpreted and enacted our own ideas.

1. *Presenting dialogue as primarily a technique for developing speaking and listening skills,* without reference to broader dialogic purposes and severed from all consideration of curricular content and context. Developing 'confident speakers and listeners' is a legitimate educational goal, and a worthy objective of dialogic pedagogy. However, casting it as the sole or even primary dialogic goal ignores the social and cognitive contexts within which confident speaking and meaningful listening are valuable activities – that is, the contexts in which pupils have something worthwhile to say and engage in an activity in which what they say matters. Creating such contexts is also crucial for successful skill development: practicing speaking and listening skills outside of a meaningful discussion is like practicing swimming outside of water.
2. *Treating dialogue as an interactional form,* often at the expense of attention to other dimensions. Best practice approaches to dialogic pedagogy often focus on surface features of interactional form, such as open teacher questions, extended pupil responses and slightly more equitable division of speaking time between teachers and pupils. However, as discussed above, these features are valued primarily as *indicators* of more essential dialogic issues such as voice, stance towards knowledge and power relations.
3. *Characterizing practice as either monologic or dialogic,* as if a chasm separated the two forms. We've found that most classroom lessons (or parts thereof) are in some respects

dialogic and in other respects much less so. For example, a lesson might exhibit critical and serious argumentation, but at the same time the relationships among pupils seem rather competitive, and the teacher controls the conversation in an authoritarian manner. Judging this lesson as more or less 'dialogic' will lead to a rather barren discussion of our pedagogical prejudices (that is, which dialogic dimension do we value most – argumentation, relationships, or empowerment?). Instead, we find it much more useful – for the development of teacher sensitivity and judgement – to investigate how the different dimensions of dialogue fit together in this case, and how the teacher and pupils manage the tensions between the multiple demands exerted by voices, critique, thinking together, relationships and power relations.[44]

4.   *Isolating dialogic pedagogy from the realities of schooling.* Dialogue, like all pedagogical practices, is necessarily constrained by the contexts in which it is enacted. For example, a number of the episodes in this book take place under the shadow of test preparations. Analysing such episodes without attending to these circumstances, or – worse – judging them to be insufficiently dialogic because they don't live up to some idealistic image, ignores the more interesting and important question of how teachers and pupils manage the tensions between their desire for dialogue and their need to live up to institutional expectations such as a high stakes test.

These final two issues point to what is for us the crux of the matter – and one of the key points of the book. Rather than seeing dialogic pedagogy as a simple and straightforward solution to a set of given problems in teaching (for example, how to inculcate speaking and listening skills), we find dialogue most powerful as a set of ideas that pose productive problems for teachers:

(a) how to reconcile or at least manage tensions between competing voices, between caring and critique, between challenging pupils' arguments and protecting their identities;
(b) how to reconcile or at least manage the tensions between idealistic dialogic goals such as critiquing orthodoxies, thinking together and democratizing power relations with the realities of school curricula, assessment and institutional roles; and
(c) how to continue to develop professionally – by honing one's sensitivity to multiple dimensions and concerns, by adding new practices to one's teaching repertoire, and by refining one's judgement about what concerns should be given priority in any given situation.

In Part 2 of the book we illustrate this approach through analysis of a series of classroom episodes. We invite readers to play with the various goals, dimensions, values, principles and questions discussed in this chapter as they consider the dialogic possibilities and challenges posed by each episode. First, in the next and final introductory chapter, we introduce you to the lead characters in the episodes and the school setting in which they took place.

Notes

1   Parts of this chapter previously appeared in Lefstein (2010) and in Lefstein and Snell (2011a).
2   The references for these books are (in the order presented): Alexander (2008b), Littleton and Howe (2010), Matusov (2009), Mercer and Littleton (2007), Myhill, Jones and Hopper (2006) and Wegerif (2007). Other influential books that have been published in the past two decades (but not in the past seven years) include Burbules' (1993) *Dialogue in teaching: theory and practice*, Nystrand and colleagues' (1997) *Opening dialogue: understanding the dynamics of language and learning in the English classroom*, and Wells' (1999) *Dialogic inquiry: towards a sociocultural practice and theory of education*.

3 See DfES (2003) and QCA (2005) for examples of the official adoption of dialogue. All content on the *Dialogic Pedagogy Journal* is freely available on-line at http://dpj.pitt.edu/ojs/index.php/dpj1/index.

4 Bauman (2001: 1).

5 The ideas we review here are rather elaborate and complex; we would struggle to do them justice in a complete book, let alone in one brief section of a chapter. Readers wishing further details are encouraged to follow up on the references in the notes.

6 Readers will note that dialogue as interactional form is the only approach for which no indicative thinker is included in the table or discussion. The reason for this is that interactional form is treated almost universally as a means to an end rather than an end in and of itself, or as an indicator of some other phenomenon that is valued. We nevertheless include this approach here because it is so common in thinking about educational dialogue, especially in best practice approaches (see pp. 25–6).

7 This is one of Alexander's (2008b) indicators of dialogic teaching.

8 Mercer (2000: 162).

9 In a review of theory and research on teaching as dialogue, Burbules and Bruce (2001) call for going 'beyond the idea that dialogue can be simply characterized as a particular pattern of question and answer among two or more people. Many instances of pedagogical communicative relations that might have this external form are not dialogical in spirit or involvement, while interactions that may not have this particular form can be' (p. 1110).

10 Bakhtin (1981, 1986) include translated collections of key works on dialogicality (see especially chapter 4, 'Discourse in the novel' and chapter 3, 'The problem of speech genres', respectively). Bakhtin also worked as a schoolteacher and teacher educator though to our knowledge he wrote only one article on pedagogy (Bakhtin, 2004). See Wertsch (1991) for a relatively friendly introduction to Bakhtin's ideas about voice and related concepts.

11 Bakhtin (1981: 337).

12 Bakhtin (1981: 293).

13 Bakhtin (1981) writes: '[C]onsciousness awakens to independent ideological life precisely in a world of alien discourses surrounding it, and from which it cannot initially separate itself; the process of distinguishing between one's own and another's discourse, between one's own and another's thought, is activated rather late in development' (p. 345).

14 There is little consensus about Socrates' method, and whether 'method' is an apt characterization. See Burbules (1990), Hare (2009), Haroutinian-Gordon (1989), Reich (1998) and Sichel (1998) for interpretations of the Socratic legacy.

15 Plato (2004: 21–2). In the interests of clarity and accessibility, we have edited Emlyn-Jones' translation. Readers are encouraged to read the dialogue, and to consult Plochmann and Robinson (1988) for a friendly guide and interpretation.

16 Vygotsky (1978: 57). We recommend Wertsch (1985) for an introduction to Vygotsky's work, Mercer (2000) for an accessible introduction to using language to think together, and Sfard (2008) for a discussion of the relationship between communicating and thinking (short version: they're two sides of the same coin).

17 Wertsch (1979).

18 Hicks (1996: 106–7, citing also Wertsch and Stone, 1985) argues that this common interpretation does not reflect the central place of learner agency in Vygotsky's theory. In her interpretation, the child does not passively internalize cultural tools, but also actively transforms them.

19 Sfard (2008).

20 Burbules (1993: 41).

21 Buber's (1937) classic treatise on dialogue, *I and Thou*, is written in a poetic, mystical style. We have taken numerous liberties in translating and interpreting key ideas here. 'Instrumental' and 'dialogic' relations are our translations of Bubers 'I-It' and 'I-Thou'.

22 In Buber's (1937) inimitable style: 'And in all the seriousness of truth, hear this: without *It* man cannot live. But he who lives with *It* alone is not a man' (p. 34).

23 Freire (1986), his most famous book, lays out his political analysis, his critique of the dominant 'banking' model of education and proposal for a dialogical alternative. Also recommended as a way into his ideas about dialogue is Shor and Freire (1987). Freire (1998) contains reflections on his later work in school education.

24 Freire (1986) writes, 'no one can say a true word alone, nor can she say it *for* another, in a prescriptive act which robs others of their words' (p. 88).

25 Ellsworth (1989).
26 See Lefstein (2010) for an elaboration of this interpretation.
27 These are *likely* rather than *necessary* tensions. We can imagine conditions under which these and other tensions dissolve, but this requires considerable imaginative powers, and suspending our knowledge of current schooling conditions.
28 For examples of renewed interest in speaking and listening skills, see DfES (2003) and QCA (2004).
29 See Fielding (2004) for an introduction to the pupil voice movement. Alexander (2008a: 122) persuasively ties the 'dialogic imperative' to global warming and other threats: 'Looking at our world as it stands at the start of the twenty first century, we can hardly argue that we as adults and professionals should debate its future, but that our children – who as the next generation of adults will inherit our problems and failures as well as our successes – should not be able to do likewise'.
30 This conception of (deliberative) democracy is based on Habermas (1989). See Michaels, O'Connor and Resnick (2008) for a good example of its application to education and classroom discourse.
31 See Furedi (2009) on uneasiness with adult authority, and Harris and Lefstein (2011) on how such changes affect classroom interaction in urban secondary schools. Such an approach is controversial, and is seen by many (including, it would seem, the current UK government) as overly permissive.
32 See Resnick, Michaels and O'Connor (2010) for a concise review of key studies, and Resnick, Asterhan and Clarke (in press) for a more detailed account of the latest research in this field.
33 IRE was first analysed by Mehan (1979) and (with variations) by Sinclair and Coulthard (1975). Cazden (2001) provides a good introduction to the study of classroom discourse. See Nassaji and Wells (2000) for an analysis of a variety of IRE forms and functions.
34 See for example the final chapter in Burbules (1993), which is also discussed in more detail in Lefstein (2010).
35 Nystrand *et al.* (1997).
36 Mercer and Littleton (2007: 51). This typology builds upon Barnes and Todd (1977).
37 Michaels, O'Connor and Resnick (2008). Elaboration of the theory, guidance for teachers and rich examples of accountable talk lessons in science and math are available in Michaels, Shouse *et al.* (2008) and Chapin, O'Connor and Anderson (2011) respectively.
38 These moves are elaborated and exemplified in Michaels, Shouse *et al.* (2008: 91). See O'Connor and Michaels (1993) for an in-depth analysis of re-voicing. On wait time see Row (1974).
39 These principles, along with the rest of the model, are explicated in Alexander (2008a, 2008b). Alexander (2003, 2004b, 2005) report on the implementation of dialogic teaching in North Yorkshire and in the London Borough of Barking and Dagenham. A major source of inspiration for his work on dialogic teaching is Alexander's (2001) comparative study of culture and pedagogy in five countries, and in particular the very different ways in which teachers and pupils interact in French and Russian primary classrooms in contrast to England and the US.
40 Alexander (2004b: 25–6). See also Alexander's commentary on Episode 2 (pp. 72–74).
41 None of these models directly confront the political dimension of dialogue (i.e. as empowerment), because they are all relatively well-aligned with existing school conditions. See Shor (1996) for a discussion of a radical and dialogic negotiation of power relations in a formal educational setting.
42 Alexander (2004a).
43 See, for example, QCA (2005), DfES (2007).
44 See Lefstein (2010) for an account of how the multiple dimensions and purposes of dialogue place multiple and often contradictory demands on teachers.

Chapter 3

Setting the scene

Working 'towards dialogue' in a London primary school

This book has grown out of research we conducted into classroom interaction and change in a London primary school during the 2008–9 academic year.[1] In this chapter we set the scene for the book by describing the background and aims of the study (which were slightly different to the aims and content of the book), the participating school and teachers, and our fieldwork in this school.

Background to the *Towards Dialogue* project

The motivation for this study, and for our continuing work in this area, was the finding that educational reforms promoting changes in classroom talk have had very little impact in UK classrooms, despite the widespread enthusiasm for dialogue documented in Chapter 2. The aim of the *Towards Dialogue* project was to help better understand why classroom interaction is so resistant to reform, and how dialogic pedagogy can be fostered and sustained; to understand, in effect, how teachers and pupils can jointly create new 'rules of the game' for interacting together in the classroom. The study encompassed two related strands: (1) a professional development programme designed to promote interactional awareness and sensitivity, and (2) lesson observations and recordings to study processes of continuity and change in classroom interactional patterns in the wake of that intervention. Practically this meant that we visited the school about three days a week over the course of the 2008–9 school year, collaboratively planning literacy lessons with the Year 5 and 6 teachers, recording literacy lessons, talking to teachers and pupils, and conducting fortnightly workshops with the teachers. We describe these research activities below, following an introduction to the school.

The focal school: Abbeyford Primary

Our focal school was Abbeyford Primary School, a relatively large community school in East London, England.[2] It is located in a London borough with a low socioeconomic profile – the majority of the pupils in the school come from white working class backgrounds – though the school is on a relatively more affluent edge of the borough, and is attended also by pupils from a neighbouring authority. We chose to work in this area, in part, because we hoped the research would have wider relevance with regard to the pressing problem of how to raise educational achievement in such settings. More significantly, the local authority had a long-standing interest in dialogic pedagogy and a history of developing and implementing pedagogical innovations. In particular, the local authority pioneered whole-class interactive teaching in mathematics in the mid-1990s, and collaborated with Robin Alexander in the

Teaching Through Dialogue Initiative in the early 2000s.[3] With the latter project, the local authority hoped to re-energize teachers' interest in the use of talk for learning. As with our study, the participating teachers reflected on video recordings of their own practice in order to identify aspects of talk in the classroom on which they could work to make classroom interaction more dialogic. We chose to work with Abbeyford Primary in particular because a senior local authority advisor recommended the school on account of its highly regarded, stable and experienced teaching staff and leadership team. Furthermore, the staff had had positive experiences in the previous *Teaching Through Dialogue* intervention and were keen to experiment with their practice.

Upon entering the school for the first time we got a sense of a businesslike environment (productive and efficient), yet at the same time the atmosphere was palpably warm and friendly. The positive atmosphere was no doubt a product of the good relationships teachers had with each other, as well as with the pupils. As visitors to the school we were immediately made to feel at ease, and it quickly became apparent (as we spent time in the staffroom, corridors and classrooms) that this was how teachers and pupils at this school felt too. It was this intangible feeling that all of the teachers commented upon when asked what (if anything) made Abbeyford unique, as in the following responses, which are excerpted from initial interviews with us:

> It's warmer … The children have a nice relationship with the teachers, the teachers have a nice relationship with each other, so, like, in the staff room, you can have – you know, it's friendly, it's chatty, whereas other staff rooms that I've been to, you sit there on your own and there's no communication and there's, you know, the vibe is not as good as it is here.

> I just enjoy it every day. I enjoy being part of the school … the staff are great, and I think that is something that is unusual, and something that would scare me about working somewhere else, where you weren't part of such a nice team of people.

> There's a nice atmosphere in this school, everyone says that, who comes in, supply teachers say that. We have got some really nice children in this school.

There was a general consensus among the staff that the pupils at Abbeyford were, on the whole, well behaved, and this was our impression too. The children we observed during the 2008–9 academic year were generally obedient, and those with whom we interacted (in lessons, in the corridors, in group discussions) were polite and friendly. Pupils had a similarly positive view of the school. In a focus group one of us conducted with Year 5 pupils, Abbeyford was described as 'the bestest school ever'. Most pupils appeared to enjoy being at school, and it was easy to understand why. The lessons we observed at Abbeyford were by and large pleasant, and often innovative in their integration of music, visual aids, noncurricular texts and dramatic performance. Teachers also often incorporated personal narratives into classroom interaction, stepping (albeit fleetingly) out of their teaching persona, and thus relating to the pupils on an interpersonal level. This seemed both to reflect and reproduce the positive relationships teachers had with their pupils.

Classrooms were organized in the traditional style, with the teacher's desk and whiteboard at the front, from which most of the teaching was conducted. Slightly less conventional was the layout of pupils' desks, which were arranged to form a horseshoe around the edges of the room, with two or three tables in the centre of the horseshoe – a full horseshoe layout not being possible due to space constraints. This layout meant that pupils could see each other (to a certain extent) as well as the teacher and the white board. While conventional for the local authority, this layout appears not to have been the norm elsewhere in the country, at least not historically. In their late 1990s follow-up to the first Observational Research and Classroom Learning Evaluation study (ORACLE), Maurice Galton and colleagues found that children were still seated in groups around tables, as they had been two decades earlier.[4] On occasions at Abbeyford, desks were rearranged to facilitate role play activities, group work or debates.

Literacy lessons lasted for between 45 and 50 minutes, with an average of 50 per cent of this time spent on whole-class discussion. Whole-class teaching typically involved one of the following activities:

- *discussion of a text* or part of a text, such as the children's book *Charlotte's Web*;
- *plenary review of group work* after pupils have collaborated to brainstorm an idea, discuss questions posed by the teacher, review each other's work and so on;
- *plenary review of pupil writing*, conducted usually at the end of the lesson where several pupils read out their written work and receive feedback from the teacher and other pupils;
- *focused discussion of an individual pupil's work*, during which pupils are encouraged to discuss the strengths and weaknesses of their peer's writing as well as areas for development;
- *shared writing*, where pupils collaborate to compose a text by voicing contributions, which the teacher then writes on the whiteboard.

Discussion was often punctuated with brief pair talk (around 30 seconds), where pupils were invited to formulate their ideas initially through discussion with the person sitting next to them. Teachers usually probed individual pupil responses with several follow-up questions. This often produced extended teacher–pupil exchanges, some of which lasted for several minutes.

The high rate of probe questions and the tendency to punctuate whole-class discussion with very brief opportunities to talk with a partner were part of what we considered to be the school's 'signature pedagogy'. Our initial intuitive sense that this was a distinctive teaching style was later confirmed by systematic comparison of the classroom data we collected at Abbeyford with a national sample of literacy lessons.[5] Table 3.1 presents some of the findings from this analysis, which included ten lessons for each of three Abbeyford teachers participating in the research (that is, 30 lessons in total).[6] This analysis focused on the whole-class element of each lesson, for which we coded every discourse move (for example, open question, probe, response, feedback). The numbers in the first half of the table show the 'rate' for each discourse move. Rate is calculated as frequency per hour to make this data comparable to the national sample. For example, if a teacher used five open questions in 20 minutes of whole-class teaching, this would be reported as a rate per hour of 15.[7] In summary, we found that classroom discourse at Abbeyford more frequently deviated from IRE format; teachers posed more open questions and probes; and pupils participated more often, and in less rigidly constrained ways. We attribute these differences to the school's prior participation in the *Teaching Through Dialogue* intervention and the local authority's attention to classroom discourse and emphasis on whole-class interactive teaching.[8] During our intervention, the participating teachers told us that they felt a transformation in classroom talk and relationships brought about by the changes they were making to their practice.

Table 3.1 Rate per hour of discourse moves: Abbeyford Primary compared to a national sample

			Abbeyford average		National sample	
Lessons sampled				30		35
Mean duration lesson (in minutes)				48		53
Mean duration whole-class teaching				24		32
Rate per hour of key discourse moves						
Teacher						
Questions						
	Open questions	16%	22	13%	15
	Closed questions	34%	46	50%	58
	Probe questions	23%	31	17%	19
	Uptake questions	4%	5	7%	8
	Repeat/repair question	22%	30	13%	15
Feedback					
	Elaborated feedback	13%	13		
	Non-elaborated feedback	87%	83		
	Total Feedback		96		65
Pupil					
	Response to teacher		169		120
	Spontaneous contribution		30		10
	Read aloud/pupil presentation		13		11
	Choral response		24		9
Percentage pupil contribution				32%		25%

They often commented positively on an emerging 'culture of talk' in the school, in which children were more willing to air their ideas and opinions in whole-class discussion. That this perceived change in culture had happened so quickly can no doubt be attributed to the school's previous participation in projects designed to promote dialogic pedagogy.

Overall, then, our impression was that Abbeyford was a productive and pleasant place to be. The head teacher, Mr Johnson, concurred, stating that he considered it a good school 'because relationships are good, the staff care for the children, the staff know the children … and most of the kids who come here are happy'. He went on to say, however, that when judged against standardized test data, the school has not always been evaluated favourably, especially in recent years. Abbeyford had been among the higher achieving schools in the local authority, as reflected in standardized test scores, but its position had slipped in the two years prior to the research. The school was ranked fifth out of 35 schools in the 'league tables' comparing local schools in 2006, but fell to twenty-ninth in 2009. School management and teachers were under considerable pressure to reverse this downward trend, and success in the standardized assessments task (SAT) tests and the upcoming governmental inspection were a major concern for all, but in particular, for the Year 6 teachers (see the head teacher's commentary in Chapter 7, pp 130–131).

Part way through the research, in January 2009, these teachers began an intense period of revision for the SATs, which their pupils were to sit in May 2009. Literacy lessons observed in the Year 6 classes during this time were devoted entirely to revising for the English component of these tests, using teaching materials provided by the local authority. During the majority of our observations in Year 6 classes, then, teachers were under competing pressures: (1) to alter their practice in line with our intervention; and (2) to prepare their pupils for the SATs, ensuring that individuals were able to perform to the best of their abilities, and that the school achieved an appropriate level of success overall. These tensions came out clearly in the planning meetings we conducted with the Year 6 teachers (see below for detail), where the consensus was that it is difficult to find opportunities for dialogue within the constraints of the SATs revision units and related materials provided by the borough (Chapter 7 looks in detail at two teachers' attempts to incorporate dialogue into the SATs revision unit on discussion writing, and Chapter 8 considers, amongst other issues, the changes in classroom dynamics brought about by SATs revision).

Fieldwork at Abbeyford Primary

The project focused on literacy teaching in Years 5 and 6 (pupils aged 9 to 11). There were three classes in each of these year groups at Abbeyford Primary, with an average of 29 pupils per class. For Year 6 literacy lessons, class size was reduced by creation of a fourth group taught by the deputy head teacher, Ms Anderton.[9] All seven teachers participated in the study. They brought with them a range of expertise and experience (see summary in Table 3.2). Ms Anderton had been teaching for 30 years – all in the same London borough – and had been deputy head teacher at Abbeyford for 11 years. Ms James had recently taken up position as Head of Year 6 and had ten years teaching experience, seven of these spent at Abbeyford. The remaining Year 6 teachers were Ms Lightfoot, who had been teaching for 16 years (eight at Abbeyford), and Ms Alexander, who was beginning her first full year as a qualified teacher (having just completed her Newly Qualified Teacher year at Abbeyford). The Head of Year 5 was Ms Leigh, who had been teaching for 11 years and also served as assistant head teacher and literacy coordinator. Mr Richards and Ms Cane taught Year 5 classes alongside Ms Leigh. Both came to Abbeyford immediately after completing their teaching qualifications (six years prior to the start of the research for Mr Richards and just one year prior for Ms Cane). Ms Anderton, Mr Richards, Ms Leigh, Ms Lightfoot and Ms James had participated in the earlier *Teaching Through Dialogue* project.

These seven teachers took part in individual interviews at the start of the research process, where they were encouraged to talk about their background, teaching experience, the school, pupils, their understanding of dialogic pedagogy and their reasons for wanting to participate in the project. All were enthusiastic about the project, and especially about the opportunity

Table 3.2 Participating teachers

	Teaching experience (years)	Years spent at Abbeyford	Number of lessons observed	Relevant chapter
Ms Anderton	30	11	6	Ch. 7, Episode 5
Ms James	10	7	14	Ch. 4
Ms Lightfoot	16	8	4	Ch. 7, Episode 4
Ms Alexander	1	1	12	Ch. 8
Ms Leigh	11	11	13	Chs. 5 and 6
Mr Richards	6	6	12	Ch. 9
Ms Cane	1	1	12	Ch. 10

it afforded them to improve the children's classroom experience. Interviews repeated at the end of the research were used as an opportunity for individuals' reflections on the academic year – challenges and high points in literacy lessons, pupil development, changes in classroom interaction – and on their participation in the study. Some of the teachers also chose to participate in feedback interviews midway through the process, in which one of us viewed with the teacher a short video clip from their classroom and discussed aspects of talk in the classroom and further directions for professional development.

The professional development programme ran from late November 2008 until mid July 2009 and included collaborative planning of literacy lessons and fortnightly meetings to discuss video-recorded excerpts of those lessons' enactment. Planning was conducted primarily in six extended meetings (three each with Y5 and Y6 teams), which took place on 1 December 2008, 2 February 2009 and 30 March 2009. In these meetings we worked with the teachers to develop three substantial curricular units. These sessions were audio-recorded and documented in field notes. In between the planning meetings we visited the school two to three times a week to observe and video- and/or audio-record participating teachers' literacy lessons, and also to spend time informally observing school life. In total, we recorded 73 literacy lessons.

We documented additional (and often more impressionistic) aspects of the school experience in detailed field notes, which we wrote up after each visit to the school. These, together with the video/audio data, formed the basis for discussion at weekly research team meetings. During these meetings we selected episodes from the lessons for use in the reflection workshops. In selecting episodes we looked for relatively positive pedagogic practice (which would not embarrass the teacher involved) that also raised interesting and important pedagogical problems worthy of further discussion. We were particularly interested in segments that included relatively dialogic moments and/or apparent shifts in interactional patterns, but we also selected episodes that addressed themes emerging from our field notes (for example, dominant frameworks for evaluating pupil writing) and/or that spoke to the teachers' own concerns (for example, the use of humour in the classroom, the extent to which revising for the SATs can be dialogic). Finally, we made sure that we used material from all the classrooms at least once. All clips were sent to the relevant teachers for approval prior to the workshops.

The reflection workshops took place every second Monday in the after-school slot reserved for staff meetings. One of us facilitated the workshops, opening each session with a short introduction that typically included something positive about the selected excerpts, and thanks to the relevant teacher(s) for agreeing to share an episode from their classroom(s). Next, we played the video and/or audio clip(s) twice and distributed a detailed transcript (like the ones used in this book). For the purposes of our research, the participants responded individually, in writing, to the clips, highlighting interesting and/or significant segments, describing what was happening in them and explaining why they found them noteworthy. Following these individual responses we elicited topics or issues that participants wished to raise, which were then discussed by the group in turn (a summary of the key issues raised in the ten sessions is represented in Table 3.3). We probed participants' ideas, asking for supporting evidence and drawing out the interactional and pedagogical implications of their interpretations. These meetings were audio-recorded and documented in field notes, and were themselves subject to detailed analysis.[10]

Many of the episodes we present in this book were used in the reflection workshops, and thus the teachers' voices are present in our analyses.[11] Although we do voice some criticisms

Table 3.3 Summary of key issues that arose in reflection meetings

	Pedagogical issues discussed	Episodes appearing in this book
1	Teacher personas/relationships Use of humour in the classroom 'Throwing in a curve ball' (i.e. leading the children into an incorrect opinion with the intention of developing the discussion) Aesthetics of teaching	Episode 1 was one of three clips used in this session
2	Pupil thinking time (how long is long enough?) Pace How to draw together pupil responses in a meaningful way	Episode 7

3	Teacher intervention
	    What impact do teacher interventions have on the discussion, on pupil engagement, on learning?
	    What kinds and levels of intervention are useful in facilitating whole-class discussion/debate?
		Episodes 4–5

4	Weaving together multiple texts and literary concepts Responding to pupil challenges Distribution of pupil participation Role of the teacher in facilitating/directing discussion	Episode 2
5	Building/scaffolding pupil disagreement Challenging a pupil's thinking in non-threatening way	Episode 8 was one of two clips used in this session
6	The SATS game Aesthetics of teacher performance Teacher's position in the classroom/spatial arrangement How to move from specific principles of pupil writing to broader principles of writing, from one pupil's work to the whole class	
7	Listening to pupils What to do with pupil error How to use pupil contributions to move the discussion forward Balancing pupils' individual needs with those of the rest of the class	
8	Importing popular culture into the classroom Models for evaluating texts	Episode 3
9	Representations of best practice	
10	Use of drama/role play Teacher's role	

of teaching in the analysed episodes, we would like to emphasize that the teachers were themselves critical of many of these practices in discussions about the episodes with us and with the other teachers, and further that most of the issues we raise are rooted in the broader policy environment in which these teachers work and against the boundaries of which they are pushing.

In this chapter, we have introduced you to the school, teachers and research project from which the episodes discussed in this book were taken. With it, we conclude our introductions, and move next into the heart of the book, a series of eight classroom episodes that offer opportunities to explore in depth the problems and possibilities of dialogic pedagogy.

Notes

1 The full name of the project is 'Towards Dialogue: A Linguistic Ethnographic Study of Classroom Interaction and Change'. It was funded by the Economic and Social Research Council (ESRC RES-061-25-0363). More information on the project, including the final report and details of publications are available on the ESRC website: http://www.esrc.ac.uk/my-esrc/grants/RES-061-25-0363/read.

2 Abbeyford is a pseudonym, as are all names of teachers and pupils in this book. There were 12 classes in the school, three in each of four year groups

3 On whole-class interactive teaching in mathematics see Luxton and Last (1998) and Ochs (2006). For more detail about the *Teaching Through Dialogue Initiative* see Alexander (2005, 2008b).

4 Galton *et al.* (1980, 1999).

5 Collected in 2001 by researchers at the University of Newcastle (Hardman *et al.*, 2003; Smith *et al.*, 2004).

6 A more detailed version of this table, and information on how the data were collected and analysed, is available on-line in Snell and Lefstein (2011).

7 For more detail about this analysis see Snell and Lefstein (2011).

8 During the *Teaching Through Dialogue Initiative*, Alexander (2008b: 45–6) reported ongoing changes in participating classrooms, including: teachers making more use of 'questions which probed and/or encouraged analysis and speculation'; greater use of 'paired talk to prepare for whole class discussion'; a 'more flexible mix of different kinds of talk – recitation, exposition, discussion, dialogue'; and 'an increase in pupil contributions of an expository, explanatory, justificatory or speculative kind'. These changes were apparent during our 2008–9 observations.

9 We use the marital-neutral 'Ms' to refer to all female teachers here and throughout the book.

10 In Lefstein and Snell (2011b) we scrutinize our own role in these workshops, subjecting transcripts of those workshops to the same kinds of detailed linguistic ethnographic analyses we apply to classroom interaction in Chapters 4 to 8. This analysis highlights the point that in viewing and discussing the video clips, not only did participants and we find different issues to be worthy of note, we also differed in how we tended to interpret or reason about what we saw.

11 Teachers, pupils and their parents gave their consent to participate in the research and for us to use the materials in publications. We also discussed with the teachers our plans for this book and double-checked that they were willing for us to use the video recordings included here.

Part II

Classroom episodes

Introduction: Practical suggestions for engaging with the episodes

Welcome to Part 2, the heart of the book. Here we present and discuss eight episodes of classroom practice. Chapters four to eight include the following sections:

1. *An introduction*, in which we acquaint you with the episode and touch on the key issues that we explore in the chapter.
2. *Setting the scene*, in which we provide crucial background information on the lesson, curricular unit, pupils, teacher and the like. We also summarize the episode in this section.
3. *Viewing the video recording*, in which we provide guiding questions for your viewing of the video recording and reading of the transcript (both can be found in the companion website, www.routledge.com/cw/lefstein).
4. *Analysis*, in which we explore some issue or issues that the episode(s) raise for us. Where available, we also summarize the Abbeyford Primary School teachers' responses to the episode in this section.
5. *Conclusion*, in which we wrap up the key issues explored.
6. *Issues for further discussion*: guiding questions for you to consider and/or discuss. Some of these relate to our analysis and its implications; some raise new issues that we did not discuss in the chapter.
7. *Commentaries*: Brief responses to the episode and/or our analysis, written by leading educational professionals and researchers.

Chapters 9 and 10 are designed to provide further material for reflection. Here we introduce the episodes and pose questions to guide your viewing of the video clips (Sections 1–3), but leave the analyses to you.

Readers can either engage with these materials on their own, or in study groups, for example in school-based learning communities, professional development workshops or higher education courses. Either way, here are a few recommendations on how to work with the materials:

1) Analyse the episodes on your own before reading our analysis. We have organized the chapters to facilitate this: the background and narrative necessary for you to make sense of the episode on your own are provided prior to and separate from our analysis. Working through each episode independent of our analysis will be more demanding, but also more rewarding.

2) Watch the episode at least twice. You might want to follow along on the transcript, or read the transcript between viewings. You will note that the transcript is organized by breath groups, rather than punctuated as in written speech. This is how we talk most of the time: not in complete sentences, rather in fragments that are bound together by intonation, timing and gestures. You will also see that we have included select non-verbal details in double parentheses and using special notations that are listed at the end of each transcript. The transcript is a work space. While we view the video we often add to the transcript, correct it, or otherwise jot down notes on it.

3) Consider what's happening in the episode, and what, if anything, is significant about it. You might want to use the guiding questions we have offered.

- Play around with the episode: watch it without sound, listen to it without looking, focus on an area away from the action, map out the development of ideas in the episode, try to put yourself in the teacher's place, or take on the perspective of one of the pupils. Have fun with it.
- Suspend your judgement until after understanding. Observers often judge classroom practice too quickly and as a result miss what is potentially most interesting.
- Focus on what is happening rather than what is missing in your opinion. A five minute episode cannot include all of your educational desires, and concentrating on what is absent from the episode will get in the way of understanding what is present in it.
- Investigate the relationships between turns at talk: how a teacher question is related to a pupil response, and how pupils' ideas are related to one another. You might want to proceed line by line, asking at each stage, 'What is happening here? Why that, now? What else could have happened, but didn't? Why not?' (See Methodology Appendix for more detail on this approach to analysis).
- Focus on the details. Everything is important. A minor change in intonation can change the meaning of a statement for the participants, so it should also be meaningful for us as analysts.

4) Read our analysis, comparing it to your own ideas. What do you think about it? Where do you agree or disagree? What are the implications of our analysis for your ideas about teaching, dialogic pedagogy or your own practice? Bear in mind that there is a wide gap separating the slow analysis of a lesson from its experience in real time. Have we gone too far in projecting our own slow experience of the lesson onto the teacher and pupils? Have you?

5) Compare your ideas to those found in the commentaries and on the www.routledge.com/cw/lefstein website.

6) Think about or discuss the further questions posed at the end of the chapter. What do you have to say about the episode? Add your voice to the book by sending us your thoughts. Give us permission to post your ideas on the website.

Further suggestions for discussing the episodes in a professional learning community, course or other group setting can be found in Chapter 12.

Chapter 4

Breakthrough to dialogue?[1]

In this chapter we employ the approaches to dialogue presented in Chapter 2 (see Table 2.1) to examine a brief episode of whole class discussion, while at the same time using the episode to probe approaches to dialogic pedagogy. We also discuss the conditions under which teacher and pupils jointly break through to dialogue.

EPISODE 1: GETTING IN TO NARNIA

In C.S. Lewis' novel *The Lion, The Witch and the Wardrobe* four children find in an old country house a wardrobe that transports them to a magical realm called Narnia. But sometimes the wardrobe was just an 'ordinary wardrobe', and did not function as a secret portal. In the episode we investigate in this chapter Ms James' Year 5 class puzzled over why the gateway to Narnia was sometimes open and sometimes closed.

Brian suggested that the wardrobe only opened on to Narnia if you believed in it. His teacher, Ms James, responded: 'Can I just disagree with Brian? Do you mind if I disagree with you, Brian?' and then proceeded to offer evidence from the story that ran counter to Brian's idea.

This response interested us for a number of reasons. First, as noted in Chapter 2, the most prevalent teacher response to a pupil answer is to evaluate it as right or wrong. Here, Ms James does not so much evaluate as *disagree*, which seems to position herself and her opinion on the same plane as Brian and his ideas. Second, she makes a bit of a show of their disagreement – even going so far as to ask for his permission to disagree. This is unusual: Why would a teacher seek permission to disagree with a pupil? What does this say about her role and responsibilities in the discussion? Third, immediately after Ms James' difference of opinion with Brian, another pupil disagreed with Ms James, and a third pupil disagreed with her. Is it possible that the first disagreement set off a chain reaction of further disagreements? And what became of those disagreements – what sort of dialogue did they ignite?[2] Finally, this exchange was one of four exchanges that explored pupils' pre-prepared answers to questions about the story, and the only one in which we witnessed a dramatic breakthrough to dialogue. How can the differences among these exchanges be explained?

This chapter looks closely at these and related questions about the instigation, development and management of a relatively dialogic stretch of classroom talk. First we set the scene by briefly describing the key stages in the lesson, and then drill down to describe the focal episode. We recommend that you read these sections before viewing the video and reading the full transcript. We next offer some guiding questions to consider in your exploration of the episode, our own analysis and two commentaries, one written by a local authority Principal Adviser and the other by a research psychologist.

Setting the scene

The lesson

The lesson from which our focal episode is drawn took place in Ms James' Year 6 classroom at the end of November 2008. The class have been reading and discussing *The Lion, the Witch and the Wardrobe* and are now nearing the end of the novel. The lesson includes five segments:

1. *Recap of recent events in the book* (4 minutes). Ms James reviews what has happened in the story so far by asking the pupils: 'Where are we up to so far? What has recently happened?' She uses pictures from a web page with an interactive map of Narnia to elaborate on the pupil summaries.
2. *Reading and discussing the text* (17 minutes): Ms James and the pupils take turns reading from Chapter 14 (the section in which Aslan goes to the Stone Table to sacrifice himself in Edmund's place – don't worry if you're not familiar with the story; we will explain details that are critical to understanding the discussion). After each paragraph, Ms James poses a question or problem. For example, 'Why are the girls following Aslan?', 'Why might Aslan be sad?', 'How does the author show that Aslan is sad?', 'How is Aslan different from the other characters?', 'Why did Aslan not put up a fight?'. She again uses the interactive map to illustrate the Stone Table setting described in the book and asks the pupils to imagine how they think they would have felt had they been there. After Ms James reads the last sentence of the chapter – the climactic moment of the book, in which Aslan is killed by the White Witch – she tells the pupils to close their books and leaves them in suspense about what will happen next. 'You're going to have to wait till tomorrow', she tells them.
3. *Small group tasks* (14 minutes). Ms James divides the pupils into groups of 3–4 participants and assigns each group two 'really important questions' that they are to discuss and prepare to report their ideas back to the class. Each group should appoint a spokesperson and a scribe. Ms James emphasizes that she's interested in their opinions, and in 'as much evidence from the text as you can possibly find'. During these small group discussions Ms James moves among the groups, checking their progress and prodding them with further questions to focus their attention on what she sees as the most salient issues.
4. *Concluding plenary* (9 minutes). Ms James and the pupils discuss as a class four questions from the group discussions: 'Aslan is a coward – Do you agree or disagree?', 'Why can't Narnia always be found in the same place?', 'Why is it significant that the White Witch's sledge is pulled by reindeer?', 'Why isn't Edmund punished for the bad things he does?'. For each question Ms James first elicits the opinion of the group who discussed that particular question, and then opens the issue to the rest of the class. Two of these discussions – about Aslan's bravery and the use of reindeer – are conventional Initiation–Response–Evaluation exchanges (see Chapter 2, p. 21) in which the teacher shepherds the pupils towards a predetermined, 'correct' interpretation. In the discussion of forgiving Edmund, two opposing views emerge, but the controversy between them is not developed. Only the discussion about why Narnia cannot always be found in the same place (recounted in the introduction to the chapter) develops into a critical exchange of ideas.
5. *Predictions* (1 minute). Ms James instructs the pupils to turn to the person next to them and discuss in pairs what they think will happen next in the story.

The episode

In this chapter we investigate the discussion of why the wardrobe passage to Narnia was not always open (in phase 4 above). The video recording and full transcript of this 2 minute and 40 second episode is included on the accompanying website, www.routledge.com/cw/lefstein. Before exploring this episode in detail, we summarize it briefly. The episode can be roughly broken up into four main stages:

1. 'What do I mean by that?' (lines 1–32)

Ms James tells the class that she asked the group sitting to her immediate left, 'Why can't Narnia always be found in the same place?' A pupil from another group, Julie, makes a puzzled face as if to say, 'What does that mean?' and Ms James asks the group who discussed the question to clarify the meaning of the question, and to provide an example in the text in which the portal was closed.

2. 'This group, why do you think that happens?' (lines 33–49)

Ms James summarizes the issue: 'When they went in there again it was all blocked up, wasn't it? They couldn't get through.' She asks the group why they think that happens. Two pupils, Ben and Sean, begin to answer at once, and Ms James nominates Sean, who hesitates for three seconds and then says, 'I don't know.' Ms James reformulates this as 'you're not sure' and gives the floor to Ben.[3] Ben suggests that 'maybe it's because they only let people in at certain times.'

3. 'But ... they let in Edmund' (lines 50–107)

Ms James accepts Ben's contribution with 'OK' and probes it with a question – 'Do you think that maybe the wardrobe only lets in good people?' – which she directs to the entire class. This leads to a series of possible explanations, each of which is refuted by someone else.

```
50   Ms James:  okay
51              do you think that maybe the wardrobe only lets in
52              good people
53   Anon:      (nope)
54   Anon:      why did (they)
55   Julie:     but she let in Edmund- they let in Edmund
56   Ms James:  so we're not saying it-
57              we- we're disagreeing with that then
58   Sean:      they only let certain people in
59   Ms James:  only let certain people in
60              bu:t if there's some-
61              we're saying they only let good people in
62              why do they let Edmund in
63              what do you think Brian
64   Brian:     I think it's if they believe in it
65   Vanessa:   yeah that's what I think
66              because (.)
67              erm Lucy-
68              Lucy wou- didn't know about it and then she (.)
69              went in Narnia and then she found out that it was there
70              and she believed in it
71   Ms James:  but can I just disagree with Brian-
```

```
72              do you mind if I disagree with you Brian
73              right
74              the rest of the children
75              they didn't really believe in it did they
76              Peter and Susan
77              they thought that Lucy was ju:st
78              being silly a bit
79              because of her age
80              and they all rushed into the wardrobe didn't they
81              when Mrs McCreedy was showing these people
82              around the house
83  Julie:     ((whispering)) they were with Lucy ((this pupil has her
84              hand up and appears eager to contribute))
85  Ms James:  and they suddenly went in
86  Julie:     because they were [with Lucy
87  Ms James:                    [but they didn't believe in it (.)
88              what do you think about that
89  Julie:     because they were with Lucy
90  Ms James:  Sorry
91  Julie:     because they were with Lucy
92  Ms James:  so they were with somebody that did believe (1)
93              ah so you think you've got to have a belief in Narnia
94  Pupils:    Yeah
95  Ms James:  to be able to get in
96  Deborah:   ((nods))
97  Pupils:    Yeah
98  Ms James:  okay
99              ((shrugs her shoulders))
100 Deborah:   yeah but what about Edmund
101 Ms James:  but what about Edmund
102             ah Deborah just said
103 Deborah:   because he went in after Lucy (.)
104             not while-
105             he didn't go in with Lucy
```

4. An inconclusive conclusion (108–14)

Following Deborah's counter-example of Edmund's solo entrance into Narnia, Ms James tells Julie that she'll 'have to sort of back down on' her argument that the wardrobe opens up to people who believe in Narnia, or are accompanied by believers. Finally, with all possible explanations found wanting, Ms James draws the discussion to an end by noting that the topic is worthy of discussion in more detail later, but that she wants to move on now to the next group's question.

Viewing the video recording

We recommend that readers now view the video recording and read the full transcript of this episode.[4] In thinking about and/or discussing the episode you might like to consider the following questions:

- What is happening here? What, if anything, stands out as particularly interesting and/or anomalous in the episode? How is this clip different from other examples of classroom interaction you've seen and/or experienced?

- Is this what you were expecting to see in a book on developing dialogic pedagogy? In what ways is it similar to or different from your expectations?
- Based on your interpretation of dialogic pedagogy, in what ways is the interaction in this episode more or less dialogic? For example, building on the discussion in Chapter 2 (see Table 2.1) you might ask:

  - *Interactional form*: Who speaks, how often, about what, to whom, and for how long? How equitable is participation?
  - *Interplay of voices*: Which voices are heard and allowed? How are they interacting?
  - *Critique*: What stances toward knowledge are being taken? Which ideas are and are not subjected to critical examination?
  - *Thinking together*: What is the quality of the thinking being articulated?
  - *Relationship*: How are participants relating to one another? What identities and concerns do they make relevant?
  - *Empowerment*: How are power relations realized? Is everyone free to say what they please? Who benefits? How are differences managed?

- What is Ms James' role in the discussion? What tasks does she perform?
- How might you explain the relatively dialogic and non-dialogic features of this episode? To what can their emergence be attributed?

Analysis: breakthrough to dialogue?

In what follows we examine the episode according to the different dimensions of dialogue discussed in Chapter 2.[5] We highlight a number of ways in which we find the episode to be relatively dialogic, focusing on the segment in which the class exchange ideas about why the wardrobe–Narnia gateway was sometimes open, sometimes closed (lines 44–113). We then proceed to consider the final question posed above, regarding the differences between this segment and the rest of the plenary.

In what ways is the episode more or less dialogic?

Interactional form

The discussion in the episode is for the most part dominated by the teacher. Ms James controls the floor – speaking when she desires and nominating the other speakers. She specifies the topic, and decides when to move on to the next question. If you highlight all her turns on the transcript you will see that she speaks most of the time (67 out of 114 lines of transcript, close to 60 per cent), that her contributions are longer and more elaborate and that she speaks after almost every pupil contribution, which suggests that most pupil talk is mediated by her.

However, while this counting of lines gives a rough indication of who speaks how often, it conceals a more complicated story. So, while the episode does display some traditional classroom discourse features, which are commonly characterized as 'monologic',[6] it also diverges from conventional structures in significant ways. A number of pupils do offer extended responses – longer, at least, than the 1–2 words typical in whole-class discussion – for example in lines 44–9, 65–70, and 103–5. Pupils participate in the discussion outside of the accepted 'Response' slot in the Initiation–Response–Evaluation (IRE) structure: for example, Vanessa follows on from Brian's response (lines 65–70); Julie repeatedly interjects, 'because they were with Lucy' during Ms James' turns; and Deborah challenges, 'Yeah, what about Edmund?' after Ms James appears to have concluded the topic (line 100). Significantly, Ms James does not communicate displeasure at such unorthodox pupil participation, suggesting that classroom norms permit such spontaneous, uninvited – yet topically relevant – pupil contributions.

Likewise, Ms James also deviates from IRE conventions: her questions tend to be more authentically open than is typical in IRE (the question with which she opened the episode is a prime example), and her use of the feedback move is more probing and challenging than strictly evaluative as right or wrong.

So, overall, while the distribution of talk in the episode is not radically different from what has been observed in traditional classroom discourse structures, it appears that the episode features some novel interactional moves. Do these differences make a difference for pupil voice, knowledge, thinking or relationships? We turn to these dimensions next.

Interplay of voices

Readers will recall that one of the main criticisms of traditional classroom talk is the dominance of the teacher's voice: not just with regard to the length of time or number of turns at talk during which the teacher can be heard physically speaking, but – more crucially – the dynamic whereby pupils attempt to replicate in their own contributions the voices of the teacher or textbook. We can see an example of this dynamic at the beginning of the episode: in lines 4–12 Ms James asks the pupils in the group that wrestled with the wardrobe question to tell the rest of the class what she (the teacher) meant. However, after establishing the meaning of the question, and further explicating it through an example from the novel (again, with a pupil providing the detail she had in mind), Ms James opened the discussion up to a lively and relatively unconstrained exchange of ideas. In the ensuing discussion multiple voices were brought to bear on the topic, with four pupils and Ms James contributing conjectures about why the gateway to Narnia was sometimes open and sometimes not, and another three pupils and Ms James responding to those conjectures. We have mapped out these conjectures and the ways in which they were contested, elaborated, supported, refuted and/or ignored, in Figure 4.1.

The figure demonstrates the myriad ways in which participants address one another's ideas. For the most part, each utterance takes seriously and builds upon the preceding utterance as voices join together to create new ideas. Conjectures #3 and #5, for example, appear to emerge out of ideas that immediately preceded them. In the case of conjecture #3, Sean's idea that the wardrobe only lets in certain people expands the preceding conjecture, according to which the wardrobe only lets in good people, to include the anomalous case of Edmund (whose goodness was debatable). Similarly, conjecture #5 (the wardrobe lets in people who are accompanied by someone who believes in Narnia) is an attempt to reconcile conjecture #4 (the wardrobe lets in people who believe in Narnia) with the contradictory evidence (it let in Susan and Peter, who didn't believe).

It is worth noting, however, exceptions to these generalizations. Most importantly, it is not entirely clear to us whether Ms James' question, 'Do you think the wardrobe only lets in good people?' (lines 51–2) is a probe of Ben's conjecture that the wardrobe only opened at certain times or an attempt to replace it with a different idea (hence the broken arrow connecting conjectures #1 and #2). Either way, Ben's contribution fell out of the

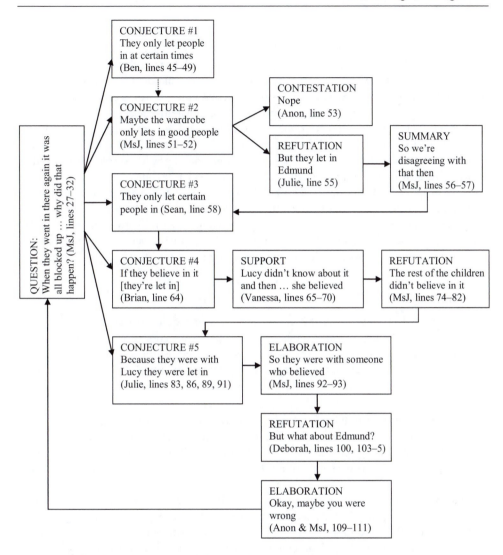

Figure 4.1 Schematic structure of the episode argumentation.

conversation, which subsequently focused on the possibility that the wardrobe only opened for certain people.

We wouldn't want to argue that such an intervention was 'wrong' or non-dialogic. There may have been excellent reasons for not directly addressing Ben's conjecture. Perhaps Ms James wanted to steer the conversation toward issues of characters' goodness and/or faith, which relate to key themes in the novel. Or perhaps she wanted to support Ben by not directly challenging his idea. While neither of these possibilities strikes us as necessarily better than addressing Ben's suggestion more directly, note that in principle both are legitimate, dialogic moves. In the terms used by Alexander in his *dialogic teaching* principles, the former alternative prioritizes the purposive criterion over the cumulative, while the latter one prioritizes the supportive criterion. Dilemmas, not deficits (see Chapter 2, pp. 23–24).

Critique

Participants display in the episode a critical stance toward knowledge, as expected in dialogue as critique, in at least four ways. First, the question discussed is authentically open in the sense that, based on Ms James' responses to pupil contributions, she does not appear to have a definitive answer in mind. Indeed, and this is the second point, it would seem that the question is also open in the sense that it does not allow for a definitive answer – it is *in principle* unknowable.[7] Thus, the class do not resolve the problem, and Ms James concludes the discussion by saying that they need to think and discuss further. Third, while Ms James plays a central role in managing the interaction, she does not assume a privileged role with regard to knowing the answer to the question she has posed. She offers a conjecture (in the form of a question, in lines 51–2), but then backs off of this five lines later when presented with evidence refuting it. Likewise, as we noted in the introduction to this chapter, she respectfully disagrees with Brian, as a peer, rather than evaluating his comment in an authoritative, teacherly manner (lines 71–82). Fourth, as noted above, multiple pupil and teacher perspectives are voiced in the extract, and the participants critically engage with most of the ideas brought forward.

Thinking together

As demonstrated in Figure 4.1, the underlying logic of inquiry in the episode is that of conjectures and refutations. Participants offer possible explanations for how the wardrobe portal to Narnia operates – that is, rules regarding when and/or for whom it opens – which other participants then test on the basis of examples from the novel. Consider the episode in light of the following characterization of *exploratory talk*:

> [P]artners engage critically but constructively with each other's ideas. Relevant information is offered for joint consideration. Proposals may be challenged and counter-challenged, but if so reasons are given and alternatives are offered. Agreement is sought as a basis for joint progress. Knowledge is made publicly accountable and reasoning is visible in the talk.[8]

Engagement is critical – participants test one another's ideas – and constructive: they offer supporting evidence, elaborations and suggestions for how to improve ideas in light of the problems raised. Relevant information and justifications are offered for every position taken. Ms James models the seeking of agreement (for example, 'so what do we think about that now?' on line 107) and gives a public account of joint progress (for example, 'so we're not saying it – we're disagreeing with that then' on lines 56–7).

Relationships

While it is difficult to comment on relationships, which take shape over long durations, on the basis of a short segment, we offer the following tentative remarks about dialogic relations in the episode (which draw also on other recordings and observations of this class). First, as noted above, we find the respectful way in which Ms James disagrees with Brian significant. She poses her ideas as a question and offers Brian the opportunity to respond to her refutation with 'what do you think about that?' (line 88). The playful spirit in which Ms James asks for permission to disagree and voices her criticism seems to encourage the pupils themselves to question and constructively disagree with ideas that arise during the discussion.

Deborah, for instance, appears at first to agree with conjecture #5 (line 96), but after giving it further thought engages more critically: 'But what about Edmund?'

Second, consider how Ms James attempts to cultivate a supportive, inclusive classroom environment by drawing in pupils, such as Sean (line 36), who are normally on the periphery of classroom discussion. This exchange merits closer attention. Ms James opens the discussion by asking the relevant group to share their response to the question they have been working on (line 33). As she nominates 'this group' she turns to face Ben. Ben is a member of the group that was tasked with answering this question, but he is not the only member; Deborah to his right, and Sean and Rob, who are sitting in front of him, were also part of the group. Based on teacher targets and our observations, we know that Ben is perceived to be an able pupil who often participates positively in class discussions, while Sean and Rob, who are seated at the front row of desks directly in front of the teacher, are viewed as lower ability. Even though Ms James verbally addresses the question to the whole group ('this group', line 33), her body language suggests that she expects the answer to come from Ben, the higher ability pupil. Ben acts as if the role of group spokesperson has been allocated to him, and begins to formulate his response, buying time with the filler 'erm' (line 35), but in doing so, he overlaps Sean who also begins what sounds like an answer ('becau:s:e', line 34). At this point Ms James stops Ben's utterance rather abruptly and offers the floor to Sean ('right Sean was just about to say something then'). Three seconds of silence follows, after which Sean replies, 'I don't know.' Ms James softens this admission by reformulating 'I don't know' as 'You're not sure' – it is not lack of knowledge but lack of certainty – and thereby protecting Sean's 'face' in front of the other pupils. She also keeps alive the possibility that he will be able to participate later: 'maybe you can add something in a moment', which indeed he does (in line 58). Rob has now raised his hand, but Ms James reverts back to Ben, who can usually be relied upon to give an answer that will move the discussion forward. How to draw in a typically quiet or disengaged pupil is complicated, since teachers' attempts to be inclusive can be experienced otherwise by pupils, and the teacher can inadvertently reinforce problematic classroom identities such as 'low ability' or 'disengaged'. Again, here we can see the emergence of the initial contours of dilemmas, between inclusion and protection, and between moving the discussion forward quickly and widening participation (see Chapter 8 for a detailed discussion of these and related issues).

In this section we have interrogated the episode according to the key questions raised by five different approaches to dialogue: dialogue as interactional form, as interplay of voices, as critique, as thinking together and as relationship. We have focused in particular on ways in which we find the episode to be relatively dialogic, though also pointing out less dialogic aspects or moments. We further highlighted some of the dilemmas the different approaches to dialogue raise for the participants, dilemmas that arise from conflicting dialogic imperatives, such as enabling and addressing voices, moving the lesson in the direction of meaningful problems and knowledge, caring for and supporting individual pupils and challenging claims.

To what factors can this breakthrough to dialogue be attributed?

We noted above that the issue discussed in this episode was one of four questions reviewed by the class in their concluding plenary discussion. Compared to the discussions of the other three questions, this episode stood out as particularly dialogic. In this section we discuss possible reasons for this relative breakthrough to dialogue.

First, since the comparison to the other parts of the plenary is instructive, we describe in a bit more detail the preceding discussion, of whether or not Aslan is a coward. A full transcript of this exchange can be found on the accompanying website, www.routledge.com/cw/lefstein, and readers may find it helpful to read it alongside our description.[9] Ms James introduced the question thus: '"Aslan is a coward", I said. "Do you agree or disagree? Give a reason for your choice." I'm going to that group first of all, and they're going to give us their opinion. But if you want to say anything – if you disagree or agree with them – you can also put your hand up and say something as well.'

The group representative reports that they decided that Aslan is brave, because he risked his life to save Edmund.

Ms James then checks five times that all agree (in lines 36, 39, 41–2, 50, 52):

```
36   Ms James:   do we agree with that
37   Pupils:     yeah
38   Ms James:   OK
39               do you think he is a coward
40   Pupils:     no
41   Ms James:   can we ever at any point say
42               that Aslan is a coward
43   Pupils:     no ((in unison))
44   Ms James:   who said yes
45               (2)
46   Sam?:       ((raises finger to slightly above the level of his head
47               - Ms James is looking the other way))
48   Ms James:   no I thought someone said yes
49               no one said yes
50               so we all agree that he's not a coward
51               OK
52               everyone in that group agree with that (.)
53               anything else you want to add to that
54               (3)
55               no
56               Sam did you have something else to say
57               no
58               OK
59               being a bit shy at the moment
```

It is not surprising, after this string of emphatic checks, that everyone acknowledges the 'correct' answer, and that no one adds any further comments when Ms James offers them the opportunity at the end of the segment (line 53). What is surprising, or at least interesting, is that Ms James both encourages disagreement – note the way she framed the question ('"Aslan is a coward", I said. Do you agree or disagree?') and her instructions to the class '… if you disagree or agree with [the group]') – and also makes it abundantly clear what the correct answer is ('Can we ever at any point say that Aslan is a coward?', and 'so we all agree …').[10] She appears to be sending mixed messages, but the specific message, that Aslan is not a coward and we cannot say that at any point, is stronger than the message encouraging disagreement in general. This may explain why Sam, who appears to hold a contrary view, is not forthcoming with his critique of the class consensus. Perhaps, after initially raising his hand, albeit timidly, he has come to interpret Ms James' 'Who said yes?' (line 44) as more of an inquisition than an invitation.

Immediately after this discussion of Aslan's (lack of) cowardice the class moved on to the question of why the wardrobe was sometimes closed (the episode analysed above). The differences between the discussions of the two questions are striking. In the 'Is Aslan a coward?' segment only one view is espoused, it is accepted by all without comment, and it would appear that the teacher's primary role is to confirm general agreement. In contrast, in the episode discussed above we heard multiple and contradictory views, all challenged and refuted, and the teacher both volunteered interpretations and disagreed with pupil interpretations.

We cannot know for certain why each segment developed in the way it did, nor do we assume that the complexity and unpredictability of classroom interaction can be explained by a limited number of factors. Nevertheless, we can surmise about a few differences between the segments that appear to be consequential here.

First, the questions posed could not be more different. The first question is a classic 'closed' or 'test' question, while the second is an 'open' or 'authentic' question, to which the questioner does not already have an answer in mind.[11] One would be hard-pressed to argue that Aslan is a coward. As the pupils point out, he sacrifices his own life for Edmund. In the chapter the class have just read, C.S. Lewis explicitly characterizes him as brave (in the eyes of Lucy), and contrasts his behaviour with that of his tormentors, whom Susan calls cowards.[12] And of course, lions are a common symbol of bravery.[13] On the other hand, we really have no idea why it is that sometimes the wardrobe functioned as a portal for Narnia and sometimes it did not; it appears that this is one of the unknowable mysteries of Narnia.[14]

The differences between the questions lead to very different roles for the teacher. With regard to the closed question, Ms James appears to be primarily concerned with making sure that everyone is on board with the correct interpretation. On the other hand, she adopts a much more adventurous and exploratory stance for dealing with the open question. However, we do not want to get carried away with this interpretation. While it is logically compelling to assume that teacher and pupil behaviour are adapted to lesson content, we have observed many instances of pupils treating apparently 'authentic' questions as closed, or *vice versa*. Nystrand and colleagues explain:

> [I]t was the *context* of each class session, built by the interactions – the classroom culture the teachers established, by giving instructions, implicitly or explicitly setting goals for the class and generally leading by example – that determined the authenticity of the teacher's questions in students' eyes. An 'authentic' teacher question would not necessarily foster student dialogue, if the teacher's rigid question–answer format suggested that interpretive student responses were not actually welcome. Conversely, an apparently inauthentic question posed during a two-way discussion about the meaning of a poem could become a genuine stepping stone to discussion if the teacher was perceived to be genuinely interested in students' interpretations.[15]

Nystrand directs our attention to the ways in which the teacher 'leads by example', and indeed in the episode we have seen a number of ways in which Ms James' responses modelled dialogic stances and behaviours: her openness to having her conjecture challenged, and the speed

---

Box 4.1 Key issues raised by teachers in the reflection meeting

1. Throwing a curveball.

I think the teacher is leading the children into an incorrect opinion, with the intention of developing the discussion, throwing in the odd curveball type thing. And ... all the kids [are saying], 'yeah, yeah', okay, they all believe – agree with the teacher. And then you've got one child who suddenly realizes there's a flaw in it, and then goes on to express this to the rest of the class, and they all agree.

2. Modelling disagreement.

You get really good examples of the teacher demonstrating how to disagree with someone, and doing it in a dignified way. So you're not taking away their self-respect, you're just disagreeing with their viewpoint. And then you get a pupil at line 100 disagreeing, saying, 'ah, but what about Edmund?' and realizing that there's a problem with the theory that the class are going along with. So, the teacher's already laid the groundwork that it's okay to disagree, but you need to explain why you're disagreeing, without saying it in so many words, and it's made wide open for another pupil to disagree, which I think is really good.

3. The importance of small group discussions.

I just generally thought the lesson, in terms of other lessons, they got a bit more out of this. They've actually – they're talking a bit more. I think the group work beforehand really helped them, they brought their ideas together there and, then, they knew what they were saying. (Comment from Ms James herself.)

---

with which she backed down from a position that had been refuted, her playful and respectful disagreement with Brian, and her general curiosity about Narnia.

The Abbeyford teachers remarked favourably on Ms James' modelling of disagreement when they briefly discussed this episode (see Box 4.1). One teacher also commended what he called 'throwing a curveball' – that is, leading the pupils down a wrong path in order for them to discover the flaws themselves. Flawed or otherwise problematic ideas are often more constructive in teaching than correct answers. By not rushing to correct problematic interpretations Ms James conferred responsibility for thinking on the rest of the class. This choice cuts through to the heart of what differentiates the episode from more traditional classroom discourse: whereas in IRE-structured recitation the teacher does most of the thinking, in the episode she shares both cognitive burden and opportunities with the pupils, many of whom readily rise to the occasion.

Conclusion

We have used this episode primarily as an opportunity to illustrate how we can use some of the approaches to dialogic pedagogy discussed in Chapter 2 as tools for interrogating a brief strip of classroom interaction. We explored dialogue as interactional form, interplay of voices, critique, thinking together and relationship. We hope that we have managed to bring these approaches to life, and to persuade you of their relevance to actual classroom practice. We hope we've also impressed upon you some of their limitations: inasmuch as they raise problems and dilemmas, rather than offering clear-cut solutions as to how teachers should act in any given situation.

Finally, we hope that we've shown that the question we posed in the chapter title – 'The question of whether or not practice counts as dialogue is something of a "curveball" question.'

The episode is in many respects dialogic, but also includes features that we would consider to be less dialogic. But we might even consider those less dialogic features to be more dialogic if we change our perspective a bit, for example by thinking about dialogue as a relationship rather than critique (or *vice versa*). Nevertheless, we would argue that the process of thinking through in what ways an episode is more or less dialogic is productive – that is, it makes us smarter about dialogic pedagogy, even if ultimately we cannot count the features and compute a dialogic 'score'.

This episode is the only one we analyse by systematically interrogating the different approaches to dialogue and the key questions they raise. We invite you to continue to play with these tools in the other episodes, even as we introduce you to new concepts and complications.

Issues for further discussion

Following analysis of the episode, readers might want to consider the following issues:

- What do you think of our analysis? What points resonate with your own interpretations of what's happening? What points seem problematic to you?
- Try analysing the episode according to the criteria or principles of one or more of the educational models of dialogue discussed in Chapter 2. For example, to what extent does it adhere to the five principles of *dialogic teaching* and/or three criteria of *accountable talk* (see pp. 22–24)?
- What do you think about the way Ms James concludes the conversation? Where might further discussion at a later date, benefiting from more time, eventually lead?
- If we're correct that there actually is no satisfactory interpretation to the problem raised – the opening of the portal is one of the mysteries of Narnia, in principle unknowable – what are the advantages and disadvantages of such an issue as a topic for class discussion?
- What questions do you typically pose after reading literature? In what ways are they authentic or closed? What sort of interpretations and discussions do they invite?

COMMENTARY

THINKING COLLECTIVELY, BACKED BY EVIDENCE
BY DAVID REEDY

This is a fascinating episode of classroom talk, and one that is an interesting contrast with the discourse which immediately precedes it.

My initial reaction to any episode of classroom talk is to ask, Is it effective? My criterion for judging effectiveness is to question whether some intended learning has taken place. Evidence for this should be found in the participants' utterances, in the overall effect of the conversation and in apparent changes to participants' thinking.

The trajectory of this episode shows clear evidence of changes in thinking. The children examine a number of hypotheses as to why Narnia cannot be entered consistently through the wardrobe: it only lets good people in (line 51), it only lets certain people in (line 58) and it only lets people in who believe in Narnia (line 64).

Each hypothesis is considered and then rejected as events in the story are cited. No definitive conclusion is reached but options have been explored and pupil's initial thinking changed. The children now know that they need to think and develop their ideas further in order to come to a satisfactory explanation.

This episode is effective pedagogically on account of specific choices the teacher makes at the beginning and throughout the conversation.

First, the question the children are asked to consider is open-ended and invites speculation and debate. It is clear that Ms James, through her responses, doesn't have a definitive answer to this question herself. Ms James' not having a clear view of her own serves to shift the balance of responsibility in this classroom onto a more equal footing. Pupils' thinking can be explored and is of worth rather than simply being judged on its proximity to the teacher's pre-formulated right answer. This does not mean that Ms James cannot challenge and move thinking forward. She does (lines 71–82, for example), but in a way that does not undermine the ethos that runs through this episode of collective endeavour ('*Do you mind if I disagree with you, Brian?*). These challenges, rooted in the pupils' preceding utterances, are crucial in prompting more focused and supported contributions from them. A classroom's ethos is created almost solely through such conversations.

This ethos of collective thinking is evidenced again at lines 98 onwards. Ms James says 'okay' and shrugs her shoulders, indicating that this particular sequence has come to an end. However Deborah feels quite enabled to interrupt with a further comment (line 100) '*Yeah but what about Edmund?*. This interruption is accepted with equanimity by the teacher and class. Disagreement backed up by evidence is clearly welcomed.

The episode's ending leaves me rather unsatisfied, without an indication of what to do now with this question. It's inconclusive. The teacher indicates they could discuss at a later stage, but when will that be and how will they remember? Perhaps a suggestion that the class will reconsider the question once they have finished reading the text, with the question written up on the wall (and added to others where an agreed conclusion has not been reached) with any further hypotheses considered if they arise.

Finally this episode demonstrates that a lesson cannot be dialogic at every turn. The discourse moves in and out of a range of forms: discussion, recitation, as well as dialogue in this case. Any collaborative developmental work in this area will be undermined by not acknowledging the complexity of classroom conversations between teachers and pupils.

David Reedy is Principal Adviser for primary schools in the London Borough of Barking and Dagenham and current General Secretary of the United Kingdom Literacy Association (UKLA). He is a former Visiting Fellow at the Institute of Education, University of London.

COMMENTARY

ART OF EDUCATION: BALANCING DIRECTION AND DIALOGUE
BY JAMES CRESSWELL

Friedrich von Schiller wrote about education: 'Utility is the great idol of the time, to which all powers do homage and all subjects are subservient. In this great balance of utility, the spiritual service of art has no weight' (2009: 4). He argued that thinking about education in terms of its utility – what we can get from it – misses its potential. For example, a utilitarian approach to education involves memorizing and regurgitating answers in order to get a grade that allows one to pass to the next level. This approach treats education as a means to an end such that personal experience and growth is bypassed in favour of the utility of educational credentials. Education can also be understood in terms of art insofar as it can involve personal experience and personal growth for its own sake rather than what it gets us. Education, just like great art, has the potential to engage people personally and help them develop as human beings. This understanding makes room for personal experience and exploration. The authors illuminate how Ms James makes such room by creating a space for dialogue. The class discussion is about discovery and engaging the material for its own sake, rather than utilitarian questioning focused on the 'correct' answer. The chapter is important because it moves us away from utility towards an artistic understanding of education.

The authors highlight that this artistic approach to education is tied to the way that the teacher empowers students by putting them on a more equal footing. In so doing, however, they downplay something important. George Steiner (2003) proposes that good teaching involves direction of students, in addition to their empowerment. Ms James' artistry can be seen in her balance between enabling a dialogical space and directing the classroom towards educational goals. The authors note that Ms James 'controls the floor', and this control can be seen in her use of voice and body to maintain a grasp on the pupils. At points in the video (e.g. lines 109–11), she raises her voice and moves toward disruptive students as the class becomes disorganized. She controls the class to keep it focussed on the topic at hand. Focussing the discussion and keeping 'control of the floor' narrows students' experience to the text and focuses their reflection. Consider also how a student is given the most power when Ms James disagrees with him as a peer (lines 71 and following). I am guessing that he is a strong student who is most like her insofar as he is able to contribute to focussed discussion and so fall in line with Ms James' educational focus. Granting him peer status is a way of acknowledging his growth towards becoming, like her, an educated adult, and a way of tacitly directing the rest of the class to emulate him. In sum, good teaching is seen in the way that Ms James artfully avoids a utilitarian mode through empowering the classroom while simultaneously focussing the classroom experience to make exploration most effective.

James Cresswell is Assistant Professor of Psychology at Booth University College, Winnipeg, Canada. He is interested in cultural psychology and how philosophers focusing on dialogue (e.g. Mikhail Bakhtin) can contribute to this field.

Notes

1 Parts of this chapter appeared in Lefstein and Snell (2011a).
2 Compare this metaphor with Nystrand *et al.* (2003: 190): 'Here we can see that, metaphorically, getting a discussion going is a little like building a fire: With enough kindling of the right sort, accompanied by patience, and along with the spark of student engagement, ignition is possible, though perhaps not on teachers' first or second try'.
3 This initial indecision about who will represent the group is discussed below, and also in Lefstein and Snell (2011a: 180–183).
4 The file includes transcripts of both the focal episode and a supplementary transcript (discussed on pp. 48–49) of the exchange immediately preceding it.
5 See in particular pp. 14–19. We do not address the political dimension (dialogue as empowerment) due to its limited relevance to this particular episode.
6 See discussion of the Initiation–Response–Evaluation format in Chapter 2, pp. 21.
7 On this sense of openness, see Harpaz and Lefstein (2000).
8 Mercer (2000: 98).
9 This supplementary transcript appears below the 'Episode 1. Getting into Narnia' transcript. Unfortunately we do not have a video recording of this segment since it took place while we changed video cassettes in the camera (the transcript was completed on the basis of the backup audio recording).
10 Another possible interpretation here is that Ms James keeps checking for disagreement because she's actually desperate for someone to disagree and thus open up discussion. While this is of course a possibility – we make no claims about what her intentions are here – the way the questions are worded seems to leave little doubt about her own position. Consider, the difference between her 'Can we ever at any point say that Aslan is a coward?' and, for example, a more searching formulation like 'Is there no point at which Aslan seems cowardly to you?'.
11 Test question and authentic question are Nystrand and colleagues' (1997) terms (see Chapter 2).
12 Lewis & Baynes (1988: 139–40).
13 See, e.g., Westfahl (2005: 475).
14 There's another way of interpreting the question, as a question about the author's purposes. For example, one might argue that the wardrobe's apparent inconsistency served Lewis' purposes, by creating mystery, and also by making Lucy appear to be crazy or a liar and thereby complicating her relationship with her older siblings. But such an interpretation sidesteps the actual question that was posed (about the rules governing the magical world of Narnia), and shifts the reading from the perspective of its children-heroes to a more adult literary analysis. This would be a legitimate line of inquiry, of course, but not necessarily as interesting to the pupils at this point in their reading of the story.
15 Nystrand *et al.* (1997: 84). See also Lefstein (2008a) for an extended example of pupils closing down teacher open questions.

Chapter 5

Responding to a pupil challenge

EPISODE 2: 'I DON'T REALLY LIKE THAT, MISS'

Ms Leigh is teaching the second of a series of lessons on writing short stories. She has just demonstrated to the class the lesson's key idea and objective – to open their stories by dropping the reader right into the action – and begins to set them the task of working in pairs to act out the opening to their own story in order to get ideas about how to improve it. Before she finishes her instructions, however, she is interrupted by an interjection from William: 'Miss, I don't really like that. I-I sort of like a bit of talk before it'. This kind of pupil challenge is relatively rare, both at Abbeyford Primary and in UK schooling more generally. In this chapter we explore how this spontaneous pupil contribution and the teacher's response to it ignited a 'dialogic spell'. We analyse in detail the interaction that followed William's challenge and use this analysis to explore the conditions that facilitate dialogue as well as the dilemmas inherent to this mode of classroom participation and learning.

Setting the scene

The lesson

Our focal episode is drawn from an extended lesson on story openers, which took place in Ms Leigh's Year 5 classroom on 7 January 2009. The literacy lesson extended over two slots in the school timetable (10.00–10.45, 11.00–12.00) in order to allow time both for drama activities (designed to help the children come up with interesting story openers) and related writing.[1] It was the second of a series of lessons on story writing that had begun the day before (Chapter 6 deals with a later lesson in this sequence, when the pupils have finished the first drafts of their stories).

The extended lesson can be broken down into eight key sections:

1. *Recap of previous lesson and introduction of new task* (15 minutes): The teacher and pupils reorganize the classroom, with the desks drawn to the edges of the room, in order to make space for a circle of chairs. The pupils and teacher sit in this circle, each pupil holding a page containing the story plan they prepared the day before. Ms Leigh recaps the previous lesson, in which they had looked at images depicting different types of weather in order to generate ideas for a short story called 'The Storm'. She tells the class that their task today is to act out the plot for their stories. Ms Leigh reminds them what a good plot looks like by referring to a visual aid, which likens a plot to climbing

a mountain: the story builds up to the main problem or dilemma and then down again to the resolution and ending.[2]

2.   *Group drama work* (20 minutes): Ms Leigh assigns the pupils to groups to work on turning their story ideas into dramatic performances. Each group goes to a different location around the school (e.g. library, school hall). Ms Leigh supervises the children in her and the neighbouring classroom, while Ms Forester, a Learning Support Assistant, works with the children in the school hall and one of the researchers works with the children in the library.

3.   *Evaluation of drama work* (6 minutes): The children return to the classroom and take up their places in the circle. Ms Leigh facilitates a discussion of how the drama work has helped pupils to organize their ideas and add more detail. She selects one pupil to explain how the drama has helped him to develop his story, and then demonstrates how this pupil's story has been transformed from a 'story mole hill' to a 'story mountain'.

4.   *Introducing a new task on constructing an opening sentence* (10 minutes): After the morning break, the pupils once again sit in the circle and Ms Leigh explains that they will now use drama to construct an effective opening sentence for their stories. Each of the pupils must write an opening sentence and then act it out for their partner. Based on their partner's feedback, they should modify their opening sentence to make it more interesting and exciting. Ms Leigh models the process using two pupil-actors. For Ms Leigh an effective story opening is one in which 'we drop ourselves right in the action to start off with and we have some speech there as well'. One pupil, William, challenges this idea, however, saying that he prefers to begin with the narrator's voice. Ms Leigh deviates from her lesson plan to explore his point of view. This is the segment we focus on in this chapter.

5.   *Paired drama activity* (17 minutes): Pupils go back to their drama spaces inside and outside of the classroom and work together to act out the openings to their stories.

6.   *Review of work* (4 minutes): The children return to the classroom and the space is reorganized such that they can sit at their usual desks. Ms Leigh recaps what they have done so far and shares with the pupils a couple of examples from the story openings she had heard in the groups she was working with. She says that these are good but challenges the pupils to make them more exciting.

7.   *Writing* (10 minutes): The children work individually to (re)write their own story openings.

8.   *Plenary* (8 minutes): Several pupils read out their story opener and receive feedback from Ms Leigh and other pupils.

The episode

In this chapter we examine closely Section 4, focusing in particular on the unintended (by Ms Leigh) discussion of the merits of 'dropping the reader right into the action' versus using the narrator's voice to open a story. Before exploring this episode in detail, we summarize it briefly. As for the preceding chapters, the accompanying website, www.routledge.com/cw/lefstein includes a video recording and full transcript of this episode. The episode can be roughly broken up into five main stages:

1. An effective story opener (lines 1–64)

The extract begins with Ms Leigh using two pupil-actors, Rachel and Terry, to demonstrate what an effective story opening might look like. At Ms Leigh's request, they go into the middle of the circle. Ms Leigh tells the class: 'Terry is going to be the narrator, and whatever Terry says, Rachel must act out'. Ms Leigh whispers something (an opening sentence) into Terry's ear and then he repeats it out loud. This first sentence is unexciting ('I was walking down the road one day') and thus elicits lacklustre actions from Rachel. Ms Leigh whispers another sentence to Terry: ('"Oh no it's a tornado" she shouted and ran') which he again repeats. Rachel acts act out this sentence more dynamically. Ms Leigh points out to the pupils that this opening is more effective because 'we drop ourselves *right* in the action to start off with and we have some speech there as well'. One pupil, William, then challenges this method of opening a story:

```
33 William:   miss I don't really like (.) that
34            I- I sort of like
35            a bit of talk before it
36 Ms Leigh:  well it depends on how you want to start your story
37            doesn't it
38 William:   ((nodding)) (yeah)
39 Ms Leigh:  so you could have-
40            you mean talk as the narrator
41            or talk as the actors
42 William:   no the narrator
```

2. An alternative story opener (lines 65–122)

Ms Leigh asks William what he would do instead to start his story. She says that she's heard Ms Forester (the class Learning Support Assistant) and Terry talking about how they're *not* going to start their story and raises the challenge of whether William plans to begin his story in this way:

```
65 Ms Leigh: what would you use to start off with-
66           your story then William
67 William:  e::r
68           ((turns around to get his story from the desk behind))
69 Harry     ((raises his hand enthusiastically))
70 Ms Leigh: because I've just overheard Ms Forester and Terry
71           having a conversation (.)
72           about how they're not going to start their story
73           let's see if he does it ((gestures to William))
74 William:  erm (.)
75           I wouldn't start it like
76           drop it straight in the action with
77           the first line
78 Mary      ((raises hand))
79 William:  as speech
80 Ms Leigh: okay
81 William:  and that
82           I would
83           have a bit of narrator talk
84           to tell you what's going on
85           and the characte:rs a:nd
86           where you are and that
87           and then get into the action
```

```
88 Ms Leigh: so you'd start off at the bottom of the story mountain
89           with the narrator directing the action
90           give me an example
91           of what you'd start off for your [story today then
92 Mary                                      [((puts arm down))
93 William:  ((looking down at paper)) erm
94           (4)
95           loads of people think nothing's going to happen
96           as they go into a tunnel
```

To counter the challenge William has made and provide a contrast to the story opener he
has offered (on lines 95–6), Ms Leigh draws upon a published novel that happens to be on her
desk (which is just behind where she is sitting). She reads out the dramatic beginning to this
story, which demonstrates her preferred method of opening a story (i.e. of 'dropping the
reader into the action'): 'Tal stretched out his hand and pulled himself up onto the next out-
thrust spike of tower'.[3] By using this book, Ms Leigh demonstrates how much more exciting
it is to begin a story right in the middle of the action (compare William's 'loads of people think
nothing's going to happen as they go into a tunnel'). William sticks to his original challenge,
however, by suggesting that sometimes books begin with 'a little paragraph before' the main
opening (lines 108–9). Another pupil, Harry, calls this 'a prologue'[4] (line 116). It isn't entirely
clear how William's point relates to the opening of the novel from which Ms Leigh has just
read, or to his earlier challenge, but Ms Leigh finds a way to make it relevant to the ongoing
discussion: 'so that [a prologue] would help *you* to have your narrator voice'.

3. 'I really want to know what happens next' (lines 123–161)

Ms Leigh then encourages Ms Forester (who is sitting next to Ms Leigh) to contribute to
the discussion: 'I just want to go back to what your conversation – because you're getting
a bit twitchy here Ms Forester. Why are you twitching?'. Ms Forester is 'twitching' because
her interest has been piqued in the novel after hearing the sentence that Ms Leigh has
read out. She tells Ms Leigh and the class, 'I really want to know what happens next'.
When asked by Ms Leigh to compare this reaction with her response to William's story
opener, it is clear that she is much less enthusiastic about William's story:

```
143   Ms Leigh:    [what did you want to know from William's story
144                [((William signals towards Harry? Harry takes his
145                  hand down))
146                (2)
147   Ms Forester: I can't even remember what his-
148                what was the beginning William
149                tell me [again
150   William:            [erm
151                many people go to a tunnel
152                thinking nothing's going to happen
153                ((Harry raises his hand))
154   Flynn:       [well yeah because you want to know what's (xxxxx)
155   Ms Forester: [well that happens every day
156                [I go into a tunnel thinking nothing's going to happen
```

```
157  Harry:        [((Raises hand))
158  William:      but then
159  Ms Forester:  that's quite normal
160  William:      but then (.) and then
161  Ms Forester:  hmmm
```

4. Dramatic narration (lines 162–185)

Building upon Ms Forester's response, Ms Leigh demonstrates how William could develop his idea to open his story with the narrator's voice by adding a hint that something is about to go wrong in the tunnel:

```
162  Ms Leigh:  so what we need to do is see if we can develop that
163             [a little bit more
164  Flynn:     [or xxxxxxxxxxxxxxx)
165  Ms Leigh:  well we could maybe have a hint from the narrator
166             earlier that there might have been something
167             that had go-
168             you know
169             ((dramatically)) the tunnel had recently been repaired
170             from the tragic accident that had killed
171             a bus load full of school children
172             (1)
173             as usual William and his father
174             went through thinking
175             nothing was going to go wrong
176             ((normal voice)) and then you've got a hint that oh
177             there's already an accident
```

5. Introduction of another text (lines 186–307)

After her dramatic reformulation of William's opening, Ms Leigh invites Harry to contribute to the discussion (he has raised his hand persistently throughout the episode and is sitting directly opposite Ms Leigh, in her line of vision). Harry introduces another text, *Necropolis*, into the debate.[5] This is a book that Harry had read outside of school and loved so much that he lent a copy to Ms Leigh, who had then also enjoyed reading it. Harry seems to suggest that Ms Leigh's reformulation of William's story is like a scene from *Necropolis*, in which the lead protagonist is almost run over by a 'massive van'. Harry does not specify in what ways these two texts are similar – perhaps the comparison is due only to the fact that both include a road accident – but Ms Leigh works with his comments in order, again, to reinforce the point that the author is giving the reader just a hint of danger, and then applies this point to William's story:

```
196  Ms Leigh:  so
197             we've got a hint then that something's going to go wrong
198             it's just a usual day for her
199             so for William's
200             he might need to open hi-
201             open his story with
```

```
202                    erm-
203                    it was a usual day-
204                    it was a day like any other
205    Harry:          but-
206    Ms Leigh:       Jonathan and his father [were driving through
207    Harry:                                  [((raises his hand))
208    Ms Leigh:       the Euro tunnel
209                    heading for France
210                    they were unaware that disaster was about to strike
211                    and that's where you can use the ellipsis that you like
212                    dot dot dot
213    William:        ((nods))
214    Ms Leigh:       because that's where you're leading the reader
215                    into thinking
216                    disaster what could it be
217                    will they crash
218                    will there be a fire
219                    will they be drowned in the tunnel
220                    what's going to happen
221                    ((signals to Harry))
```

At first Harry does not understand what Ms Leigh is getting at: 'Miss but when it says it, nothing does go wrong, a man saves her' (lines 223–6). Ms Leigh elaborates, demonstrating how the author is building up 'the suspense and the interest in the story' (line 305–306).

6. *Another attempt at beginning the task is thwarted* (308–37)

After further interaction between Harry and Ms Leigh related to *Necropolis*, Ms Leigh attempts to bring the discussion to a close so that pupils can get on with their task: 'right, I'm actually going to stop you there because otherwise we're not going to have time' (lines 308–9). But William poses another challenge: 'well something sort of goes wrong in that the truck's about to hit her' (lines 321–2). This prompts Ms Leigh to give further clarification of what 'suspense' means:

```
321    William:        well something sort of goes wrong
322                    in that the truck's about to hit her
323    Ms Leigh:       does it actually go wrong
324    William:        s- sort of
325    Ms Leigh:       okay and is that a hint of danger
326                    that's what I mean by suspense
327                    it's a bit like
328                    you know if I stand behind you
329                    and you're talking and doing something you
                       shouldn't be
330                    all of a sudden you kind of get that
331                    aa::hhh feeling
332    Pupils3&5       ((laugh))
333    Ms Leigh:       'she's behind me'
334                    and the hairs on the back of your neck stand up
335                    that's what we mean by suspense
336                    we're waiting for something to go wrong
```

Viewing the video recording

We recommend that readers now view the video recording and read the full transcript of this episode. While viewing for the first time, think about what (if anything) stands out as particularly interesting. You might like to consider the following questions:

- What is happening in this episode? How do you know? How is this clip similar to or different from other examples of classroom interaction you've seen and/or experienced? For example, is it usual, in your experience, for pupils to challenge the teacher's authority? And, when this happens, how do teachers typically respond?
- How does Ms Leigh respond to pupil interventions that deviate from her plan? What are the advantages and disadvantages of the tactics she employs?
- Based on your interpretation of dialogic pedagogy (including your reading of Chapter 2), in what ways is the interaction in this episode more or less dialogic?
- Which pupils participate most actively in this part of the lesson? Are there any pupils who do not participate at all? How do you define 'participation'?
- What possibilities does the seating arrangement open up? What problems does it pose?
- How are the various texts – pupil-written, dramatically performed, and published – used in the episode? What are the advantages and disadvantages of juxtaposing so many different texts?
- What opportunities for learning are made available to pupils through this discussion?

Analysis

In this section we'll focus on three issues. First, we introduce the notion of a 'dialogic spell' and apply it to the focal episode. Next, we look in detail at the different texts introduced into the discussion, published novels as well as pupil writing, and attempt to track their contribution to the line of inquiry Ms Leigh pursues. Finally, we draw attention to the dilemmas highlighted in this episode, and suggest they may be inherent to all teaching and learning.

A 'dialogic spell'

Martin Nystrand and colleagues have highlighted the important role of pupil questions in igniting what they term a 'dialogic spell': a 'pedagogically rich sequence of teacher–student interaction' in which relatively monologic, traditional patterns of classroom interaction give way to more dialogic forms of discourse.[6] We were drawn to Episode 2 because it seems to us to be a good example of a dialogic spell, one that begins not with a pupil question, but with a pupil challenge: 'Miss, I don't really like that. I-I sort of like a bit of talk before it' (lines 33–5). A pupil challenge may be even more powerful than a pupil question in igniting a dialogic spell because this discourse move gives rise instantly to the cognitive tension necessary for productive dialogue. It is not enough simply for a pupil to make a challenge however; the teacher's response is critical. For a dialogic spell to occur, the teacher must make space for the pupil's ideas. This is not necessarily easy, however, especially if conducting the lesson according to a predefined plan. In this case, Ms Leigh had set out her preferred model of story opening (dropping the reader in the action), which was to act as a model for the pupils' next task. The lesson would have proceeded in the intended direction but for William's challenge, and importantly, his teacher's uptake of this challenge.

We see traces of the original lesson plan in Ms Leigh's initial response to William's challenge, in which she quickly moves to incorporate his comments within her predefined aims and structure. She begins to talk immediately after William's challenge, rationalizing his response with 'well it depends on how you want to start your story, doesn't it' (lines 36–7). The tag question at the end of her utterance ('doesn't it?') constructs agreement or shared understanding (which William affirms by nodding and saying 'yeah' on line 38). She then continues with 'so you could have-', but stops herself mid-sentence in order to request clarification: 'you mean talk as the narrator or talk as the actors?' (lines 40–1). With this request Ms Leigh demonstrates a willingness to slow down the lesson in order to properly understand William's point, as well as openness to this potential new line of enquiry. Her use of 'talk' rather than 'speech' (which she had used previously in her summary on line 32) echoes William's utterance and further signals her uptake of the point he has made. She is now beginning to make a space for the pupil challenge, and we see her fully commit to this space when she asks Rachel and Terry to sit down on line 63, and gives William the green light to continue, asking 'what would you use to start off with- your story then' (65–6). William's input is now being taken seriously and the scene is set for a potentially dialogic deviation from the lesson plan.

Ms Leigh allows William to put forward an alternative (and conflicting) perspective on story openings. From this point on, there isn't a single, predefined, 'best' way of opening a story; rather there are competing perspectives, and both teacher and pupils are active in weighing the merits of different strategies for opening stories. William's own ideas are subject to challenge and are tested by both Ms Leigh and Ms Forester. On lines 70–3, the test is whether or not William will start his story in the way that Ms Forester and Terry have already decided that they would *not*. Ms Leigh says, 'because I've just overheard Ms Forester and Terry having a conversation about how they're *not* going to start their story. Let's see if he does it'. Ms Leigh, Ms Forester and Terry all share knowledge to which William is not privy, but William does not appear threatened by this. He simply gives his own example of a story opening. On line 143, Ms Leigh invites Ms Forester to compare William's opening with another story, this time a published novel that she had read over the Christmas holiday. Ms Forester reveals that she 'can't even remember' what William's story opening was (even though he read it out loud only a few seconds earlier). The comparison clearly does not work in William's favour. The teacher responds to William's challenge, then, not by appealing to her own knowledge as sole authority, but by drawing upon a number of other sources of knowledge, including Ms Forester and a published author.

Pupils also challenge each other in this episode and build on each other's responses. In lines 292 and 321–2, for example, William challenges Harry's assessment of the opening to the book *Necropolis* (which Harry had introduced into the discussion on line 186). Harry had said earlier (on lines 223–7) that nothing actually goes wrong in the scene he recounted because the character of Scarlet is saved from being run over, but William contests this ('something sort of goes wrong in that the truck's about to hit her'), and in doing so, he pushes forward the discussion of suspense and foreshadowing that runs through the interaction.

This discussion of story openings has clearly moved beyond traditional recitation, in which pupils are expected to take on the teacher's ideas, into a more open exchange of ideas. The teacher asks 'authentic questions'[7] (that is, questions for which she does not have a pre-specified answer in mind, for example, lines 40–1, 65–6) and demonstrates to the pupils that she is interested in their ideas and thought processes, not merely in their ability to recall previously given information. As a result, the discussion of story writing opens up to include multiple and conflicting voices. The voices of Ms Leigh, Ms Forester, Terry, William, Harry and a variety of texts are all woven into the discussion (the role of these texts is discussed in detail below). The possibility of there being multiple voices in the classroom, of which the teacher's is merely one and is not necessarily dominant, is at the heart of dialogic pedagogy.

This dialogic spell may, at least in part, have been facilitated by the spatial arrangement of the room. In his summary of the contexts and conditions that facilitate dialogic teaching, Robin Alexander highlights teachers' willingness 'to change classroom layout to meet the requirements of different kinds of learning task and different kinds of learning talk' as a key criterion.[8] Ms Leigh was quite unusual in her willingness to do this. In this focal lesson, tables and chairs were rearranged on more than one occasion in order to suit the activity. This was commonplace in the lessons we observed in Ms Leigh's classroom, but relatively rare in other classrooms in this school (likely due in part to space constraints that made rearranging the furniture difficult). The alternative spatial arrangement meant that pupils could see each other as well as the teacher and learning support assistant (LSA). A circle seating arrangement also sends out a more egalitarian message – all participants are on an equal footing – and this influences the nature of the relationships that develop between teacher and pupils during classroom discourse[9] (though the arrangement in this episode was a bit more complicated – see 'dialogic dilemmas' below). It is much more difficult to achieve this sense of equality if the teacher stands at the front of the room while the children sit in ordered rows.

There was certainly something about this particular classroom context which meant that William felt comfortable and confident enough to challenge the teacher. The circle arrangement was likely part of this, but so too was the fact that Ms Leigh had a supportive and congenial relationship with this pupil (and indeed with the other pupils in the class). This relationship is crucial to facilitating the production of cognitive tension (and thus dialogue) in this episode: not only does William feel able to challenge the teacher, but he is also able to withstand challenges to his own position. William knows that the extent to which his ideas about story writing are 'correct' is not the issue; what is important is that his ideas are a springboard from which he and his peers can learn more about the craft of story writing. He has learnt this through his previous interactions with Ms Leigh and other pupils in this classroom.

From an aesthetic point of view, the circle made possible the drama of the opening sequence in which Rachel and Terry acted out alternative story openings. This spatial arrangement (and the eye contact it facilitated) also augmented the sense of performance and drama created by Ms Leigh's retelling of both William's story and *Necropolis*. The video shows that the pupils' interest piques at lines 236–53 when the teacher acts out her own experience of reading the opening to *Necropolis*, sitting up in her chair and using exaggerated hand gestures. Harry then mirrors these hand gestures in his version of events on lines 257–70.

A web of texts or a coherent line of inquiry?

A number of texts are woven into the discussion. They include a specific example of pupil writing (William's story), published novels (Ms Leigh's holiday reading and *Necropolis*), and generalized examples (texts which drop the reader right in the action, texts where there's a bit of talk before, texts which have a prologue). The movement between these texts is not linear; there are shifts back and forth between texts and associated topics (for example, narrator voice, prologue, suspense). In order to show how these texts and topics interact, we have represented the movements between them visually in Figure 5.1. The complicated arrangement represented here highlights, first and foremost, the teacher's skill in keeping all of these different texts and ideas in play. Nothing is closed down prematurely. So when Harry introduces the book *Necropolis* into the discussion on line 186, Ms Leigh finds a way of comparing this text with William's story, describing how both might make use of foreshadowing (i.e. 'a hint'). And later, on line 275, she extrapolates from Harry's summary of *Necropolis* to general techniques that writers might use to ensure that the reader is engaged with the story's characters right from the beginning.

Ms Leigh works hard to chain pupil responses and the texts and ideas they invoke into a coherent line of enquiry. This effort is what Robin Alexander calls the 'cumulative' principle of dialogue ('teachers and children build on their own and each other's ideas and chain them into coherent lines of thinking and enquiry' – see Chapter 2, p. 24), and it is easy to see from this episode why Alexander describes it as the most challenging of his five principles of dialogic teaching. The teacher has to process each pupil's response, interpreting it in relation to her knowledge of the pupil and his/her level of current understanding and relating it to previous responses, and then decide how best to use it in order to push the discussion and pupils' thinking forward. All of this in a matter of seconds. This is a daunting task, one made all the more difficult by the unpredictability of pupil responses. William's challenge is certainly unexpected, but so too are many of Harry's contributions.

When Harry introduces *Necropolis* for the first time (on line 186), he claims coherence by prefacing his utterance with 'Miss it's like …', thus suggesting that his comment relates directly to Ms Leigh's dramatic re-formulation of William's story (on lines 165–82). But the reference of Harry's 'it' is ambiguous. Is he making a comparison between the opening to *Necropolis* and Ms Leigh's retelling of William's story? Or does his comment refer further back to Ms Leigh's initial point that a good sentence opener drops the reader right in the action (lines 30–2), for this is how *Necropolis* begins: 'The girl didn't look before crossing the road.'[10] Either way, it's important to keep in mind, that the other pupils have not read *Necropolis;* thus Harry's contribution moves the discussion away from the common ground of William's story and towards Harry's own literary preferences. In trying to better understand this new turn in the conversation, we found it useful to pay attention to the social (as well as ideational) aspects of the talk. This is the final column in Figure 5.1. We have already noted that the book Harry introduces into the conversation, *Necropolis*, is not one that the whole class have read. Harry had read the book and then lent it to Ms Leigh. Similarly, the holiday reading that Ms Leigh introduces on line 100 was also given to her by Harry. These texts are not just materials for exploring issues related to suspense and foreshadowing, but are also tools for managing social relationships. It may be that Harry is attempting to establish or demonstrate his privileged position in the classroom as a pupil who shares books (as well as ideas, likes and dislikes) with the teacher. Because of their shared knowledge of *Necropolis*, Harry and Ms Leigh are able to engage in a shared interpretation of this text in lines 239–73. The extent to which other pupils can join in with this is of course less straightforward (this point is taken up in 'dialogic dilemmas' below). William and Harry were centre stage in this interaction perhaps in part because they had direct and privileged access to some of the texts being discussed.

The cumulative dimension of dialogue becomes intertwined with the interpersonal dimension (or what Alexander terms the 'supportive' principle of dialogue). To ignore or down play Harry's comment would risk undermining his enthusiasm, but to run with it threatens the coherence of the discussion, especially from the perspective of the other pupils. Ms Leigh finds a compromise. She draws Harry's response into the cumulative line of enquiry she is constructing. We might summarize this line of enquiry as follows: Ms Leigh begins the episode by telling the class that the best way to open a story is to drop the reader 'right in the action to start off with' and 'have some speech there as well' (lines 30–2). This is challenged by William, who is keen to use the narrator's voice instead. Ms Leigh takes on board William's point about the narrator's voice and suggests that he use this voice to give 'a hint' that something is about to go wrong in his story (lines 165–82). In doing so, Ms Leigh concedes the specific point (that a story should begin by dropping the reader right in the action) but manages to maintain the general point (that the children must find ways to make their story openings more exciting in order to engage the reader).

When Harry gives his description of *Necropolis* on lines 186–95, Ms Leigh makes it relevant to her re-formulation of William's story by showing that the author of *Necropolis* is giving the reader 'a hint then that something's going to go wrong' (lines 197–8) and demonstrating how William could use the same technique in his story (lines 199–221). When Harry challenges her (on lines 223–7), Ms Leigh takes this line of enquiry further by explaining that 'a hint' builds up 'a bit of suspense' (line 237). Keeping all the texts in play, she then demonstrates how this applies to *Necropolis* (lines 239–56). Harry responds with his own description of the same event. His contribution doesn't appear immediately relevant, but Ms Leigh *makes* it relevant by summarizing: 'the writer used that then to make sure that you were involved in the story, you got engaged with the character'. She explains later that this detail at the beginning 'helps to build up suspense and interest in the story' (lines 302–6). Throughout this episode, then, Ms Leigh pursues her main point (that pupils need to find ways to create interest in their story openers) but manages to incorporate pupils' spontaneous responses. She creates a sense of cumulation and manages to tie everything together, even when Harry and William threaten to pull the lesson in the opposite direction.

Dialogic dilemmas

In many ways, the focal episode is a textbook example of a dialogic spell: a spontaneous pupil challenge followed by extended interaction between the teacher and that pupil, with the rest of the class listening attentively; multiple (and conflicting) perspectives on a curricular topic; pupils building on each other's responses; and so on. At the same time, the episode raises a number of dilemmas. We've already noted some of these. At the beginning of our analysis, we highlighted the dilemma posed by a spontaneous pupil challenge: should the teacher stick to her lesson plan or pursue (potentially narrow and less relevant) pupil interests? And we also touched upon the tension between constructing a meaningful, cumulative line of enquiry and maintaining positive social relations (both being essential aspects of dialogic pedagogy).

The dilemma that most occupied the Abbeyford teachers when reflecting on this video clip was the extent to which pupils not directly involved in the action (which included almost everyone apart from William and Harry) were really engaged (see summary of participating teachers responses in Box 5.1). These pupils were well behaved, but were they

	Texts				
Lines	Pupil writing	Texts in general	Real books	Key ideas	Social dimension
1	Dramatized text #1 (1–13)			Purpose of opener to excite the reader	
10	→				
20	Dramatized text #2 (14–32) →			Drop reader right into the action	
30	Challenged (33–51) →W→	Texts where they talk a little beforehand		Opening with narration?	W expresses personal opinion
40		(33–51) →			
50				The purpose of the drama task	
60	W's story (67–96) →	← → ← T			W has privileged position as storyteller
70	→	→ T		An idea for how *not* to open a story	Threat to W
80	T				
90	→	↑ ↑ →		Story mountain	
100	↑	'Often they put a little paragraph before' (108–22) T/LSA →	Holiday reading (98–107) ← W ←		H has special relationship with T
110			↓	Prologue	
120			'I really want to know what happens next?' (127–41) →	Narrator voice	
130	T	↓ ↓ ↓	← T	Creating suspense	
140	What did you want to know from W's story? (143–61)	↑	↓		
150	Improving W's story (162–84) →	↑	↓		Threat to W
160		↑	↑	But then … and then A hint … (foreshadowing)	
170	H→ ↑	↑	→		

Line	Texts	Topics	Social relations
180			
190	*Necropolis* (186–98)	Foreshadowing	H displays literary knowledge and claims privileged position
200	So for W's story (199–221)		
210			Change of roles (from teacher–pupil to readers of shared text)
220	But nothing does go wrong (*Necropolis*) (223–306)		
230			
240		Suspense	H mirrors T's response – claims special connection?
250		Slowing down / speeding up pace	
260			
270		Engagement with characters	T resumes role of teacher
280			W challenges H
290		Suspense /interest in the story	
300	Right, I'm going to stop you there (308)		T re-establishes connection with class
310	...So what I want you to do (313)		
320	W: Something does go wrong (321–36)	Hint of danger, suspense	
330			
340			

(T=Teacher, W=William, H=Harry, LSA=Learning Support Assistant)

Figure 5.1 Weaving of texts, topics and social relations.

really paying attention? Responses from participating teachers (and other educational practitioners and researchers with whom we have shared this video clip) have been mixed. Several
shared a concern that too many pupils appeared not to be following the discussion – perhaps
could not follow it because of the complicated layering of ideas and texts – and thus were not
learning much from it. Others saw evidence of pupil engagement in their gaze and body
language (e.g. nodding of heads, eye contact with speaker), suggesting that these pupils
might actually be actively listening to and reflecting on the discussion. The way the classroom is organized, making all pupils visible and giving them unobstructed access to the
centre stage action, certainly maximizes the potential for this kind of silent participation.
Some conceded that the pupils did appear to be engaged but felt that this was more likely
to be due to the drama and movement that accompanied the discussion rather than the ideas
discussed.

We cannot know for sure what (if anything) the pupils in this classroom learned from
this particular discussion of story openers, but the episode raises a more general dilemma
for teachers seeking to promote dialogic pedagogy in their classrooms. On the one hand,
part of what makes this episode dialogic is the sustained interaction between the teacher
and just a small number of pupils. If Ms Leigh had attempted to open out the discussion
to include all members of the class, the dialogic spell would likely have dissipated. When
all pupils are involved in a class discussion it is very difficult to maintain a coherent line
of enquiry (consider how difficult this was with responses from just two pupils).[11] On
the other hand, if pupils not involved in centre stage talk feel excluded from classroom
discourse they may become disengaged from their learning. How might we resolve this
conflict?

Box 5.1 Key issues raised by teachers in the reflection meeting

1. Pupil participation and engagement.

   a) *I think there was concern about how few children actually spoke. That was the only thing
   is that there was, as you say, dialogic talk going on, but the rest of the group, class, weren't
   involved. And that was the only concern. I mean, they were well behaved, I'm not saying they
   weren't, but they just switched off, would they have got much from that?*

   b) *They seemed to follow it really well, though, when you looked at them. Because I was quite
   surprised, I would imagine, or I'd expect, normally, that if you get two kids talking for that
   length of time, I would normally switch off, but that's very good. I was watching some kids
   and their faces, and they were literally sort of like nodding along and shaking their heads, but
   you do wonder whether they've got really good ideas that they're not –*

   c) *Because there's pupils talking, children are maybe less likely to just switch off. The teacher's voice,
   you know, constantly going on, going on, then, you know, they're more likely to get bored and
   frustrated, but maybe because it's – they can relate to what they're saying more … But I think,
   generally, yeah, he did talk a lot, didn't he, William? He's got a lot to say. But it was valid.*

   d) *I know it made a difference to William and Harry's writing … But I was just sort of concerned, as a writing task, how much the other people got out of the editing, how much did they
   put speech or suspense into their openers.*

2. Raising the status of talk in the classroom.

   a) *I think because Harry talks quite a lot, he's really into – he's really into his reading and his
   writing, amazing stuff that he comes out with, but he's kind of raised – I don't know if doing more of the talking has actually made it a higher status thing now, because William was*

desperately trying to jump in and say, 'oh, yeah, well I know what Harry says.' And Brett, who was actually sat next to him, watching him, was going, 'oh yeah, I see what you mean now.' And, actually, it's really amazing, it's something that they all want to do.

b) *Now [since the intervention on dialogic pedagogy], like you say, in this culture, now they are much more aware that they can put their opinion across and it will be valued and it will be appreciated, and we are making much of a point of making them talk*

c) *It might be that sort of a few months of someone like Harry, who's talking for England, just establishes it as something you do.*

3. Stance towards knowledge.

a) *I think it really helps the fact that you've got a kid here, as well, was it William, who challenges your idea at the beginning, they can see that, 'well, that doesn't have to be right, then, I can have my ideas, I can have my thoughts', and, 'oh no, Miss, that's not good.'*

b) *They're much more willing to sort of say, 'well, do you not think maybe this should happen instead?' Or, 'why do you think – why do we need to include that'. They actually sort of engage at, I suppose, the higher level of actually questioning what they're doing.*

c) *They seem to have a certain amount of respect for each other's opinions, as well. Whilst you still get the occasional butting in that was going on, they know when to stop, I've found.*

4. Arrangement of the classroom/position of teacher.

It's very easy when you're teaching, or when you're discussing something like that, that you pick the children that are in your sightline, the one that you can see going like that, because you can see the movement of their arm, rather than the child who you can see on their face, the lightbulb's just switched on, you might not see that, because they're not in your sightline. So, the teacher moving might help, as well.

We would argue that genuine thinking and involvement from just a few pupils is better than a superficial discussion that includes contributions from all children. The challenge, however, is to find ways to ensure that it is not the same pupils who participate in every lesson. One point to bear in mind in this endeavour is the physical positioning of pupils in the classroom. We have already outlined the advantages of the non-traditional seating arrangement in the focal episode, but we should now also consider the possibility that this arrangement inadvertently skewed the conversation in William's and Harry's favour. Both pupils were sitting directly opposite the teacher and both were in her immediate line of vision. This made it easy for William to get the teacher's attention in the first place, and difficult for Ms Leigh to ignore Harry's persistently raised hand. Also, how might the dynamics of the interaction have changed if the learning support assistant were sitting at the other end of the circle, rather than next to Ms Leigh? Attention would certainly have moved to the opposite end of the circle when Ms Leigh asked her to comment on William's story, making it potentially easier for pupils at that end of the room to contribute to the discussion. Finally, it is worth making the (perhaps rather obvious) point that the 'circle' is not really a circle at all, but an oblong with a narrow tail to one end (the size of the room, the furniture and the speed at which they were rearranged militated against achieving a perfect circle). Again, this oblong shape made the space inhabited by Ms Leigh, William and Harry the natural centre for the discussion, and perhaps negated some of the advantages of a circular seating arrangement (e.g. that all pupils are on an equal footing).

On this occasion, there are no inherent problems with the way pupils are positioned; indeed it had advantages. It sets up a stage for the main action that all pupils can see.

William takes up his place on this stage and adopts an almost heroic role, challenging the authority of the teacher. Ms Leigh sets him up in this way ('I've just overheard Ms Forester and Terry having a conversation about how they're *not* going to start their story. Let's see if he does it'), putting the spotlight on William. He rises to the occasion and the ensuing drama seems to keep most pupils engaged (or at least they give the appearance of being engaged). All of this happened informally. The pupils had not been given designated seats; in fact, earlier in the lesson, before the children left the class for the morning break, William and Harry had been sitting in different positions. As teachers, we may be able to find ways to formalize what happened here in a way that brings different pupils onto centre stage each time.

We noted above the important role played by the different texts brought into the discussion, suggesting that William and Harry may have been centre stage because of their privileged access to these texts. Again, this is not in and of itself a bad thing; on the contrary, Ms Leigh's bonding with the boys in her class around their mutual love of books is relatively exceptional, at least if we're to believe public pronouncements about the problem of 'getting boys into reading'.[12] More generally, using pupils' out-of-school knowledge and experiences can be highly productive (as we argue in Chapter 6). Varying the types of texts referenced in class discussion, however, in order to touch upon different pupils' areas of interest and expertise, may be another way to change participation structures.

There are, of course, things that teachers cannot (and would not want to) change, such as Harry's obvious enthusiasm for literature, which is what prompts his introduction of *Necropolis* and his general exuberance in this extract. It may appear that Ms Leigh indulges Harry in allowing him to talk at length about *Necropolis*, but it became clear during the course of our intervention at Abbeyford Primary that his enthusiasm for reading was infectious in this classroom. Ms Leigh herself made the point that Harry had raised the status of reading and of talking in this class, acting as a role model for other pupils (see also comments 2(a) and 2(c) in Box 5.1). There may be other ways of utilizing the confidence and enthusiasm of pupils such as Harry and William. In a later lesson we observed in Ms Leigh's classroom, for example, she set up small group work such that the most talkative and confident members of the class (including Harry and William) were group leaders. The leaders had an important task; they were instructed to make it their 'secret mission' to ensure that everyone in their group spoke at least once. Taking this one step further, they could also have been instructed to appoint a different member of the group to act as spokesperson when it came to reporting the group's work back to the whole class. This person would then have their time 'on stage' interacting with the teacher.[13]

Finally, we need to take account of the fact that pupils, as well as teachers, are engaged in a learning process when schools aim to make their classes more dialogic. They need to develop new ways of talking and participating in lessons, which includes learning to listen to others, make room for alternative points of view and give other pupils time to think. These may be new skills for some (if not all) pupils and will take time and effort to acquire. Robin Alexander refers to these skills as a repertoire of 'learning talk' and stresses that if we don't give due attention to learning talk as well as teacher talk, 'the intellectual and social empowerment that dialogic teaching should be able to offer may remain limited even when in other respects talk displays dialogic properties.'[14]

Before closing, it's worth considering a final dilemma, which has been implicit throughout much of the discussion in this chapter, but never explicitly stated; that is, the tension between complexity and manageability in whole-class discussion. Look again at the video and transcript and consider the options available to Ms Leigh at lines 36, 90, 98, 124, 143, 228, 273, 315. Which option does Ms Leigh take and what is the impact of this choice? Which action would you have taken? And how would this have changed the following interaction?

If you're like the many teachers with whom we've shared this episode, you probably suggested that, at some or all of these key moments Ms Leigh might have attempted to close the discussion down, or at least reduce the complexity by summarizing one or two key points before moving on. She does not do this, however. At each juncture, Ms Leigh *adds* to the complexity by incorporating new texts or new directions to the discussion. On line 98, for example, she introduces a new text out of the blue (the holiday reading that was sitting on her desk), which only a few pupils in the class had read. She uses it to make a comparison between the dramatic opening of this text and William's lacklustre story opening. The discussion becomes more complex as a result, but with it, richer: the introduction of the holiday reading opens up the discussion of foreshadowing and suspense.

At the same time, however, the discussion becomes ever more unwieldy. While it appears that Ms Leigh has a grip on the flow of ideas, we might question to what extent pupils in the class are able to follow. It is perhaps not surprising that most pupils (that is, those other than William and Harry) did not participate more, since they would have had to pick up on the relevant connections among the texts and topics raised in order to establish some coherence for themselves (and some may have needed more help than others to do this).

Conclusion

We have presented this episode as an example of what a 'dialogic spell' might look like. It has all of the right ingredients. Ms Leigh presents her version of how best to open a story, but not all pupils unquestioningly accept this. William challenges the teacher, and by taking up his challenge Ms Leigh facilitates a discussion in which competing points of view are tested. Ultimately, Ms Leigh retains control of this discussion, steering it in a direction that enabled her to cover key topics (e.g. suspense and how building suspense through action at the beginning of a story is an effective way to engage the reader), but that does not make the interaction any less dialogic. She covers the key learning points from her lesson plan, but rather than just telling the children what she wants them to know, she allows them (or at least some of them) to take part in jointly constructing knowledge.

A number of the pupils responded to the themes and topics that arose in the diversion caused by the student challenge, but many remained silent. We have considered some possible reasons for their silence. Perhaps the discussion become too complicated, with its references to multiple ideas and texts, leaving some members of the class unable (or unwilling) to contribute more fully. Perhaps some felt that they couldn't compete with the dominance of Harry and William. Or perhaps most were following the discussion attentively and learning both from its (pupil-led) structure and content. Whatever the reason, their silence could be viewed as a problem, especially given the emphasis in English schooling on inclusion and whole-class participation (see Chapter 8 for further discussion of this issue). We have argued that meaningful discussion between just a few pupils is better than token recitation that involves everyone in the class. But, we need to ensure that it's not the same pupils dominating classroom talk time and time again (see Chapter 6 for further analysis of the impact of dominant boys). Classroom culture will be important in this respect. An atmosphere that is collaborative rather than competitive is likely to encourage pupils to listen to others instead of vying to get across their own point of view. Fostering this kind of culture may include introducing explicit ground rules for talking in the classroom and helping pupils to develop a full repertoire of 'learning talk'. It may also require direct teacher intervention (for example, in changing seating arrangements to facilitate contributions from less confident pupils, and conversely to limit contributions from more dominant pupils). Less explicitly, this kind of culture develops when pupils come to internalize their teachers' ways of interacting. For example, Ms Leigh demonstrates to the pupils that she is genuinely interested in their ideas when she allows William to challenge her authority on the topic of story writing. She takes pupil contributions seriously, which, importantly, includes probing and challenging them to test their merit rather than offering ritualistic praise. As a result she creates an atmosphere of mutual respect, which is a critical condition for classroom dialogue.

Issues for further discussion

- What do you think of our analysis? What points resonate with your own interpretations of what's happening? What points seem problematic to you?
- Is this kind of dialogue replicable given that it began with a spontaneous pupil challenge? What conditions make is possible for a pupil to raise a challenge and/or ask a substantive question?
- How can we strike the right balance between sticking to the lesson plan (and thus ensuring appropriate curriculum coverage) and taking account of pupils' own ideas and responses?
- How can we encourage children to listen to one another?
- What other strategies can be used to ensure that all pupils (not just those who are dominant) regularly participate in these kinds of productive teacher–pupil interactions?

COMMENTARY

TRIUMPHS AND DILEMMAS OF DIALOGUE
BY ROBIN ALEXANDER

For the moment let's suspend questions about those who speak and those who don't. Concern about the balance of oral participation in this episode is understandable and I shall comment on it. But the transcript commands attention to what is said, and here we find dialogic pedagogy of a high order.

Thus, exemplifying Nystrand's gloss on those 'authentic' questions that generate the richest gains in pupil learning, Ms Leigh undoubtedly gets pupils 'to think, not just to report someone else's thinking' (Nystrand 1997: 72). She re-formulates, or as Michaels and O'Connor would say, 'revoices', pupil contributions to check whether her understanding accords with theirs and to clarify and extend their ideas (Michaels and O'Connor 2013). She challenges pupils to justify their assertions and counters their hypotheses with her own. They in turn challenge her, showing that classroom dialogue entails real argument rather than stage-managed discussion in which pupils merely play the dialogic game.

Yet the lesson consistently advances the teacher's intentions. This is as it should be: whatever direction classroom talk takes it must in the end be – to apply my most basic dialogic test – *purposeful*.

It is also founded on mutual respect. There's a seriousness to the exchanges that has no truck with the arch and patronizing teacherly voice that too often dominates primary classroom discourse and is dialogue's antithesis. Equally, the discussion's forward impulse stems not from Ofsted's misconceived notion of 'pace' but from shared commitment to the value of the task. Other dialogic criteria are met: there is genuine *reciprocity* of word and thought, while the pupils' readiness to talk as they do stems from the teacher's having established a climate which is demanding yet *supportive*.

All this favours *cumulation*, talk that 'chains ideas into coherent lines of thinking and enquiry' (Alexander 2008a: 38). Cumulation, as Adam and Julia note, is not a linear progression from existing understanding to new, but a more complex set of discursive and cognitive moves backwards, forwards and sideways. The trick is to nurture grist-to-the-mill divergence while maintaining forward momentum.

It is a mark of this teacher's mastery that she achieves this and – as Adam and Julia also note – when confronted by the growing complexity of the layers of meaning being uncovered she doesn't channel discussion into safer, blander terrain but adds to those layers and keeps them all in play. Such teaching demands a lively intelligence as well as skill.

So far so good. Now to the concern raised in Box 5.1. If one attends to the transcript one marks the dialogue that learning requires; if one responds to the video's visual cues one notices the silence of the majority. In assessing whether this really is a problem we should consider the evidence as a whole, for in combination the utterances of the few and the behaviour of the many test the final dialogic principle, *collectivity* – 'teachers and children address learning tasks together, whether as a group or as a class' (Alexander 2008a: 38). This principle arose from lesson observations in countries where there is more whole-class teaching than in Britain, but its character and values are very different (Alexander 2001). Set against such international evidence and what we know about human learning, the claim that children in this episode aren't 'involved' simply because they don't speak can be challenged on three grounds.

First, teaching is a collective act. Every child is manifestly an individual but in classrooms children share space, time, tasks, routines and much more, and they learn from each other as well as from the teacher. Second, knowledge co-construction and Vygotskian accounts of human development show us that young children's classroom learning is not only collective in this obvious sense but is also best conceived as a social process. Third, if children are taught to think about what they hear they will be as 'involved' as when they answer questions: to extend Nystrand's maxim, authentic dialogue gets *all* pupils to think, not only those who speak. For in a book about dialogic pedagogy we should remember that there are internal as well as external dialogues – Vygotsky's 'inner' and 'outer' speech – and that humans habitually but silently converse, reason and argue. It is therefore perverse to insist that only vocalized dialogue demonstrates engagement. What matters is how external and internal dialogues relate, how one inhabits – or inhibits – the other.

To reinforce the idea of collective engagement through speaking, listening and thinking in combination, teachers may draw on three procedures. First, they may ask a few children to articulate their thinking while others listen. The principle here is that 'the child who ... works through a problem, aloud and at length, is less an individual being tested and compared with others than their representative' (Alexander 2001: 454). Second, they may opt for extended exchanges with a few children rather than brief exchanges with many, on the provable grounds that in their learning outcomes such exchanges are more productive. Third, instead of insisting that in a given lesson all children must speak, however briefly, dialogic teachers may use the day or week as their unit, ensuring that over a longer period every child has an opportunity for the probing exchanges for which the research evidence calls and which we see exemplified here. However – a crucial proviso – those who do not speak *must* listen and think. Fully engaged listening is as critical to the repertoire of learning talk as those vocalized elements like questioning, explaining, arguing and justifying (all of which are also evident in this episode).

So what we have here is not an organizational failing to set against Ms Leigh's oral success – though we might ask about the girl in the far corner whose attention wanders or the two who are so dazzled by the sun that they can't concentrate and of course what the silent children are thinking about – but an example of the dilemmas that teaching by its nature creates. In this instance, how should one adult distribute her time, attention and interaction in order to maximize the learning of 25–35 children? Should she try to be everywhere at once, interacting fleetingly with each child in hope of securing their 'involvement', behaviourally if not cognitively? Should she heed the evidence about the talk that matters and opt for extended exchanges with fewer children? Should her repertoire include both strategies, and if so when should each be deployed? And what, before and after this one lesson fragment, did Ms Leigh do?

This brings us back to the discussion of 'practice' and 'best practice' in Chapter 1. Both are intrinsically problematic partly because they entail operational dilemmas of the kind exemplified here and partly because the practice of education is itself a dialogue, for it stands at the intersection of voices political, pragmatic, evidential, conceptual and ethical (Alexander 1997: 284; 2008b: 121). Values send us in one direction, a classroom's human and physical circumstances in another, anxiety about inspection, accountability and national tests in a third, evidence about the conditions for effective teaching in a fourth and so on. It's our job as teachers to reconcile such competing imperatives while striving to keep children's learning and wellbeing paramount. That's education. That's life.

Robin Alexander is Fellow of Wolfson College at Cambridge University, Professor of Education at University of York , and Chair of the Cambridge Primary Review Trust. He has produced over 260 publications, including Culture and Pedagogy *(2001 – winner of the AERA Outstanding Book Award),* Essays on Pedagogy *(2008),* Towards Dialogic Teaching *(2008) and* Children, their World, their Education: final report and recommendations of the Cambridge Primary Review *(2010).*

COMMENTARY

WRITING *IN* THE TALK
BY GEMMA MOSS

The analysis rests on what the talk does: the space it creates to make links and generate cumulative thinking, in which contributions extend and explore an idea. The common anxiety recorded from observers of the video is that the uneven knowledge base brought to this exchange silences many. It is not clear what the spectators in the classroom gain from listening, or even who is doing so. Yet when the teacher begins to unpack the sequence of events in *Necropolis* (line 236+), attention in the class shifts. Everyone seems to be grabbed by her plot summary, in a way in which they were not by the 'drop straight into the action' sentence she read aloud earlier.

All of this suggests another potential analytic focus – not on the dialogue in the classroom and the orchestration of its many threads, but on the substance under discussion: writing. How does writing feature in the talk? Does the absence of writing *in* the talk – the teacher does not scribe her model opening sentence on a board, for instance – matter? How do the children in the classroom orchestrate their attention across modes, from the writing task they have been set to the representation of their story ideas in drama, to the composition of an opening sentence? How helpful is the mode-switching to realizing the writing? Text and sentence level aspects of the writing task layer into the talk unevenly, intertwining in complex ways. Follow the act of writing into the exchange and different orientations emerge.

The teacher initially focuses on using a single sentence to hook readers immediately into the action. But William's challenge seems preoccupied with how to stage the plot and its potential twists. He is clear that he doesn't want to start with dialogue, but does not bring a fully fledged opening sentence to the discussion, and when pressed to produce one fumbles from 'loads of people think nothing's going to happen as they go into a tunnel' to 'many people go to a tunnel thinking nothing's going to happen'. This is more like a mini summary of a first scene than an opening sentence. Yet by line 162, Ms Leigh is beginning to chain sentences into a plot sequence, bringing her focus more in line with both boys'. The work done by a single sentence is replaced by consideration of the larger shapes in the text, and this shadows back into a consideration of suspense and plot twists, connected to the opening of *Necropolis* and its use of these devices. This is thinking on the hoof in which technical and informal terms slide by, as those most involved in the conversation try to find common ground, exchanging different reference points. What is unusual is the extent to which the teacher engages on equal terms with her interlocutors in doing this. What makes it potentially awkward pedagogically is the difficulty of articulating clearly enough for others what is really going on. What can the spectators take away from this encounter? Scripting the talk onto a board as it progresses would visually represent the shifts in attention to writing, from the tight structure of a single opening sentence to the looser organization of plot. This might have changed the dynamic here by making the exchange more transparent to others. It would also have made more visible and open to discussion the different forms writing takes as it is applied to different tasks: 'organizing thinking', recording ideas, sketching out a plot sequence, representing speech on the page or enticing a reader into a scenario that is not yet fully shown.

It is hard to focus on writing without seeing the words. Real time scripting of the talk would have added another dimension to dialogue in the classroom.

Gemma Moss is Professor of Education at the Institute of Education, University of London. She has extensive experience of researching classroom literacy practices using ethnographic tools, and is the author of Literacy and Gender: Researching Texts, Contexts and Readers *(2007) Routledge.*

COMMENTARY

A CHALLENGE (?) IN THE INTEREST OF DIALOGUE BY GREG THOMPSON

In viewing the video and reading the authors' analysis, a rather singular question comes to mind: When seen in the context of this classroom, is William's question really a 'challenge'?

As a speech act, a 'challenge' is no simple thing. Minimally, one imagines it involving the putting at risk the selves of both the challenger and the challenged. In the video we see two possible examples of this (William, line 33; Harry, line 223). Yet, both examples seem to lack an element of risk on either the part of the challenged or the challenger. Neither William nor Harry appear anxious as they pose their questions. Nor do they seem to have bad intentions (as one might expect of a student seeking to 'challenge the teacher's authority'). Furthermore, the teacher does not seem to be bothered by these questions and her engagement with them functions as a kind of implicit reinforcement, suggesting that this behaviour is actually appreciated. This hardly seems the stuff of a challenge.

It is further noteworthy that of the three appearances of the discourse marker 'Miss', two introduce disagreements and one introduces a constructive contribution. This fact that their disagreements are prefaced by 'Miss' at least suggests that these disagreements may be seen by the students as tokens of a type of speech acts we might call 'constructively contributing' to the conversation.

But all of this is precisely the point of dialogic pedagogy – to create a classroom context in which what would otherwise be seen as 'challenges to the teacher's authority' become 'constructive contributions' and opportunities for talk. This is the stuff of good dialogic pedagogy.

Yet, in the interest of dialogue (!), and in accord with the teachers who viewed and commented upon this segment, I would like to push the point further and ask: can we imagine developing a dialogic frame that can enable more students to engage with the dialogue?

However masterfully done, Ms Leigh primarily engages in dialogue with just two students, William and Harry. The author's note 11 speaks to this issue by describing what Robin Alexander identified as the key difficulty with efforts to include the voices of many students, namely that such inclusionary efforts resulted in 'an emphasis on participation at the expense of engagement and thematic continuity.'

Is this necessarily the case? Can we not imagine 10- and 11-year-olds building, with the teacher's guidance, a local interactional context in which many voices are heard but all are working towards thematic continuity? This is certainly no easy task, but it seems like a very worthwhile one – helping students to develop in themselves the habits and practices central to dialogic pedagogy.[15]

At the risk of disagreeing with (challenging?) the very thoughtful and insightful analysis of the authors, these seem like questions worth asking.

Greg Thompson is a Visiting Assistant Professor in the Department of Anthropology at Brigham Young University and is an Affiliated Researcher with the Laboratory of Comparative Human Cognition at University of California, San Diego.

COMMENTARY

THE IMPACT OF DIALOGIC TEACHING TECHNIQUES – A TEACHER'S PERSPECTIVE BY LAURA HUGHES

It wasn't until I read this chapter, with its analysis, that I realized that I had been challenged on many levels. My authority had been questioned by William's interjection, as had my expertise, and rather than being affronted, it pleased me greatly. First, he had the self-assuredness to voice a controversial opinion in front of his peers, second he had confidence that he would be listened to and finally, due to the culture of the classroom, his opinion was placed on a par with my own.

By this point in the school year, and as it was the second time that I was involved in a dialogic project, I had an understanding of the practical aspects of achieving conditions for talk such as: challenging subject matter, classroom organization, creating a listening culture and planning the content that might be covered as a year group. With all this in mind, it was still difficult to see though that the pupils were learning something from this newly applied teaching strategy.

William's statement then is evidence that what was really changing was the pupils as learners. They were shifting from being passive absorbers of knowledge to being more critical of what was presented to them, analyzing how it fitted with their understanding and developing the language to justify their opinions. From nine- and ten-year-olds this is quite a feat and in my opinion, what school is really about. It is about the understanding of knowledge deemed important to our current culture, delivered through a prescribed curriculum, but it is also about the enjoyment of learning and building the basis of a lifelong habit of enquiry. This harnesses children's natural curiosity and supports the development of the self through confidence gained by analysis of what is being presented so that opinions can be justified and although they might be refuted, the interaction will in itself be learnt from, rather than the self damaged by being challenged. A moral dimension is also developed as pupils begin to connect with what they are learning and are able to defend or oppose opinions, rationalize and modify their understanding and take action so that they are not passive learners.

I had the pleasure of teaching a number of the children in this class again in the following year as they were preparing to leave the school and enter secondary education. This unusual position, at least in this school, meant that I was able to see improved social relationships in the year group, greater independence and a large amount of care for each other. Ultimately it was difficult to produce a summative numerical assessment of what the pupils had gained from involvement in the project, other than looking at National Curriculum levels in Speaking and Listening. Looking at the pupils as they left us though it was evident that the cohort was more orally confident, happy to challenge and be challenged and engaged with their world.

Laura Hughes is the teacher who appears in this chapter's focal extract. She graduated as a teacher from University of Lancaster in 1998. During the research process she was the Assistant Head Teacher of the large Inner London school described in this book, and later moved on to become the Deputy Head Teacher there. She is a Certified Teacher of PSHE and is currently studying for a Masters in Education.

Notes

1 Robin Alexander has found that time in primary school literacy lessons tends to be devoted to reading and writing, rather than oral work, and that when oral work does take place it often involves teachers talking and pupils listening, leaving little time for pupils to collaborate with each other (Alexander 1995: 155–6). Maurice Galton and colleagues' ORACLE studies (1980, 1999) found a significant *increase* in time spent on oral English between 1976 and 1996 (from around 6 per cent to 30 per cent), due to the overall increase in whole-class teaching; but in line with Alexander's point, it was still teachers who did most of the talking: 'As was the case 20 years ago, teachers talk *at* rather than *with* children during class teaching (Galton *et al.* 1999: 183).

2 See the following web link for an example of the story mountain: http://www.primaryresources.co.uk/english/pdfs/StoryMountain_TL.pdf

3 This is the opening of Garth Nix's book *The Fall* (published in 2000 by Scholastic), which is the first book in Nix's *The Seventh Tower* series.

4 It's not entirely clear how relevant the idea of a prologue is to this discussion, but this kind of labelling is a common activity in primary schooling. It could be that this is a momentary diversion into the label guessing game that pupils are familiar with before getting back to the literary discussion.

5 *Necropolis* is the fourth novel in Anthony Horowitz's *Power of Five* series (2008, Walker Books Ltd).

6 Nystrand, Wu, Gamoran, Zeiser, and Long (2003: 136).

7 Nystrand, Gamoran, Kachur and Prendergast (1997). See also Chapter 2.

8 Alexander (2008a: 188).

9 Robin Alexander (2008a: 101) also makes this point. All of the participating teachers at Abbeyford arranged their classrooms in a semi-horseshoe layout (full horseshoe not being possible due to space constraints – see Chapter 3), likely due to the school's previous participation in Alexander's *Teaching Through Dialogue* project.

10 Horowitz (2008).

11 In Robin Alexander's international comparison of classroom discourse he found that interactions in English primary classrooms 'tended to be brief rather than sustained, and teachers moved from one child to another in rapid succession in order to maximise participation, or from one question to another in the interests of maintaining pace rather than developing sustained and incremental

lines of thinking and understanding'. Such classrooms stifled the emergence of meaningful and cognitively demanding interaction because of 'an emphasis on participation at the expense of engagement and thematic continuity' (Alexander 2008a: 105). Set against Alexander's data, Ms Leigh's interaction with William stands out as being unusually dialogic, and thus we must be careful not to rush too quickly to accusations of inadequate pupil participation without considering the wider context; such accusations are routed in the ideology of inclusion and whole-class participation which is dominant in UK schools (see Chapter 8).

12 See Moss (2007) for an analysis of this debate, and discussion of how literacy, gender and attainment intertwine.

13 Of course some pupils (e.g. those who are very shy) will resist taking part in centre-stage talk. For these pupils, it may be better if their time spent interacting with the teacher came in small teacher-led group work or one-to-one.

14 Alexander (2008a: 117–18).

15 These questions all hang on an important question of development, namely, at what age are kids able to understand thematic continuity well enough to know how to build it?

Chapter 6

Importing popular culture into the classroom

EPISODE 3: 'SO WE'RE GOING TO HAVE *X FACTOR*'

A brief reference to popular culture led to momentary disruption of the norms, roles and interaction customary in Ms Leigh's Year 5 classroom. This event took place in a January literacy lesson, in the middle of a unit on writing short stories about a storm. Prior to this lesson the pupils wrote first drafts of 'timed stories' (written under conditions of limited time to simulate the national tests), which Ms Leigh assessed, providing pupils with their assessment levels and targets for improvement. The pupils then redrafted their stories. In the lesson we discuss in this chapter, they shared their targets, after which one pupil, Harry, read out loud his first draft. Ms Leigh then announced:

> We're going to be your judges now. So we're going to have *X Factor*. We're going to decide marks out of ten for how much Harry has improved in the second version of his story.

Ms Leigh's reference to the televised talent show *X Factor* was received by a number of pupils with enthusiastic exclamations. One pupil, William, raised his arms above his head in the trademark 'X' sign and hummed the show's theme tune. Harry removed his jumper, readying himself for the contest. Later, when Ms Leigh asked pupils to decide 'How many marks out of ten do you think we should give Harry for the improvement to his story?', Harry held up both hands and projected a perfect score of 10 around the room in the manner of an *X Factor* contestant pleading with the audience for telephone votes; William responded by showing Harry a nil sign.

This was the first time Ms Leigh had introduced *X Factor* into her classroom, and we were intrigued by pupils' immediate and positive responses to the mere mention of the televised talent show. This chapter examines closely how the episode unfolded, asking: How, if at all, did the introduction of *X Factor* bear upon teaching and learning practices in this classroom? In recent years enthusiasm for the pedagogical and social potential of the mixing of popular culture with school-based activities has grown. We use this *X Factor* episode as an opportunity to explore the alleged advantages and complexities of importing popular culture into the classroom. The chapter also raises issues about how to arrange and facilitate peer assessment, when and how to intervene in pupil dialogue, and what should be valued in pupil writing.

Setting the scene

The lesson

The lesson from which our focal episode is taken can be broken down into the following four sections:

1. *Review of previous work and pupil targets* (8 minutes). Ms Leigh recaps the previous lesson and asks for a show of hands about which kinds of targets pupils have been assigned: V targets for vocabulary issues, C targets dealing with connectives, O targets for sentence openers, and P targets for punctuation. She then calls on individual pupils to read out their targets and answers questions about targets that do not fit neatly into the VCOP scheme (we discuss this scheme in greater detail below).
2. *Feedback on Harry's story* (19 minutes). This is the *X Factor* episode introduced already (and which we will examine in detail). One pupil, Harry, shares his stories and targets, and the rest of the pupils assess and discuss his improved version.
3. *Group work* (20 minutes). Pupils review their stories with a partner, discussing how they responded to their targets and other ways of further improving their stories.
4. *Plenary conclusion* (6 minutes). Ms Leigh calls upon one pair to share their work, and this leads into a discussion of how to build tension in a story and engage the reader. Ms Leigh congratulates the pair and the rest of the class on their progress.

The episode

In this chapter we examine the second section, in which the pupils use *X Factor* as a way of assessing and discussing Harry's stories. Before exploring this episode in detail, we summarize it briefly. As for the preceding chapters, the companion website www.routledge.com/cw/lefstein includes a video recording and full transcript of this episode. We recommend that readers review the summary below before watching the video for the first time. The episode can be roughly broken up into three main stages:

1. Presentation of stories and introduction of X Factor (lines 1–130)

Immediately before the focal episode (and accompanying video clip) begins, Ms Leigh calls upon Harry to tell the class why he is keen to share his story. Harry says that it is because he knows he can make it much better, probably improving to a 4b or 4a (in national assessment levels). Ms Leigh replies playfully, 'Let us be the judge of that' and asks the rest of the class to face Harry and 'give him a stare'. She asks him to first read out the targets she had set him based on the first draft of his story, which were as follows:

> To be a level *4b* you need to:

- read back over what you've written at the end of a paragraph to add in the words that are missing and affect the meaning of the plot;
- keep working on using details and action but aiming to reach the ending of the plot so that all issues are resolved (even if this means changing your mind to shorten the second bit of action you want to use).

Following a brief discussion of these targets and how Harry might be able to over-come the problem of finishing his stories in the allotted time, Harry reads out the first version of his story (Figure 6.1). William comments that he wants to hear what happens next, but Harry tells him, 'You want to hear this one!' referring to the second version of his story. This is where the focal episode begins. Ms Leigh says to Harry, 'Okay, so we're going to be your judges now' and tells the class, 'We're going to have *X Factor*. We're going to decide marks out of ten for how much Harry has improved in the second version of his story.' Harry then reads his second story out loud. Ms Leigh projects this text (Figure 6.2) on the board and instructs the pupils to discuss in pairs what they thought of the second story, and the extent to which it had improved upon Harry's first draft. These consultations last about 30 seconds, after which the pupils all turn to face Harry and raise their hands to display their scores (see Figure 6.3). At this point, almost all eyes are on Harry, and more than half the class have their backs to Ms Leigh, who is located at the front of the room (off screen, beyond the right edge of the drawing). Harry rises out of his chair and surveys his scores, commenting enthusiastically about the nines and tens.

2. Pupil assessments, explanations and related discussion (lines 131–397)

Harry receives feedback from six pupils, three of whom are nominated by Harry, while the others are nominated by Ms Leigh, who also offers her own evaluative comments. Most of this discussion revolves around the question of whether the description, and in particular the quantity of descriptive words, is better in the first or second version. William, who is chosen by Harry to be the first pupil judge, begins this line of reasoning. It is perhaps useful to note that William and Harry were friends, but also keen competitors in classroom tasks, and because they were confident, outgoing pupils, they were at the centre of many of the classroom discussions we observed (see, for example, Episode 2):

```
132  Harry:      excuse me
133              explain why you've only give me a five
134  William:    because
135  Pupils:     ((laughter))
136              ((most pupils put down their hands))
137  William:    becau:se in the first story y-
138              you had more descriptive (.) words
139              and you didn't ex-
140              in the second story you didn't [explai:n the:
141  Julie:      ((to neighbouring pupil)        [(xxxxxxxxxxx)
142  William:    man who was changing the weather
143              and
144              the characters (.)
145              a:nd
146              in the other one-
147              because in the first one you had (.)
148              better descriptive words
149              in that one you had more
```

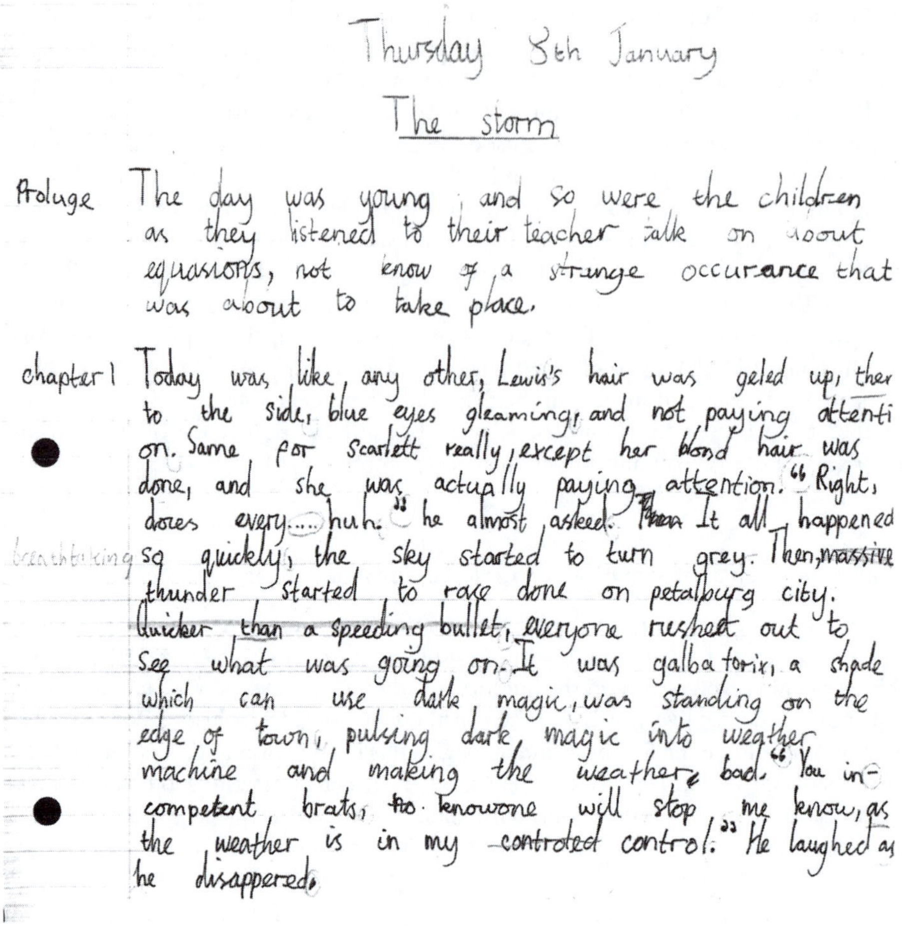

Thursday 8th January

The storm

Proluge The day was young, and so were the children
as they listened to their teacher talk on about
equasions, not know of a strange occurance that
was about to take place.

chapter 1 Today was like, any other, Lewis's hair was geled up, then
to the side, blue eyes gleaming, and not paying attenti
on. Same for Scarlett really, except her blond hair was
done, and she was actually paying attention. "Right,
does every...... huh." he almost asked. Then It all happened
so quickly, the sky started to turn grey. Then, massive
thunder started to race done on petalburg city.
Quicker than a speeding bullet, everyone rushed out to
See what was going on. It was galbatorix, a shade
which can use dark magic, was standing on the
edge of town, pulsing dark, magic into weather
machine and making the weather bad. "You incompetent brats, no knowone will stop me know, as
the weather is in my controled control." He laughed as
he disappered.

Figure 6.1 The first draft of Harry's story.

Harry begins to respond, just as Ms Leigh calls upon Julie, whom she caught whispering during William's turn (line 141), to share her thoughts with the class. She quotes William (almost) directly: 'yeah like because h- the better- the first one was better because he had like more descriptive words but in that one he didn't like describe the person who was changing the weather much' (compare with lines 137–8 and 140–2). Ms Leigh challenges this line of criticism, first by calling on a pupil, Tamara, to comment on the *quality* of the words chosen, then by highlighting some words that she felt were particularly advanced:

```
163   Ms Leigh:   [Tamara
164               what did you think about
165               the quality of the words that he used
166   Tamara:     they were quite good
167               but (2)
```

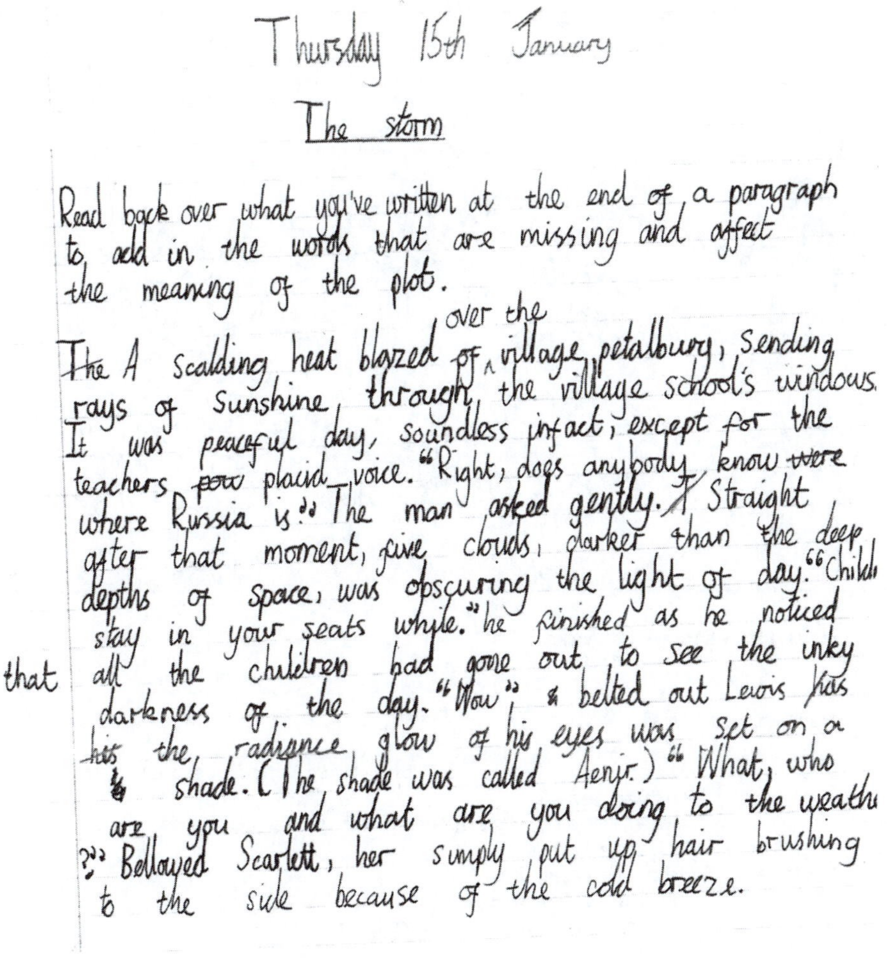

Thursday 15th January

The storm

Read back over what you've written at the end of a paragraph to add in the words that are missing and affect the meaning of the plot.

The A scalding heat blazed of over the village, petalbury, sending rays of sunshine, through the village school's windows. It was peaceful day, soundless infact, except for the teachers placid voice. "Right, does anybody know were where Russia is?" The man asked gently. Straight after that moment, five clouds, darker than the deep depths of space, was obscuring the light of day. "Child, stay in your seats while." he finished as he noticed that all the children had gone out to see the inky darkness of the day. "Wow" belted out Lewis has the radiance glow of his eyes was set on a shade. (The shade was called Aenjr.) "What, who are you and what are you doing to the weath? Bellowed Scarlett, her simply put up hair brushing to the side because of the cold breeze.

Figure 6.2 The second draft of Harry's story.

168		he could've used like more <u>descriptive</u> words
169	Ms Leigh:	give me an example
170	Tamara:	li::ke (2)
171	William:	(some xxxxxx)
172	Ms Leigh:	(come on) William you've spoken now
173		so for example
174		my <u>personal</u> choice
175		I really liked e:r
176		scalding ((*pointing out words on the visualizer*))
177		er blazed
178		peaceful
179		placid
180		and there's another one
181		[obscuring
182	Pupil:	[what does placid mean

Figure 6.3 Harry surveys his marks.

```
183   Ms Leigh:   calm
184               radiance
185               I thought actually the word choices were very
                  advanced
186               what would you have preferred to have seen
187   Pupil:      obscuring
188   Tamara:     erm more like (.)
189               I don't know really
190               it's just hard to explain
191   Ms Leigh:   okay
192   Harry:      you can say it's rubbish
193               I don't mind
194   Ms Leigh:   would you say that
195   Tamara:     no
196   Ms Leigh:   why not
```

Ms Leigh continues to question Tamara about the vocabulary in Harry's stories, pointing out that Tamara is very similar to Harry, in that they both have excellent vocabularies. Ms Leigh positively evaluates Harry's word choices, and in particular, the way he has described the character of Scarlett, the phrase 'her simply put up hair' being applauded for saying a lot about the character. The discussion of vocabulary continues when Harry chooses his next pupil judge, Gina, who felt that Harry's vocabulary was 'like level 4 or 5'. Ms Leigh probes this response by asking Gina: 'Why? What did it do for you as a reader?' Harry is then invited by Ms Leigh to choose a final judge. With some resignation, he selects Callum, who is enthusiastically projecting a score of four in Harry's direction:

```
283    Ms Leigh:        right Harry we've had
284                     a girl and a boy
285                     so now somebody else who's given you
286                     not a ten out of ten
287                     not a five out of ten
288                     [>come< o::n who's going to give Harry some
                        honest feedback
289                     [((Callum changes from six fingers to four))
290    Callum:          me ((moves hand in Harry's direction))
291    Harry:           er ((looks around the room))
292    William:         four ((points to Callum's hand))
293                     (2)
294    Harry:           Callum go on
295                     why did you give me a four
296    Callum:          er well like
297                     you never really explained as much
298                     [as like the first one
299                     [((Rachel and William raise their hands))
300    Harry:           I didn't get up to there [peo:ple
301    Callum:                                   [yeah but you c-
302                     (2)
303                     okay
304                     you could have like done the characters
305                     like you and the Ms Leigh or whatever you
                        were
306                     [or was you even in it
307    Harry:           [((looks back at first version of story on
                        his desk))
308                     oh you mean describe the Ms Leigh [and stuff
309    Callum:                                            [yeah
310    Harry:           aw right yeah
```

Harry acquiesces to Callum's criticism and then demonstrates orally how he might have added more description of one of the characters, but Ms Leigh challenges the idea that more description is necessarily better, demonstrating how minimal descriptive details can provide excellent characterization without slowing down plot development (lines 62–326).

3. Conclusion (lines 398–416)

At the end of the segment Ms Leigh summarizes the discussion by asking, 'Do we all generally agree [Harry's] story improved from yesterday?' (lines 404–5). The pupils assent, and William initiates a round of applause for Harry, who asks, 'Should I bow?' (line 411).

Viewing the video recording

We recommend that readers now view the video recording and read the full transcript of this episode.[1] While viewing, think about what (if anything) stands out as particularly interesting and/or anomalous. You might like to consider the following questions:

- What is happening here? How do you know? How is this clip different to other examples of classroom interaction you've seen and/or experienced?

- How do participants organize the classroom space? Where is attention being directed and how does it shift over the course of the episode?
- What do you think is motivating pupils' feedback choices and manner? How does Harry respond to them?
- What is Ms Leigh's role in this interaction? Are there any marked shifts in pupil roles?
- Which version of the two stories do most of the pupils prefer? How does this compare to Ms Leigh's position? Which version do you prefer?

Analysis

The lesson described in this chapter was among those selected, in the first instance, as basis for a one-to-one feedback conversation with Ms Leigh in mid-March 2009; ten weeks later, the *X Factor* episode was discussed in a reflection meeting with all seven participating teachers (a summary of the issues voiced by these teachers can be found in Box 6.1). We also used this episode as a basis for a number of presentations at academic meetings and conferences, and ultimately wrote up our analyses in an article published in *Reading Research Quarterly*.[2] We were interested in this episode because it raised for us the following questions:

- What social, discursive and pedagogical possibilities did *X Factor* open up or close down? How were these possibilities and/or challenges taken up and managed by participants?
- What are the advantages and disadvantages of importing popular culture into the classroom?
- How should we assess pupil writing? What counts as a good story? How can we help pupils become better writers?

We address these issues in the following discussion. In doing so, we build upon research on popular culture in classrooms and the concept of 'discourse genre', which we have found very helpful in making sense of what happens in this episode. We begin by explaining our use of discourse genre, and characterize and contrast the two genres that interact in this lesson: whole-class feedback and *X Factor*. We then briefly review the alleged advantages of importing popular culture into the classroom, and question to what extent the *X Factor* episode presents cause for celebration. We examine the ways in which pupils and teacher draw upon and manage *X Factor*, as well as the more conventional school discourse genre of class feedback on pupil writing, and explore the consequences of mixing popular culture with school knowledge in this case. Finally, we investigate the development of the ideas about Harry's stories and writing more generally.

Contrasting discourse genres: whole-class feedback and X Factor

Different spheres of social activity (for example, classroom lessons, television talk shows, dinner parties, doctor–patient consultations) are associated with particular ways of using language and interacting. We come to recognize and understand these patterns through multiple experiences over time. For example, most of us have some memory of our first day at school. We might recall feeling overwhelmed by difference – the classroom regime is quite distinct from that of the home – and daunted by the introduction of a new set of

Box 6.1 Key issued raised by teachers in the reflection meeting

Pupil participation.

I was trying to work out what is the level of engagement of the children, but now that I've watched it a few times, I think, using the X Factor sort of format really got them interested in what they were doing, they were quite keen to participate, and they were sort of fiddling around just before they went to put their hands up. So, I thought that was quite a good way to get them motivated with doing analysis. But I wanted to double check what the level of involvement was with all the children

Level of detail in pupils' answers.

I was interested to find out how detailed the children's answers were … Tamara, the first one, has got a reading age of about 16, and she's really bright, really into her writing, really top notch sort of English student. And yet when I asked her what do you think could be improved, she couldn't give me a detailed answer, she just said, 'yeah, probably better words.' And I wanted to see if that was because of how much time I'd given her to think it through, or whether it just because it wasn't, you know, a particular format that worked for her.

Julie, for example, she is in my focus group, so, she's slightly below average, and when I asked her, 'what is it that you think could get better?' she had an answer for me, and she could say to me, 'well, I like this word, this one and this one.' But she couldn't give me anything that was more in depth than that, and that's why I'm so interested in the detail of the answers. Is it because of the way that I'm asking them? Is it because they don't have the subject knowledge? Or is it something else?

Level of ability.

They always come back to, 'oh, choose better words,' which, I suppose, when you've got like a mixed ability class, is what they're going to focus on. Is it entertaining? Is it interesting? Do I understand this? If it's too highbrow, too many commas, too many – you know, they just don't access it, at all.

Is it a bit difficult because Harry is a brighter child? If you had chosen a kind of average story, with the child working on it, could they have been able to analyse it better?… because Harry is quite articulate, that it doesn't leave much to the children who are of a lower ability.

Gina, I mean she's fairly bright, isn't she? And for a long, long time, she just said, 'really, really good. Really good.' And I don't think they do have the words to say anything different. I don't think they can give anything more than that, sometimes.

She did get there in the end, didn't she? She said it builds up a picture. And then, the first half, I thought, 'oh well, she did know really,' and then the second time I watched it, I thought, well, is that just a prepared answer? I think she's heard someone say that before.

Frameworks for evaluating pupil writing.

And that could have been the one point where the lesson could have gone off to actually focus on, well, you're thinking about the reader all the time when you're writing … But maybe that's something that I need to do more of, as well. What does it do for the reader? Why is it good? What does it make me think? What does it make me feel? What should you have there instead?

> *If you've got two people reading one story, as it's so open to interpretation, you need to be able to pick some technical elements, vocabulary choices, construction, as well as plot development and characterisation, so that you can actually say, this is better than this, because*
>
> Positive learning environment.
>
> *I think, on the positive, you've got a great working environment, the children obviously feel comfortable that they can challenge each other, they take on criticism and they're used to it, but they don't take it personally, and they're thinking of improving their work. So, it's a very comfortable environment in there.*
>
> *They love the class, don't they? And all – the majority are engaged. You've got a really nice way with them, I like the humour and the way they respond to that.*

rules to regulate classroom behaviour (e.g. raising a hand to bid for permission to speak, addressing the teacher with title plus surname). But very quickly we come to understand the rules and regularities associated with schooling and how they differ from those at home (and from the supermarket, doctor's surgery, peer-group and so on). This is because these rules and regularities are relatively stable and enduring, and as a consequence of repeated experiences, we internalize the ways of speaking and acting that are expected in a particular social context; so much so, in fact, that we might police others' behaviour when they break away from these expectations (as when a child reprimands a fellow pupil for calling out without permission in class). These relatively stable ways of communicating are what we, with others, refer to as 'discourse genres'.[3] We find this a useful concept in thinking about interaction because it helps us to make sense of the speaking context. A single utterance might be interpreted quite differently in different contexts. Consider, for example, the meanings associated with a command like 'Sit down' when uttered in the head teacher's office or in an army barracks compared to in a friend's living room; the meanings evoked would be different again if used as part of a classroom game in which the winner is the person who remains standing, or when directed to a pregnant woman by a kindly passenger offering to give up their seat on a busy train or bus.

The context cannot be taken for granted, however; it is negotiated (and renegotiated) by speakers as they interact together. For example, the formality and frostiness of a head teacher's office might dissipate, being replaced with congeniality, if the head teacher and nervous parent summoned to meet with her suddenly realize that they had known each other as children – all at once the discourse associated with an official meeting turns into friendly banter and the rules of interaction change. The notion of discourse genre helps us to see which contextual frames are relevant at different points in an interaction. We hope that our use of this term will become clearer when applied to the classroom interaction outlined above.

The interaction in Ms Leigh's classroom is clearly recognizable as an instance of the literacy lesson feedback discourse genre: it is based on a recognizable topic (writing short stories); has recognizable roles (teacher and pupils); and is structured according to recognizable frameworks for assessment (national curriculum assessment standards). Evoking one or more dimensions of a genre calls to mind the other dimensions, and invites participants in the interaction to think about an utterance and/or social situation in terms of the genre evoked, in this case whole-class feedback in a literacy lesson.

Class feedback on individual pupil's written work was a relatively common activity in Ms Leigh's literacy classes, part of the routine lesson sequence used to develop pupils' writing skills. Feedback was usually given in the final few minutes of the lesson, in which several pupils read out their written work and received comments. Ms Leigh typically provided detailed individual feedback, and also often gave other pupils the opportunity to evaluate the work of their peers. In most cases, this peer feedback was directed by Ms Leigh (e.g. 'Spot the interesting technique that Carl has used'; 'Is there anything you would change about Rachel's word choices or the style she's writing in?'). The focal episode does not fully adhere to the norms and practices associated with the genre of feedback in Ms Leigh's lessons. For example, peer assessment is not always directed by Ms Leigh in this episode. On a number of occasions it is Harry who elicits comments from his peers (e.g. lines 132–3, lines 294–5). That this is unusual is indicated by initial pupil laughter (e.g. line 135). There appears to be a gap, then, between generic expectations and what actually occurs in this lesson. Upon reflection, we think these divergences are due to the introduction of another genre, *X Factor*.

UK readers will be familiar with *X Factor*, a highly popular British television music talent show in which would-be pop stars audition in front of a panel of celebrity judges in order to demonstrate that they have what it takes to be a successful recording artist – the allusive 'X Factor'. Indeed, readers from around the world are likely to have encountered the show in one of its many local guises: *Pop Idol* (the UK predecessor), *American Idol, Canadian Idol, Nouvelle Star* (France), *Ídolos* (Brazil) and *Super Star* (Arab world). These shows share a common format: aspiring pop artists audition to compete in a series of live television shows; each week individuals perform for the studio and television audiences, and their singing abilities, technique, appearance, star quality and so-called 'likeability' are critiqued by music industry judges; after each show a telephone vote from the audience at home decides the fate of the performers – the contestant with the fewest votes is eliminated from the competition. *X Factor*'s creator, Simon Cowell, was also a judge on the panel, and his trademark harsh but allegedly 'honest' comments have become a defining characteristic of the show.

In addition to their role as arbiters of talent, the celebrity judges also act as mentors, each responsible for a group of contestants, for whom they offer advice on song choice, performance, styling and so on. Ultimately there is only one prize – a million pound recording contract – and the fierce competition between the finalists is encouraged by the judges, who often draw explicit comparisons between performers, strive to elevate their own mentees and attack others.

Teachers and pupils at Abbeyford Primary were familiar with *X Factor*; indeed, the school hosted its own *X Factor* talent show in July 2009, in which each year group performed a song and were judged by a panel of staff members. *X Factor* and related shows were also a regular topic of conversation at the school, and the general consensus was that Cowell's were the best critiques, a necessary evil that ultimately helps contestants to improve.

Upon initial consideration, *X Factor* appears to be quite different to the genre of feedback in a literacy lesson, but there are also a number of similarities. In Table 6.1 we systematically compare these two genres as a first step towards understanding how they might interact together in a literacy lesson. The table highlights that at the level of central task there is a good deal of overlap. Both involve the evaluation of a performance (written work in the case of class feedback and a singing performance in the case of *X Factor*) and provision of feedback for improvement. Both genres also embody the assumption that everyone cannot be equally excellent – some performances will be better than others, and assessments and rewards will be meted out accordingly. Only one of the *X Factor* contestants will win. Similarly, primary school pupils understand that assessments of their work (whether recorded privately by the teacher or publicly as part of whole-class feedback) are used to rank them relative to their peers. Most are aware of the class hierarchy and their place in it, and thus being asked to read out a piece of work poses both the opportunity to show off and the threat of humiliation.

There are differences, however, in many of the other dimensions outlined in Table 6.1, including, significantly, the bases for and object(s) of evaluation. Within *X Factor*, contestants are judged on the basis of their personality and moral character in addition to (and sometimes at the expense of) consideration of their actual performances. Within schools, in contrast, teachers are advised to focus feedback on the pupil's performance rather than on who they are, because overly 'personal' feedback, oriented to the pupil's 'self', can distract from the substantive issues.[4] Further, while *X Factor* judgements focus almost exclusively on the immediacy of the performance, classroom evaluation is part of a process of continuous assessment, which takes account of an individual's previous performances and level of ability, and the expectation is that pupils will improve week on week.

Before applying this understanding of the two discourse genres to Ms Leigh's classroom, we turn in the next section to a brief review of the potential advantages of importing popular culture into the classroom.

Should we import popular culture into the classroom?

A major challenge in communicating academic knowledge and language is their isolation from the everyday knowledge and discourse that pupils bring with them from the home and their peer groups. This gap is particularly acute in the case of children from disadvantaged and marginalized backgrounds.[5] Popular culture can provide a bridge between the everyday 'funds of knowledge' that children bring with them to school and academic knowledge.[6] This bridging enables pupils to use everyday experiences and discourse to make sense of and build academic knowledge, and moreover, to see the potential relevance of school knowledge to their everyday lives.[7] Introducing popular culture also has the potential to challenge official discourse and knowledge, and to expand their boundaries through the integration of non-academic concepts and experiences.[8]

Reporting on research based in a school serving a socially and economically disadvantaged area of the US, George Kamberelis highlights the progress made by two fifth-grade pupils, Kyle and Max, when their use of popular cultural discourses was embraced by their teacher.[9] Working together on the dissection of an owl pellet, for example, Kyle and Max used their advanced knowledge of popular culture (for example, drawing upon surgery discourse common to television series such as *Chicago Hope* or *ER*) to engage in a challenging scientific activity. The boys channelled this mixture of home and school knowledge, or what Kamberelis refers to as 'hybrid discourses', into their written report, which was praised by their teacher for its creativity and later became a model for the whole class. The boys had been perceived initially as outsiders with poor behaviour and inappropriate interests, but following this event

Table 6.1 Contrasting discourse genres

	Feedback in a literacy lesson	*X Factor*
Social field	Education/schooling	Entertainment/television/music
Central task	To evaluate and improve a pupil's written work	To evaluate and improve a contestant's stage performance
Participants and roles	Teacher and pupils	Celebrity judges/mentors, contestants, coaches and audience
Purposes	*Teacher*: to improve an individual piece of pupil writing; to teach the rest of the class about qualities of good writing; to produce an institutionally adequate lesson; categorize pupils according to national standards of achievement *Pupils*: to perform well, be accepted by peers, get through the lesson	*Producer/judges*: to produce an entertaining show (as indicated in viewer ratings, which lead to advertising revenue); to organize contestants according to their relative talent, and promote the best performers to the next level *Contestants*: to win the show and/or launch a career in the entertainment industry
Sequential structure/stages	Will typically include the following (though not necessarily in this order): • discussion of targets/criteria • sharing of pupil work • judgement and/or interpretation of the work • suggestions for improvement • conclusion	Will typically include the following (usually in this order): • review of contestant's participation in competition so far (through edited clips) • contestant's stage performance • critique of performance by judges (with some suggestions for improvement) • interview with contestant (who then has the 'right-to-reply' to the judges' comments)
Topics/themes	Issues arising from pupil written work that are salient to the official curriculum	Contestant's performance (but this focal point often overridden by discussion of judges' own careers, arguments between judges etc.)
Interactional norms	Speaking dominated by the teacher, who also allocates the floor; primarily recitation	Speaking dominated by judges; host allocates the floor to individual judges, but judges also assume the power to self-select; lots of interruptions and overlap
Social relationships	'Emotionally flat' (Goodlad, 1984). Pupils are emotionally invested in peer relations, but these are downplayed in the public spaces of lessons	Emotionally charged. There is a competitive relationship between judges, but to their own acts, judges provide support and guidance in their role as 'mentor'
Language use	Polite or at least disciplined; use of standard grammatical forms	'Brutally honest' assessments of a contestants' potential; highly emotive responses
Evaluative criteria	National curriculum attainment levels and related learning objectives, divided into word, sentence and text levels	Does the contestant have the 'X Factor'? This encompasses musical talent, personality (e.g. genuineness, likeability), and moral character (e.g. humility, niceness)

they began to be admired by their peers for their 'creative genius', and the teacher came to realize that the children's references to popular culture were often academically productive.

The above example highlights another advantage of popular culture, its potential to disrupt conventional power relations, both by affording pupils from marginalized linguistic and cultural backgrounds greater opportunity for participation in classroom discourse – enabling their voice – and by creating a space in which the teacher and dominant pupils' voices are less dominant. Drawing upon popular culture in the classroom might thus cause shifts in habitual classroom roles and interactional patterns, facilitating more equitable and open dialogue. This, in turn, may create a more inclusive classroom community, by affording increased opportunity for a greater number of pupils to identify with and inhabit positions within classroom discourse. Jackie Marsh and colleagues conducted a project designed to use popular culture and new technologies to develop the early years curriculum (e.g. basing whole units on popular children's television programmes). Teachers reported that children who had not previously participated in class suddenly found a voice, becoming more engaged in classroom activities and more popular with their peers.[10] Likewise teachers can use popular culture discourse genres to signal their solidarity with pupils, through their shared participation in out-of-school discourses and practices.

For these reasons, educational researchers and practitioners are generally very positive about the educational and emancipatory potential of discourse genre mixing or hybridity – whereby school-based discourse genres *inter-mix* with everyday and popular culture genres.[11] The *X Factor* episode exhibited some of the processes outlined above, and to a certain extent presented cause for celebration, but we saw the episode as being potentially much more complicated. We wondered, for example, how the tensions between the two genres were managed by participants in the interaction. How, if at all, did *X Factor* shape conventional classroom feedback in this episode, and *vice versa*?

How did participants draw upon and manage the two discourse genres?

William and Harry are the pupils most obviously attuned to the *X Factor* genre. It carves out a space for these boys to take on unconventional roles and assume non-pupil interactional privileges (standing up, nominating pupils, interrupting). Harry rises to the occasion, performing for the class and winning their appreciative laughter. Likewise, William takes great pleasure in the role of pupil–judge when selected by Harry to give the first round of feedback. William gives Harry a score of five out of ten (which is rather low relative to the other pupils' scores) and evaluates Harry's first story as being better than the second because he claimed it had 'more descriptive words' (line 138), 'better descriptive words' (Excerpt 1, line 148), and overall greater explanation of character (lines 140–4). This assessment draws upon the resources of the school feedback genre: William's comments refer to specific elements of Harry's stories (e.g. line 142) and tap into shared frameworks for assessment (which highlight the importance of descriptive vocabulary). William's rather critical assessment of Harry's second story may also draw upon his experience of *X Factor*. *X Factor* contestants who appear overly confident or arrogant (an accusation that might be levied at Harry) are usually 'put back in their place' by the judges' sobering comments. By adopting the critical stance of an *X Factor* judge, while also drawing upon his knowledge of the school-based genre, he is able to orient both to the classroom task of peer assessment, and to his social relationship with Harry (recall that the boys were friendly competitors). Note also that rather than grading Harry on the improvement he made to his story through the redrafting process (as Ms Leigh had requested), William is actually evaluating which version of the story is better. This focus on categorical judgment rather than on the process of improvement is more in keeping with *X Factor* evaluative criteria than school assessments, and it sets the tone for the following discussion. This shift in focus threatens to undermine the school ideology of continuous improvement, according to which feedback and editing necessarily lead to better writing (and better writers) – we return to this point later.

Other pupils in the class also orient to the *X Factor* genre, most noticeably when invited to give their initial scores to Harry, which evokes a flurry of excitement. The presentation of numerical scores is not a feature of *X Factor* (numerical grading is more in keeping with the classroom feedback genre) but the public show of approval (or indeed disapproval) *is* part of this genre, and the children enthusiastically embrace this element, projecting their scores in Harry's direction and calling out his name in a bid for his attention.

Some pupils adopt more conventional classroom roles. When Tamara is called upon to speak by Ms Leigh, their interaction is situated firmly within the genre of classroom feedback. This is evident in the extended interrogation that Ms Leigh conducts, her use of the whiteboard on lines 175–81 (which focuses attention on her and on the front of the classroom, rather than on the pupil-contestant Harry), and the various strategies that Tamara employs to evade her teacher's questions, including the use of pauses, hesitation and fillers such as 'like' (lines 170–1, 188, 202–3), and stock excuses ('I don't know really, it's just hard to explain', lines 189–90). By line 191, Tamara's strategies appear to have worked and Ms Leigh moves to end the exchange with 'Okay'. Harry prevents closure of the topic, however, when he interjects with 'You *can* say it's rubbish. I don't mind' (lines 192–3). Harry's interjection reframes Tamara's hesitation from insufficiently elaborated pupil response to overly sensitive (and hence not appropriate for *X Factor*) judge response. It can also be seen as an attempt to refocus attention on the *X Factor* game and on him as contestant. Harry speaks without permission, in keeping with the interactional privileges awarded to him by the *X Factor* game, and uses a term ('rubbish') that is more fitting in *X Factor*-style judgements than in traditional classroom feedback. Ms Leigh co-opts Harry's comment but moves back into the frame of conventional teacher–pupil talk. She asks Tamara 'Would you say that?', and 'Why not?' (lines 194 and 196). Tamara is unsure of how to respond, perhaps in part because of genre ambiguity.

Overall, Ms Leigh shifts in and out of *X Factor* according to competing pedagogical goals. For example, after her interrogation of Tamara, Ms Leigh is about to select the next speaker in accordance with traditional classroom discourse norms and participant roles ('Okay Callum what did you give-', line 239), but stops herself ('oh sorry, I shouldn't do that should I?', lines 240–1) and transfers authority to the pupil-contestant Harry ('Harry, you had two more choices for people who gave you marks', line 243), in keeping with the '*X Factor*' rules she set up at the beginning of the activity. It is significant that Ms Leigh did not establish for herself a legitimate participant role in *X Factor*: she is neither host nor contestant nor judge. This means that when she needs to discipline a pupil who is not paying attention (lines 151–3) or move the discussion onto a different topic (e.g. away from *quantity* to *quality* of descriptive words, on lines 163–5) she has to shift out of *X Factor* and into conventional teacher recitation mode. When she can see that pupil interest is waning (evident through pupil gaze and body positioning), she shifts back to *X Factor*, and takes it up a gear: 'Come on, who's going to give Harry some *honest* feedback?' (line 288).

Ms Leigh's call for 'honest feedback' is not simply a request for the next pupil-judge; rather it appears to invite a certain kind of pupil response. Within *X Factor,* 'honest' often means Simon Cowell-like harsh criticism, and there's some evidence that this is what Ms Leigh is trying to invoke in the stress she places on 'honest' and in the elongated vowel sound of 'o::n', which makes Ms Leigh's 'come on' sound like something of a rallying call. So the expectation is not simply that pupils should bid to give the final round of feedback, but also that the resulting evaluation should be 'brutally honest'. Watching the video carefully, we see Callum (who is sitting directly opposite Harry) respond to this. He reduces his score from an original six fingers to four during Ms Leigh's utterance and appears eager to speak – his right hand, which displays the score, is outstretched towards Harry, and he pleads, 'me' (line 290). William, who is sitting next to Callum, points to the latter's score and exclaims, 'four'. Harry surveys the room, studiously avoiding Callum's gaze (even though Callum is sitting directly between Harry and Ms Leigh). When he fails to find a socially acceptable alternative, Harry rather begrudgingly selects Callum. The resignation audible in the statement 'Callum go on then' (line 294) is in marked contrast with the playfulness of his earlier 'Excuse me, explain why you've only give me five' (lines 132–3).

Callum responds to Harry's question on line 295 by bringing the discussion back to the issue of character description, echoing the idea originally expounded by William that more is better (lines 297–8). Callum does not appear entirely comfortable, however: he hesitates, using the discourse marker 'well', and stalls with the filler 'like'.[12] Harry responds defensively and with more than a hint of exasperation, appealing not just to Callum but to the whole class to cut him some slack: 'I didn't get up to there, people' (line 300). As he speaks, Harry's body tenses and he holds out his hands, palms up, in a beseeching gesture. Callum has been asked to take on a role usually reserved for teachers, and has also arguably been encouraged to take a more negative evaluative stance by Ms Leigh; that this feels slightly awkward and out of the ordinary is indicated through Callum's hesitations and Harry's tense and exaggerated response.

Pupils take an active role throughout the entire episode, but ultimately, Ms Leigh retains control of the discussion. She stops pupils from interrupting during her more didactic exchanges (e.g. line 172) and on a few occasions prevents the pupil-contestant Harry from having his 'right-to-reply' (e.g. lines 150, 163), but she accepts *X Factor*-style comments that contribute to her pedagogical aims (e.g. lines 192–4). She decides which genre conventions are and are not possible in this situation (e.g. lines 288 and 416, respectively), and makes it clear when she feels that it is time to move away from *X Factor* completely and on to the next classroom activity (lines 398–401). This decision to move on to the next activity – to attend to other lesson goals – is at least in part motivated by the sense that time was running out, a point that Ms Leigh emphasized in discussing the episode with the other teachers.

The possibilities and problems of using popular culture in teaching

From our conversations with her, and from her actions in the lesson, it appears that Ms Leigh's primary motivation in mentioning *X Factor,* and in sustaining it as a salient frame of reference, was to attract pupils' interest, especially through orchestration of dramatic confrontations of contestant and judges.[13] This ploy was largely successful, as evidenced, for example, in pupils' heightened engagement both when giving their scores at the beginning of the episode (see lines 101–27 and Figure 6.3) and then again before the appointment of the third judge (lines 283–94). Almost everyone's involvement in the activity intensified with the mention of *X Factor*. A clear advantage of importing popular culture in this instance is therefore that it capitalizes on the passion pupils have for *X Factor*, bringing this same enthusiasm to bear on the school curriculum. On the downside, there are peaks and troughs in this enthusiasm throughout the episode, with intense involvement only really sustained by a few key individuals (especially Harry, William and Callum).

Try viewing the video clip again focusing on just one pupil, preferably one who does not appear in the written transcript. We did this for Jessie (see Figures 6.4 and 6.5), who does not contribute verbally to the feedback activity. Silence does not in and of itself signal a lack of engagement and/or learning so we turned to other signs of attention, such as shifts in bodily orientation, gaze and gesture. At the beginning of the *X Factor* episode, Jessie appears to be an active member of the class: she enthusiastically projects her score of nine in the air, smiling and laughing along with the other pupils (Figure 6.4). Just over four minutes later, however, this enthusiasm has clearly dissipated: she appears slumped at her desk, head resting on her hand, eyes down (Figure 6.5). Jessie's ennui seems to be shared by the other girls sitting on her table. Analysis of the video record shows that the levels of attention and involvement for these girls were not always well-aligned with the 'key events' as experienced by Ms Leigh, Harry, William and Callum. So, for example, in lines 251 and 259 William and Callum laugh at the teacher's joke about her voice, but Jesse ignores the second joke and only smiles mildly at the first, while the other girls do not react at all. This hybrid classroom event thus appears to be experienced differently by different participants at different times.

A second (perhaps unintended) advantage of importing *X Factor* into the classroom is that it opened up a range of discursive possibilities. The episode displays significant shifts in

Figure 6.4 Jessie and the other pupils present their scores.

Figure 6.5 Jessie displays non-interest in the class discussion.

interactional patterns relative to other lessons we observed in Ms Leigh's classroom (and elsewhere in the school), including high incidences of extended pupil utterances and pupil–pupil exchanges (not directly mediated by the teacher). These discourse patterns seem to indicate a move towards more open classroom dialogue. On a number of occasions, the discussion breaks away completely from traditional recitation mode, with Harry (rather than Ms Leigh) initiating questions and pupils responding directly to him. Classroom space is used differently, with attention periodically shifting from the traditional front-of-room teacher focus to pupil focus, and much of the action centred on Harry as contestant. In this way, conventional classroom power relations are disrupted: pupils respond to one another directly, without teacher mediation (e.g. lines 132–4, 192, 244–5), freely challenge one another (e.g. line 300), and resist their teacher's ideas (e.g. that the second story had improved from the first version).

However, on further investigation, our enthusiasm for these changes was somewhat tempered by consideration of the complexities of the event. The introduction of *X Factor* created a space in which the teacher's voice was less dominant, but the pupils who filled that space were the very same boys who were normally most dominant in this classroom. Harry's unconventional role as '*X Factor* contestant' clearly granted him non-pupil interactional privileges. William also participated actively in this unconventional discourse genre – he spoke out of turn and was extremely active nonverbally. He was reprimanded once (line 172, at a point where Ms Leigh had moved into traditional classroom recitation), but otherwise his exuberance was tacitly accepted by the teacher. Several other pupils participated actively in the lesson – bidding enthusiastically for turns, calling out, gesturing, engaging other pupils in dialogue – but some had to be drawn (sometimes reluctantly) into the discussion by the teacher (see Ms Leigh's interactions with Julie, Tamara and Karen). In this class, the more active pupils were generally male (though this was not the case in other classrooms observed during the study).

Based on our observations of other lessons in this classroom and on our conversations with Ms Leigh, we know that Harry, William and Callum, in particular, were very often the centre of attention and the focus of classroom interaction. Because of their dominance, these boys were in a better position than the other pupils to exploit the opportunities presented by importing popular culture in this instance. *X Factor* needs confident performers, and in this context, that role naturally fell upon Harry, William and Callum. It was these boys who fully engaged with the *X Factor* genre and with the interactional privileges it afforded them; so although discourse genre mixing led to shifts in classroom power relations, these shifts did not involve empowerment of traditionally marginalized pupils in this case. Patricia Duff has made the point that particular care should be taken in linguistically and culturally diverse classrooms, where pupils (especially recent immigrants) may come with different cultural models and experiences. Pupils who do not have access to the popular cultural models evoked in classroom discussion/activities may be inadvertently excluded from participating in the lesson.[14]

We have focused so far on the motivational, and especially, interactional opportunities afforded by the importation of popular culture. We turn now to the substance of these interactions, and consider ways in which the introduction of *X Factor* shaped opportunities to learn.

What were they talking about? The development of ideas in the episode

The central point of contention in the episode was which of the two story versions contained the better description. The dominant opinion, voiced by William, Julie, Tamara and Callum, was that the second version was inferior to the first because it had fewer descriptive words, less advanced vocabulary and inadequate character description. This criticism was disputed by Gina, who claimed that the second story contained 'really good description ... level 4 or 5 in vocabulary', and by Ms Leigh who cited some 'very advanced' words. Our own analyses of the stories align with those of Tamara and Ms Leigh: systematic comparison of the descriptive words used in the two versions reveals that there were *more* adjectives in the second version, and in terms of quality, many of the word choices in the second version appear to fulfil implicit criteria presented by the pupils for high level descriptive words.[15] This raises questions about how William, Julie, Tamara and Callum arrived at their assessment, and what it was based upon. In this section we explore the conflicting evaluations, where they came from, and how they were developed in the episode.

The pupils' evaluations – both negative and positive – appear to be based upon an implicit set of criteria for assessment of story value, according to which:

- more character description = better story (e.g. lines 140–4, 256, 304);
- more descriptive words = better character description (e.g. lines 155–9); and
- more advanced words = better description/better story (e.g. lines 137, 148, 168, 245–54).

This way of thinking about writing quality appears to be widespread in English primary schools, and is inadvertently promoted, alongside competing approaches, in policy documents and supporting materials. Underlying this formula is the assumption that the value of a word is predetermined, based on its obscurity, specificity and/or length, rather than its suitability to the particular context of use. We call this an 'essentialist' theory of word value, since it problematically locates value in the word's essence, irrespective of the way in which the word is used or received by the audience.[16]

One way in which these ideas have entered the classroom is through the VCOP scheme of assessment. Within this scheme, four key aspects of 'good' writing are identified – Vocabulary, Connectives, Openers, Punctuation – and in each area the items are hierarchically ordered into attainment levels (which are displayed visually in a pyramid structure). According to this scheme, for example, 'exciting' and 'so' are level one words while 'formidable' and 'outstandingly' are level five. VCOP pyramids are displayed prominently in the classrooms and are often referred to by the teachers (and also by pupils themselves). Prior to the focal extract, Ms Leigh spent ten minutes discussing the written feedback she had given the pupils on their timed stories in terms of VCOP targets (e.g. asking for a show of hands to indicate who 'had a V-type target … a C target'). The pupils were thus primed to judge Harry's writing using this frame.

The two versions of the story were read out loud in class only once, and just one of them (the second version) was displayed on the whiteboard, which was only partially visible to most of the pupils. These conditions might explain why the few references to the stories were vague. It may have been difficult for pupils to see or remember Harry's stories, but VCOP – and associated evaluative framework – were on the tips of everyone's tongues. VCOP is implicit, for example, in William's judgement that the first story had 'better descriptive words' and explicit in Gina's later, opposite statement that the description in the second version 'was like level four or five in vocabulary' (line 153). These diametrically opposed views might be explained if we consider another available resource: *X Factor*. We have already seen that William was well tuned to the *X Factor* genre. In taking up his role as first pupil-judge, he appears to have based his response (at least in part) upon the model of *X Factor* judges, especially Simon Cowell and his combative critical stance, hence William's lower than average score and critical assessment of Harry's second story. With limited access to the texts, Julie, Tamara and Callum appear to have taken William's lead, basing their answers on his evaluation (in Julie's case almost word for word).

Ms Leigh challenged the pupils' evaluations in three ways.[17] First, she gave counter-examples of 'very advanced words' (lines 175–85) from the second draft, which she favoured, and asked Tamara, 'What would you have preferred to have seen?' (line 186). Note that this strategy questions the pupils' application of essentialist criteria to Harry's word choices, but does not challenge the essentialist theory of word value itself. Next, she probes Gina's positive assessment of Harry's vocabulary choices, which are a re-voicing of some of Ms Leigh's own 'personal favourite' words from a few moments earlier, asking what the description did for her as a reader. In such a way, she challenges Gina's appeal to an essentialist notion of high level vocabulary, adding a new criterion about rhetorical effects. Gina answers, 'It makes you think that … she's really nice and pretty. You want to know more about her because … you've described her so well' (lines 260–4). Gina's recourse to stock responses like 'you want to know more about her' (line 263) do not give Ms Leigh much to work with in pursuing this line of enquiry, though perhaps *X Factor* could have been a useful guide at this point. Consideration of the subjective gut reactions offered by *X Factor* judges might have provided a bridge between Gina's existing knowledge of evaluative frames and related vocabulary and the kind of reader response that Ms Leigh was trying to promote.

Finally, towards the end of the episode, after Harry has acquiesced to Callum's criticism, and demonstrated orally how he might have added more description of one of the characters (which earned him appreciative laughter from some of his classmates), Ms Leigh challenged the idea that more description is necessarily better (lines 326–44). The problem with the kind of additional descriptive detail Harry proposed (e.g. quiet voice, thick glasses) is that it does little to advance the plot. *National Literacy Strategy* guidance on characterization specifically discusses this problem, which is common in pupil writing:

> Many young writers find it hard to build up characterisation. They muddle this with character description, which is dropped into the story in one chunk, e.g. 'Tom came into the room. He was a tall boy with dark hair. He wore blue jeans and talked with a deep voice. He had trainers on ...' The problem with too much description is that it can interfere with the narrative.[18]

Ms Leigh's discussion of how 'a simple phrase ... actually helps to give you lots of character details' echoes this advice. Moreover, in her comments, Ms Leigh highlights an important difference between the two stories. While in the first story character description is direct (e.g. *Lewis's hair was geled up, there to the side, blue eyes gleaming and not paying attention*), in his second attempt Harry developed character through action and dialogue (e.g. *'Children stay in your seats while,' he finished as he noticed that all the children had gone out.*). This latter example serves to demonstrate the shortcomings of an essentialist approach to evaluating description and vocabulary. Harry uses no adjectives in this description, and the words chosen appear 'simple' and 'lower level'. However, they are quite effective at painting a relatively rich picture of the ineffective and out of touch teacher while also moving the plot along.

The *X Factor* activity opened up a potentially productive space for the emergence of multiple perspectives on story writing. Ms Leigh and Gina disagreed (for different reasons) with the evaluations offered by William, Julie, Tamara and Callum. This could have led to a more in-depth discussion of how different language elements contribute to narrative effects, thus shifting the focus from specific feedback on a single pupil's work to a more general discussion of story writing relevant to the entire class. This does not happen, however. Following her extended analysis of the phrase 'her simply put up hair', Ms Leigh calls upon a final pupil-judge, Karen, and then wraps up the activity with 'do we all generally agree his [Harry's] story improved from yesterday?' (lines 404–5). This is a rather curious account of the discussion, since the question of which story was better had been contested throughout and was never resolved. Ms Leigh mentioned multiple goals for this lesson in her discussions with us, including encouraging pupils to engage in a process of continuous editing and redrafting to improve their work. Ms Leigh's summary of the discussion makes sense in the context of this goal. It also makes sense within the context of the ideology embedded within the classroom feedback genre in UK schools more generally: pupils should be rewarded with praise for presenting their work, and feedback-and-redrafting necessarily leads to improvement. It would not have been easy for Ms Leigh to relinquish control and explore the children's suggestion that the first story was better than the second because the challenge to the pedagogical aims might have been too costly.

Finally, we can note the way in which Ms Leigh had to step out of the *X Factor* inter-actional frame in order to make any substantive points (see for example lines 172–81, 266–82, and 326–62). One of the problems she experienced in the lesson was that, in the way she set up the activity, she had no legitimate role as an active participant in *X Factor*. Thus, every teacherly contribution to the discussion was at the same time a disruption of the alternative discourse genre she had introduced. Ms Leigh's sensitivity to this fact is indicated in her re-formulation on lines 240–3: 'Oh sorry, I shouldn't do that should I?'. This comment may also indicate her sensitivity to the change in classroom dynamics brought about by her extended (over two minutes, from lines 163 to 238) interaction with Tamara. When we focused our attention on members of the audience (rather than on the speakers), and on non-verbal communication, we observed a slide in the pupils' attention during this period of traditional teacher–pupil recitation. By line 188, very few pupils are orienting their gaze and posture towards the speakers; a number of them yawn, look down at their desks and/or hold their heads in their hands. When Ms Leigh reacti-vates *X Factor* (line 243) and allows Harry to select his next judge, however, the children re-engage with the lesson, craning their heads and shifting position in order to see the speaker. In summary, *X Factor* opened up the possibility for more open pupil dialogue, but created problems for Ms Leigh in terms of how she might usefully intervene in this dialogue.

Conclusion

X Factor created new opportunities for pupils in Ms Leigh's Year 5 classroom, but it also posed some problems. First, although the introduction of *X Factor* created a space in which the teacher's voice was less dominant, the pupils who filled that space (William, Harry and Callum) were the very same boys who were normally most dominant in this classroom. On reflection, this dynamic is not surprising: their central position in the classroom facilitated their exploitation of the opportunities afforded by the introduction of *X Factor* into the lesson.

Second, the introduction of *X Factor* led to changes in interactional patterns and partici-pation structures. For some participants, however, enthusiastically embracing their new *X Factor* role meant taking on an *X Factor*-ish critical stance, which was not necessarily con-ducive to thoughtful comparison of the two stories. The interactions around William's and Callum's critical comments, though exuberant and at times entertaining, were problematic *vis-à-vis* engagement with the substantive issues. In a sense, Harry's, William's and Callum's displays of hyper-engagement mask the superficial ways in which the class engages with the issue of characterization.[19] There is perhaps an inherent tension in any lesson between increasing pupil interest and participation on the one hand, while engaging pupils deeply and substantively in learning academic content and processes on the other. Our analysis of the *X Factor* episode has demonstrated further that there may be aspects of popular culture, such as critical stance and categorical judgments, which are counterproductive to the kinds of academic learning opportunities most helpful to pupils.

Third, Ms Leigh possessed no clear role in the *X Factor* game as it played out in this lesson, and as such could not intervene to probe pupils' ideas or offer her own interpretations without 'stopping' the game. Throughout the episode, Ms Leigh juggled the competing goals of engaging pupils, giving them voice, managing participation, advancing new perspectives on story quality and getting through the lesson.

Finally, while the pupils and Ms Leigh drew upon and mixed various elements of both classroom feedback and *X Factor* discourse genres, we hypothesize that not all elements could be readily combined, and that choices in this regard are to an extent regimented by the school context. Most crucially, inasmuch as pupils recruited *X Factor*, it was to manage social relations, try out identities and entertain the classroom audience; but the content of their evaluations of writing quality relied upon established assessment frameworks (more and better descriptive words, VCOP and national curriculum assessment levels). *X Factor* afforded a degree of playfulness, but the game did not (and perhaps could not) impinge upon what really matters in the reigning ideology of primary schooling in the United Kingdom. Such regimentation is shaped by the institutions of accountability in education: the national tests, league tables, inspectorate and performance management. Working in a school with falling test scores and an impending inspection, Ms Leigh was not in a position to deviate significantly from curricular contents and assessment structures perceived to be crucial for success in the national tests. This context may help explain why *X Factor* only gained limited traction in the lesson, despite the pupils' enthusiasm.

Although some of the problems Ms Leigh encountered are likely specific to *X Factor*, we suggest that this challenge of managing multiple goals, and the ways in which popular cultural resources interact with these goals, is inherent to the practice of teaching more generally. Although teachers may be tempted to bring popular culture into their classrooms to draw pupils into the lesson and facilitate change in interactional norms, they thereby may also introduce less helpful discursive resources and frames of reference. Indeed, the same resources that make popular culture attractive as a means of motivating pupils to engage in classroom activity (such as their entertainment value) may, in many cases, also be counterproductive for meaningful and substantive academic learning. This is not an argument against the use of popular culture, but rather a recognition that any intervention on pedagogy, which integrates multiple and often conflicting concerns, will involve trade-offs and the introduction of new dilemmas.

Drawing upon popular culture can be a fantastic way of sparking pupil enthusiasm and increasing levels of motivation, but activities involving popular culture require careful preparation and thought on the part of the teacher if they are to promote meaningful learning. There isn't a one-size-fits-all solution. Popular cultural texts are complex and multidimensional. Educators need to be sensitive to this complexity and consider each instance of popular culture in the light of their specific pedagogical goals and the particular social and cultural context of their classroom.[20] Mapping out the dimensions of the popular culture genre being adopted against those of the classroom task (as in Table 6.1) could be a useful starting point. Where are the points of commonality and of contrast? Which dimensions of the popular culture genre appear most useful/suited to the pedagogical aims?

Episode 3 demonstrates, of course, that teachers are not able to dictate precisely which elements of a popular culture discourse genre will be exploited by pupils, and in what ways. Nevertheless, attention to the social and discursive associations that accompany discourse genres as they enter the classroom (as outlined in Table 6.1) may help alert us to both potential problems and productive possibilities. For example, one aspect of *X Factor*, which was untapped in the lesson, was the similarity between *X Factor* judgments as intuitive, gut reactions, and the sort of unfettered reader responses Ms Leigh tried to encourage at points in the lesson (e.g. line 258). Another useful resource might have been to draw upon the participant role of mentor rather than judge, and thus charge the pupils with giving Harry advice on how to improve his writing for the next round of assessment.

Issues for further discussion

Following analysis of the episode, readers might want to consider the following issues:

- What do you think of our analysis? What points resonate with your own interpretations of what's happening? What points seem problematic to you?
- Is importing popular culture a good strategy for making classroom practice more dialogic? What are its advantages and disadvantages? What dilemmas does it raise?
- What popular culture programmes, games, texts, etc. most interest your pupils? What interactive possibilities and learning opportunities might they offer? And how might you incorporate them into your teaching? Which children are likely to respond most readily to such activities? What might be the disadvantages?
- What do you value in the texts (novels, short stories, news articles, letters, advertisements and so on) you encounter outside of school? What do you value in pupil writing? Are there any differences between these two sets of evaluative criteria? If so, why might this be the case? What do your pupils value in their own and others' writing?

COMMENTARIES

WRITING: HARD SLOG, OR ENGAGING AND ENTERTAINING? BY ROXY HARRIS

The authors draw attention to the contrasts between the genres of popular culture (*X Factor*, in this case) and the 'conventional school discourse genre of class feedback on pupil writing'. They also suggest that one benefit of utilizing popular cultural genres in the classroom is a greater degree of engagement from pupils. But what if this is all that it achieves? What if the exercise does little or nothing to improve pupils' writing? Would it still be worth doing, and what damage might it do to pupils' understanding of the nature of writing in a school context?

There was a time in UK society when popular culture struggled for recognition and when its introduction in a school classroom setting was a daring and innovative act. However now popular culture and celebrity popular culture in particular, saturates most aspects of life outside school. Where else, if not in a school classroom, are school age children to be able to gain some respite from the norms and aesthetics of this pervasive culture? One central message of *X Factor* is that success, admiration and wealth are connected only loosely, if at all, with hard work or precision in developing the craft of singing. On the other hand, all skilled professional commercial and academic writers know that developing the craft of writing *is* a long-term project requiring hard work, great precision and attention to detail.

In the video clip a number of the pupils seem capable of producing evaluative comments expressing general likes or dislikes (in quasi-*X Factor* style) of aspects of Harry's writing; but their comments aren't directed to a precise place in the text. The teacher *does* attempt on several occasions to make highly specific comments about Harry's writing and to direct the pupils' attention to an exact place in the text using the whiteboard. It is not clear that at these moments the pupils can know to which place in the text, exactly, the teacher is referring, or that they can dwell on the pedagogic point she is making. Would not line numbering of the text shown on the whiteboard, be required, as a minimum, to achieve the necessary precision? It is noticeable that one girl, at the table nearest to the whiteboard appears to have her back to it at all times, and the boy at the bottom right of the video clip rarely appears to look at the screen. One could argue, then, that pupils in this episode reinforce their affiliation to the popular cultural genres epitomized by *X Factor*. They express personal likes and dislikes not accountable or tightly linked to supporting evidence. The genre of writing in school, though, concerns exactness in the selection and placement of words, phrases, sentences towards the construction of whole texts. This process involves prolonged hard work and attention to detail, and may not involve much immediate pleasure. When popular culture is included in the mix, are pupils misled into expecting that learning to write is entertaining?

Roxy Harris is a Senior Lecturer in Language in Education at King's College London. He is the author of New Ethnicities and Language Use *(2006) and co-author of* Urban Classroom Culture *(2011).*

COMMENTARY

'LOADS OF REALLY GOOD WORDS' BY JANET MAYBIN

The authors make very useful points about genre mixing. In thinking about what was actually achieved in the discussion of Harry's work, however, I also want to foreground the importance of the language available to these children for talking about differences between the two versions of his story (henceforth V1 and V2). This language links their work to the VCOP scheme and the national curriculum criteria but does not enable them to articulate what it is that they like about V1, and find problematic with the apparently more polished V2.

First, I have to admit that I, like some of the children, strongly preferred Harry's first version. Events are related through his distinctive, laconic voice: 'The day was young and so were the children', and the story is focalized closely through Harry's perceptions and viewpoint ('quicker than a speeding bullet, everyone rushed out to see …'). The writing is more pacy and exciting in V1, appealing to an audience of peers who would appreciate the contrast between inattentive Harry with his gelled hair and the 'good student' Scarlett with her 'done' hair. Child readers would also understand that a teacher 'talk(ing) on about equations' was probably boring, without needing this to be spelt out more explicitly, as is suggested in lines 353–7.

However, the teacher in the video extract is skilfully shifting students towards the kind of writing which will be positively evaluated within the national SATs, focusing here on the vocabulary part of the VCOP scheme. In terms of descriptive words V2 is seen by the teacher and some students as better than V1 because of 'very advanced' word choices like 'scalding, blazed, peaceful, placid ... obscuring' (176–81), evocative phrases like Scarlett's 'simply put up hair brushing to the side because of the cold breeze' (233–4) and speech tags like 'bellowed' (384). Variations on 'descriptive words', 'good words' and so on in fact provide the only criteria that the students and teacher use in this extract to analyse, discuss and evaluate versions 1 and 2 of Harry's writing (see lines 138, 156, 168, 197, 209–13), apart from vague references to more 'explaining characters' (140–4, 158–9) and 'explaining' (297) in V1. This tendency to focus on individual words limits their capacity to explain what they find good or problematic about the writing.

One problem with the atomized linguistic approach in the national English curriculum which is behind this focus on words, is that it can lead to meta-level description and grading of the ingredients of writing at the expense of a more holistic understanding and assessment of its effects. Thus Tamara suggests that Harry's V2 is 'like level four or five in vocabulary' (253) and Karen (366–7) says she liked 'the speech tags, the adverbs'. However, an individual word cannot be assessed as if it were being used in isolation. Words are effective in relation to the context in which they are used, in their contribution to the overall interest, sense of place, time and mood, characterization and plot development in the story. From this point of view I would suggest that V2 could be seen as rather full of heavy description which slows down the unfolding action, and involves some awkward juxtapositions. Would the teacher really ask 'gently' where Russia is? Would Scarlett with her simply put-up hair 'bellow' a question to the 'shade'? Confronted with a 'galba torix' 'pulsing dark magic into weather machine' (V1), are we interested in Scarlett's hair anyway? The arresting, racy genre of the V1 is almost lost in Harry's attempt to extend his descriptive vocabulary in V2.

When William (137–49) says that Harry explained the man who changed the weather and the characters better in V1 he is responding to the succinct, clever snapshot of Harry's and Scarlett's contrasting appearances and characters, and to the 'galba torix''s taunt and laugh which convey its power and evil intentions directly to the reader. However, when the only way children have to talk about Harry's writing is in relation to discrete elements of descriptive vocabulary, 'it's just hard to explain' what is wrong with V2 (Tamara, 190). Harry may have 'loads of really good words' (197) but what is significant is 'the way he put it' (229). V1 has 'better descriptive words' for the children not because of their individual ascribed levels and difficulty, but because of the way Harry weaves them together. Children need a framework and language of description that can address such subtle higher level effects which they are already employing in their own writing practice.

Janet Maybin is a senior lecturer in Language and Communication at the Open University. Originally trained as a social anthropologist, she has written extensively for Open University courses in language and education and also researches and writes on children and adults' informal language and literacy practices.

COMMENTARY

WEAVING POPULAR CULTURE: TOWARDS KNOWLEDGE BUILDING
BY DENNIS KWEK

In 1930, anthropologist Gladys Reichard studied Navajo culture by living with a Navajo family and learning to weave. She learned how to use weaving implements such as the shuttle which linked threads from side to side of the pattern. As she became proficient, she appreciated how individual threads connect together, over time, into a strong, coherent whole: 'A good weaver ... never considers how much work a pattern is. She sees it as a finished whole and exerts herself to accomplish the ideal' (Reichard 1934: 112).

Like a weaver, teachers make connections all the time between academic knowledge and pupils' interests, experiences and prior knowledge. Analogies, examples, metaphors, and contrasting cases can aid in making connections to promote deep understanding. Teachers may also connect previous, current and future lessons to link old and new knowledge. Such weaving of knowledge can engage and motivate pupils, but more importantly, weaving helps pupils to make personal connections and to see learning as 'building on'. Philosopher John Dewey argues that weaving engenders 'the best type of teaching' as it 'puts the student in the habitual attitude of finding points of contact and mutual bearings' (Dewey 1916: 192) between knowledge that is new and old, academic and out-of-school.

However, for connections to be effective, teachers need to be mindful of their quality and purposes. Here, I suggest there are differences between 'shuttling' and 'weaving'. Shuttling refers to making connections that are spontaneous, temporary, unplanned, superficial, have no direction nor do they build knowledge. Examples are recaps, brief summaries and poorly articulated connections. In contrast, weaving involves connections that are purposeful, planned and sustained over time, and that build multiple threads of knowledge into a coherent whole. And like a good weaver, the teacher has to consider the short-term lesson objectives and the long-term aims of what she wants her pupils to learn, know and become, and weave towards these aims.

Due to its complexity, weaving problems can occur. Pupils may latch onto the wrong characteristics of the analogy or example, multiple popular culture references may confuse rather than engage, connections may not explicitly refer to curricular objectives. Problems can be minimised if teachers design weaving during their lesson planning. In this episode, rather than the off-the-cuff, momentary use of *X Factor*, Ms Leigh could consider not only how *X Factor* could be weaved into this lesson in a more integrated manner, but throughout the entire unit as well. Not only could she use the suggested comparison table, she could highlight to the pupils the key characteristics of *X Factor* that are relevant to the learning at hand, rather than leaving pupils to decipher what they are. Over several lessons, different pupils could be assigned roles as judges or mentors, maintaining the dialogic patterns but expanding the participative opportunities. As peer feedback was a key focus for introducing *X Factor* and a potential learning outcome, the teacher could provide pupils with a better understanding of how feedback could be used to improve writing.

Ultimately, it is important to recognise that weaving can be imperfect. However, if the direction is consistent and design adhered to, the overall weave can contribute to productive learning.

Dennis Kwek is a Senior Research Associate at the Centre for Research in Pedagogy and Practice, National Institute of Education, Singapore. He is investigating the practice of 'weaving' in Singapore classrooms, a pedagogical model of connected learning across different types and forms of knowledge.

COMMENTARY

WHAT DID I LEARN AT SCHOOL TODAY?
BY LAURA HUGHES

After you've been teaching for a while it is rare to spend time thinking not just about what you're doing, but why you're doing it. As a participant in this research the opportunity to reflect upon my teaching was interesting but also a little threatening, particularly as it was to be done with my peers. Group reflection was not a tool that we had used before and as a conclusion was not always reached, it was at times frustrating, particularly when trying to isolate what could be done to improve standards in the classroom. However, the discussions in themselves raised the profile of pedagogy and made us more creative in planning learning opportunities for pupils.

The main concern that we had as practitioners was that dialogic episodes in themselves usually only involved very few children. This led us to continually return to questioning the impact that dialogic strategies had on the remaining majority of the pupils. Viewed in isolation, the lesson reported upon here rightly questions the engagement levels of pupils. It would appear that the teaching strategy has a minimal impact on the class as a whole, and this in turn means that the drive to raise standards was not being met as progress could not be seen. It is worth remembering however that this is one episode and that the objective of the lesson was again covered in several future lessons.

The spur of the moment decision to use the *X Factor* format came from previous experiences I'd had of groans of complaint in response to lessons where work was analysed and then redrafted. As such, it immediately engaged the pupils and gave them a familiar framework in which to operate, and interest in the learning task was immediately provoked, however, it was difficult to sustain this. Again, we return to the problem of reaching the majority of pupils for the majority of the time. As pupils have been taught in particular styles common to UK schools, they have become accustomed to them and arguably they produce results. Is this though simply because it is a learned way of learning, meaning that the use of contemporary culture would not be immediately regarded as a learning opportunity by the pupils themselves? I viewed it as one of many different teaching techniques that I employed in the hope of reaching each pupil across the year that I taught them.

Understanding the limitations in impact of the use of popular culture due to my negotiable role, the mixing of discourses and their rules as well as the analytical level of working has given me the opportunity to reflect upon the strategies that I employ and their effectiveness. In the process of learning about the impact of talk in all its forms, I have found that what seemed like a good idea at the time would have had greater power had I understood how to manage its use in the classroom. I'm pleased to say that I'm still learning too!

Laura Hughes is the teacher who appears in this chapter focal extract. She graduated as a teacher from University of Lancaster in 1998. During the research process she was the Assistant Head Teacher of the large Inner London school described in this book, and later moved on to become the Deputy Head Teacher there. She is a Certified Teacher of PSHE and is currently studying for a Masters in Education.

Notes

1 In addition to Ms Leigh, two other adults can be seen in the video. They are a teaching assistant (who appears at the left-hand side of the classroom, towards the back) and a student teacher (who is sitting at a desk at the front left of the classroom). Neither participate actively in the class discussion.

2 Lefstein and Snell (2011c). We further reflected on the processes of analysis and interpretation that went into writing this article in a chapter written for the forthcoming *International Handbook of Interpretation in Educational Research Methods* (Snell and Lefstein, in press). See Snell and Lefstein (2012) for an early version of this chapter.

3 Our use of the term is inspired primarily by Mikhail Bakhtin (1981, 1986), and the way his concept of speech genre has been taken up in linguistic anthropology and linguistic ethnography. In particular we have been influenced by research conducted by Jan Blommaert (2005), Charles Briggs and Richard Bauman (1992), William Hanks (1996), Janet Maybin (2006) and Ben Rampton (2006). For a more detailed exploration of the discourse genre concept, and the scholarship upon which we have based our ideas, see Lefstein and Snell (2011c).

4 John Hattie and Helen Timperley (2007) review the research evidence for the effectiveness of feedback directed toward the task, the learning process, pupil self-regulation and the self as a person. This latter category of feedback directed toward who the pupil (for example, smart or slow, diligent or lazy) is shown to be the least effective type of feedback.

5 Jackie Marsh (2008) makes the point that popular cultural texts may be the primary source of out-of-school literacy practices for these pupils.

6 On the importance of 'funds of knowledge' acquired in the home or community, see, for example, Moll *et al.* (1992).

7 Teo (2008). See also Dennis Kwek (2012) on the 'weaving' of academic and non-academic knowledge.

8 See, for example, Barton and Tan (2009).

9 Kamberelis (2001).

10 Marsh *et al.* (2005).

11 Often referred to as 'hybridity' or 'third space'. For a review of this literature see Lefstein and Snell (2011c).

12 Drawing upon the frameworks available within Conversation Analysis, we might say that Callum's utterance is marked as a 'dispreferred response'. (See Conversation Analysis literature on preference organization, for example, in Hutchby and Wooffitt, 1998).

13 Jackie Marsh (2008) outlines four key motivations, and associated models, for using popular culture in classrooms. These are: (1) Utilitarian model: using popular culture to encourage greater engagement with school work; (2) Cultural Capital model: using popular culture to provide a bridge between the

home and the school (particularly for children from disadvantaged backgrounds); (3) Critical model: using popular culture to develop pupils' skills as critical readers and writers; (4) Third space model: bringing together the different cultural spaces children inhabit to create new knowledge, reshaping both academic discourses *and* out-of-school knowledge. According to Marsh's categories, Ms Leigh's invocation of *X Factor* here is utilitarian.
14 Duff (2004).
15 For the detail behind this analysis see Table 4 in Lefstein and Snell (2011c: 57).
16 For an extended discussion of essentialism, and for the development of an alternative, 'rhetorical' approach, which we argue is more productive educationally and more sound linguistically, see Lefstein (2009).
17 We speculate that there may be at least three reasons Ms Leigh defended the second story: she preferred its advanced vocabulary and/or more sophisticated approach to characterization; she sought to promote the narrative of improvement through redrafting; and she sought to protect Harry from his peers' criticism.
18 DfES (2001).
19 The pupils' activity might be characterized as 'procedural display', defined by David Bloome and colleagues (1989) as teacher and pupils' display to one another 'procedures that count as doing a lesson', though they are not necessarily related to learning.
20 Marsh (2008).

Chapter 7

The teacher's role in classroom debates

The Year 6 teachers decided to conclude the winter term with a pupil debate about whether or not football on the playground should be restricted during lunchtime and breaks. In a planning meeting, one of the teachers, Ms Anderton, voiced some concern that in her previous experience in organizing classroom discussions of this nature the activity 'didn't get off the ground' because all the talk still went through the teacher. She challenged herself and the others to encourage the pupils to talk directly between themselves, without the teacher mediating and controlling the discussion.

Two weeks later, in the debate conducted in her classroom, Ms Anderton sat at the back of the room as pupils argued about how the playground should be divided between football and other activities. The debate clearly got off the ground. Indeed, at times it appeared as if Ms Anderton might be *too* successful: the pupils were so passionate about the issue that they frequently deviated from the terms and topic of the debate. One of the boys cursed, another argued that school would be a 'crummy place' without football, and one of the girls repeatedly raised her voice to lay into the boys, at one point angrily exclaiming, 'girls can't just make space for boys; boys are not the biggest thing in the world.' These heated exchanges offered the sort of mutual engagement and feisty participation that Ms Anderton had been working to orchestrate. But they also threatened to deteriorate into a not-so-dialogic shouting match. Moreover, they posed a formidable challenge for the teacher: How to maintain order without stifling the debate?

In this chapter we look at this and another debate in two Year 6 classrooms. The topic of playing football on the school playground at lunch time attracted considerable interest and concern, and led to many pupils' spirited involvement in the activity. In both cases the teacher moved to a relatively peripheral role in the debates to allow for more pupil participation in the discussion and greater pupil control over its course. This positioning led to interesting dynamics as the pupils assumed responsibility for conduct of the debates, but were unable to manage them effectively for an extended period of time. The two teachers dealt with this problem differently: one moved quickly to resume control at the first signs of trouble, while the other intervened minimally from the back of the room. Despite these differences, we were struck by a common dynamic: in both cases, pupils were most engaged and the interaction was most dialogic when the teachers assumed more marginal positions, and these sequences tended to subside when the teachers intervened to encourage and/or steer the debate. This raises a possible paradox for developing dialogic pedagogy: the more teachers attempt to actively promote dialogue, the less likely the pupils are to engage in it. We explore this paradox, and its implications for the teacher's role, along with other issues about structuring and conducting classroom debates, in this chapter.

A final note about chapter structure: the chapter is organized slightly differently from the preceding chapters because it presents and contrasts two episodes, rather than just one. First, we describe the Year 6 planning meeting at which we decided to conduct the debates, and which forms background to both episodes. Then we present and discuss each episode in turn, including sections on setting the scene, guiding questions for viewing the video and analysis. We conclude the chapter with a discussion that draws together the analyses of both episodes, questions for further discussion and three guest commentaries from Abbeyford's head teacher, a literacy consultant and an educational researcher.

Classroom debates in the shadow of SATs revision

The idea of debating restrictions on football playing was born in a planning meeting we conducted with the Year 6 teachers in December, 2008. We were entering SATs preparation season, which the teachers saw as constraining opportunities for dialogic pedagogy. However, in order to experiment with dialogic teaching, and also, no doubt, in order to not disappoint us researchers, the four Year 6 teachers perused the local authority guidance in search of suitable opportunities to engage in dialogue.[1] The SATs revision programme primarily involved review of features and practice in writing in the key genres assessed in the Year 6 tests, including letters, persuasive texts, play scripts, explanations, instructions, news reports, narrative and discussion texts. As the teachers and we leafed through the guidance we looked for issues that pupils could productively talk about, and among other topics, decided to conduct debates at the end of the autumn term as preparation for writing discussion texts in the beginning of the winter term. Discussion texts, also referred to as argument texts, involve presenting a problem and a proposition for addressing the problem, laying out arguments and related evidence for and against the proposition, and concluding with the author's own position. This format appeared to the teachers particularly well suited for dialogic teaching, since it captures many of the features we seek to develop in a dialogic discussion: consideration of multiple perspectives, development of arguments and formulation and defence of one's own position.[2]

In thinking about topics for debate, we sought out questions that were open – that is, propositions for which there are at least two legitimate positions, and there's likely to be actual disagreement within the class; charged questions – that is, they strike an emotional chord, have the potential to incite pupils' passions and spur their involvement; and, finally, issues for which there was a real audience that pupils could appeal to.[3] The curriculum guide suggests two discussion text topics: Is smoking bad for you? And should football be restricted? We preferred the latter topic since the topic of smoking is not really open (defending smoking is not a legitimate position within the school setting), and since the football issue was more likely to be meaningful for the pupils – they could potentially act on the basis of conclusions drawn in the debate. The local authority guidance includes the following example of a discussion text on the issue of restricting football:

> Our class have been debating whether football should only be allowed to be played in the school playground on Mondays, Wednesdays and Fridays because our playground is quite small in the winter when we can't use the field.
>
>   The people who don't like playing football say it is unfair that the game takes up a lot of space in the playground. They say they cannot walk around because they get bumped into and hit with the ball. They also say it is scary for little kids.

The footballers' opinion is that most people like playing so they should be allowed to. If they cannot practice the school team will get worse and they wouldn't win many games. Also they will not enjoy school if they cannot play with their friends.

I think that football should be allowed every day because most people like it and it is good fun.[4]

The local authority guidance, which the teachers customarily followed, called for using this and similar texts as an opportunity to identify key features of the genre being studied (in this case discussion texts). We decided instead to use the topic as a focal issue for a classroom debate – thereby to prioritize substantive engagement with the issue over technical compliance with genre conventions. Pupils would first think and talk about the issues in an oral debate, and subsequently write discussion texts on the topic.

We didn't delve into the specifics of how the debates would be conducted, and indeed the two teachers whose football debate lessons we recorded, Ms Anderton and Ms Lightfoot, organized and managed the debates in their respective classrooms in different ways. In this chapter we look at how these two debates unfolded. First we consider each episode in turn, and then discuss the similarities and differences between them, and key issues arising. We begin with the discussion in Ms Lightfoot's classroom, which is to a certain extent easier to follow than the debate in the other classroom.

EPISODE 4: DEBATING FOOTBALL IN MS LIGHTFOOT'S CLASSROOM

Setting the scene

The lesson

This lesson was composed of five segments:

1. *Introduction to debating* (7 minutes). Ms Lightfoot introduces the topic of debating, alternating between posing a question for pupils to discuss in pairs and collecting and probing their answers. First, she asks what it means to debate something, and collects and displays on the overhead projector pupil answers, including 'to disagree', 'argue about something', 'different ideas', 'putting across your viewpoint/[learning about] a different viewpoint'. She then asks why you might want to engage in debate, and again gives the pupils a minute to discuss in pairs before collecting answers. One pupil suggests that a debate might be useful for finding the right answer, which prompts Ms Lightfoot to introduce the idea of debate topics for which there is no right answer, and give the class a further 30 seconds to consider (again, in pairs) why one might want to discuss such a topic with others.
2. *Discussion of the sample discussion text* (reprinted above) (17 minutes). Ms Lightfoot uses the sample pupil text as the basis for review of the main features of the discussion text genre, focusing on text structure and the functions of each of the different sections (opening statement, arguments for and against, conclusion). Throughout, the discussion is punctuated with brief stretches of pair talk, for example about why it is important in a discussion text to include arguments for and against the proposition.
3. *Small group discussions about playing football on the Abbeyford Primary playground* (8 minutes). Ms Lightfoot asks the pupils to reflect on the issue in small groups: Should

the school restrict football playing to certain days? She directs them to come up with arguments specific to their own situation, which, she says, may be different from that of the school considered in the sample text.

4.   *Whole-class debate of the topic* (10 minutes). The class first discuss ground rules for the discussion, specifically how to signal they have something to contribute, and the importance of talking to and facing one another. Ms Lightfoot directs the front row of pupils to turn around and face the rest of the class, forming a circle with three pupils seated in the middle. Next, she asks them to close their eyes and vote on the issue. When the debate begins, pupils at first appear unsure of what to say and how to participate. However, the discussion picks up when one of the pupils introduces the idea that football be played with softer balls. The episode discussed in detail below begins at this point in the debate.

5.   *Reflection on the debate and on what the class have learned about discussion texts* (10 minutes). Ms Lightfoot concludes the debate by asking the pupils to vote again on the issue, again with eyes shut, and then queries who has changed their mind and why. The class then return to the list of debate characteristics and discuss the extent to which the debate they conducted featured those elements.

The episode

We have chosen to focus on four and a half minutes from the middle of the debate, because it captures nicely the dynamics we observed as Ms Lightfoot shifted between different positions in managing the discussion. For convenience sake, we divide this episode into four segments. Before exploring this episode in detail, we summarize it briefly. As for the preceding chapters, the accompanying website includes a video recording and full transcript of this episode. We recommend that readers follow the summary below before watching the video for the first time.

1. Softer balls? (lines 1–30)

At the beginning of the segment the pupils are talking between themselves, with no overt involvement on the part of their teacher, who indeed is out of the camera frame at the beginning of the clip, and moves to the door to attend to business taking place outside the room (lines 9–15). During this time, the conversation focuses on the problem of non-football playing bystanders being struck by the ball, and in response a few of the girls propose that football be played with softer balls. Toward the latter half of the segment (from line 16, approximately), the discussion begins to disintegrate, with the eight pupils on the right side of the screen talking to each other excitedly, but with the other half of the class stranded outside of the conversation.

```
 1    Natalie:   yeah also I think there should be soft balls
 2               because erm
 3               like it was saying over there
 4               loads of people
 5               when they're walking around they get hit by the balls
 6    Tom:       yeah but when you have soft balls
 7               you can't really play with a soft ball
 8               it's- not really fun to play with
 9               ((Ms Lightfoot walks across the room and opens
10               the door to speak to someone in the corridor))
11    Jessica:   no but if- [if it's hard it (will hurt you)
```

```
12   Kaylee:              [yeah but Tom some people (are thinking
13                        that all balls are this hard) and people
14                        get sent to the office
15            ((Ms Lightfoot re-enters room and shuts door))
16   Jessica:   because [the (xxxxx)
17   Harriet:           [(xxxxxxxxxxx)
18   Natalie:             [yeah true but-
19              and to be honest
20              (lighter) balls are quite softer to play with
21   Kaylee:    [and-
22   Jessica    [yeah but
23              it should be- it should be like
24   Kaylee:    [hard well not too hard
25   Jessica:   [if it- if it- if it's too hard
26              ((Ms Lightfoot sits down amongst the pupils))
27              because Debbie was just saying
28              she got hit on the head with a (.) hard [ball
29   Natalie:                                            [yeah
30   Jessica:   and she had to go to the office
```

2. Is that an argument for or against? (lines 31–58)

Ms Lightfoot intervenes, asking Jessica, who had been speaking, 'Can these people here hear what you're saying?' Jessica shakes her head in response, and is instructed by her teacher to 'face everyone'. Another pupil attempts to enter the conversation, but Ms Lightfoot stops him, noting that it's still Jessica's turn. Jessica repeats her point that football should be played with softer balls so as to minimize injuries. Ms Lightfoot questions whether this comment is on topic: 'Is that an argument for or against restricting where football is being played?' and concludes that it's a slightly different topic.

3. Proposals for dividing time and space (lines 59–125)

Next, four pupils present a series of proposals for how to address the situation: Allan and Christopher propose dividing up the days between football and other activities; Tom suggests dividing the days between teams; and Natalie suggests dividing the playground between football and non-football areas with a spray-painted boundary.

```
59   Ms Lightfoot:  what were you going to say Allan
60                  tell everyone your point of view
61   Allan:         well if we don't play football
62                  and it's like
63                  Tuesdays and Wednesdays
64                  and then
65                  it would be fair for the children
66                  who don't really have enough space
67                  and then football
68                  (xxxxx one day)
69                  and then children would be able to
70                  have [more space
71                       [((Christopher raises hand; Ms Lightfoot
72                  motions to lower it, which he does))
73   Allan:         and then like
74                  the next day there'd be football
```

```
74                      and then
75                      and then
76                      ((Christopher and Natalie raise hands discreetly))
77    Allan:            the football people could play football
78                      [so that's like (different days)
79                      [((Ms Lightfoot says something very softly to
80                      Christopher, who gets up and closes the door. She
81                      then signals to him that it's his turn to talk?))
82    Christopher:      on Mondays we could do
83                      football
84                      and then on Tuesdays we can do a different sport
85                      and then on Wednesday br- perhaps a different sport
86                      then on Thursday football
87                      and then
88                      Friday football or a different sport
89                      er
90    Ms Lightfoot:     ((softly)) ask som-
91                      ask someone who's got their hand up
92    Christopher:      Tom
93    Tom:              I think there should be-
94                      I think
95                      if you want to
96                      play football
97                      you get into a team with your friends
98                      and they have a league
99                      and if it-
100                     you have two teams playing every (.) day
101                     so there's (.) not
102                     so you can use a little less space for football
103                     because there's not as many people playing
104                     in one day
105   Natalie:          ((whose hand has been up since line 76, motions))
106   Tom:              Natalie
107   Natalie:          I think there should be like
108                     like spray painted an area
109                     of a particular area for them to play football in
110                     so that erm
111                     they don't like
112                     maybe allowed to go past that line
113                     if they want to play football
114                     because some people can get hit
115                     and there's not really that much space
```

4. Equipment considerations (126–65)

Ms Lightfoot asks what days the pupils are given playground equipment, and suggests bringing that into the conversation. Natalie develops this idea, suggesting that on equipment days 'there's not really much point playing football because we've got ... really good equipment ... brand new equipment.' Christopher responds by returning to the question of soft balls: 'the footballs we have are flat, and if you kick [them] really hard and it hits someone – flat balls tend to like cane when [they] hit you.' His solution is 'soft and bouncy balls'. Ms Lightfoot accepts this point, and asks what Christopher thinks of Natalie's idea that they not play football 'on the days you've got the equipment bags out there?'

5. Tell everyone that (166–76)

Christopher says something inaudible – to us at least, but presumably also to others, since Ms Lightfoot instructs him to tell everyone. He says, 'I don't know', smiling sheepishly. Ms Lightfoot presses on, offering him a template: 'Tell everyone what you think. Say I think that …'. Christopher meets her gaze and smiles, but says nothing. She exclaims, incredulously, 'You don't know what you think?' He says, 'no', laughing. Ms Lightfoot says in an exaggerated tone, 'Oh dear', and laughs, along with Christopher and other pupils.

Viewing the video recording

We recommend that readers now view the video recording[5] and read the full transcript of this episode. While viewing, we suggest you consider some or all of the following issues:

- What is happening in this episode? How do you know? What, if anything, stands out as particularly interesting and/or anomalous? How is this clip different from other examples of classroom interaction you've seen and/or experienced?
- What sort of discourse genre (see Chapter 6) are the pupils engaged in? What are its rules and roles?
- How does Ms Lightfoot position herself – both physically and *vis-à-vis* the content and conduct of the discussion? How, if at all, are changes in her positioning related to changes in pupil participation?
- Finally, what are the key points of agreement and disagreement in the discussion? Who is pulling the discussion in which directions, and how?

Analysis: getting off the ground or falling apart?

In analysing this episode we focus on the issue raised at the planning meeting of how to get the discussion 'off the ground' – that is, how to encourage the pupils to talk directly between themselves, without teacher mediation and control.

At the beginning of the episode we witness a breakthrough into such a discussion structure (see lines 1–30). Throughout this 35-second sequence the pupils face and speak to one another without any teacher intervention. Moreover, there is a marked shift in the tone of the interaction after Tom's turn in lines 6–8. Watch again the way the pupils talk and listen to one another in lines 1–8 and 11–30. As Natalie speaks in lines 1–6, she swivels around to address everyone, and formulates her argument in a complete and complex sentence. The other pupils sit quietly and face her, with the one exception of Jessica, who leans forward to say something softly to the girl sitting across from her. Tom begins talking immediately after Natalie has finished her sentence, latching his contribution onto hers. It sounds as if someone else tried to come in at the same time (perhaps Jessica or Kaylee?), but promptly withdrew as Tom claimed the floor. Again, while Tom speaks, almost all pupils face him, sitting quietly. Natalie, Tom and the others' participation here is generally in line with our expectations about how pupils should behave in classroom discussions.

However, the tenor of the conversation changes markedly after Tom completes his turn. Pupils lean forward (some of them out of their seats; see Figure 7.1) and their speech overlaps. They talk more rapidly, and in sentence fragments, completing one another's turns. Kaylee, Jessica, Harriet and Natalie primarily address themselves to Tom, and ignore the rest of the

Figure 7.1 Line drawing of interaction at line 14. The pupils on the right side of the frame, especially those shaded in grey, lean forward and talk animatedly; the pupils on the left and in back are for the most part stranded from the discussion.

class (prompting Ms Lightfoot's intervention). They are more animated than is typical in classroom discussions; indeed, their participation here seems more characteristic of a casual conversation among friends than an academic discussion in school.

What precipitates this shift in forms of participation? One possibility is that the topic of softer balls, and especially Tom's position that 'you can't really play with soft balls', is of greater interest than the previous topic of whether and when football should be restricted. A second possible factor is that this is the first time in the discussion that a pupil has directly disagreed with another pupil's position. Up until this point (and later in the episode), the discussion resembles a survey of various opinions, not really engaging directly with one another. Tom, on the other hand, directly responds to Natalie, arguing against her suggestion to use soft balls because they're 'not really fun to play with'. Perhaps part of what gets Kaylee out of her seat is Tom's implication that footballers' fun should take precedence over the risk of injuring bystanders. Finally, the conversational shift takes place precisely at the moment in which Ms Lightfoot pokes her head out of the classroom in order to speak to someone in the corridor.[6] Her momentary absence appears to contribute to transformation of the classroom into a less formal, less structured space.

The conversation reverts back to more conventional, school-based discourse patterns after Ms Lightfoot intervenes on lines 31–41. Though ostensibly her intervention is geared toward facilitating direct communication between pupils ('face everyone'), the actual effect of this and her subsequent interventions is that almost all pupil communication now passes through the teacher. Ms Lightfoot's involvement in the discussion takes a number of different forms:

- providing feedback on pupils' ideas (for example, querying Jessica on the relevance of her comments in lines 47–53, or accepting Christopher's idea in lines 157–9);
- posing questions to the class, for example, 'What does everyone else think?' (line 118) and 'What day do you have equipment on?' (line 126);
- facilitating the transfer of the floor (for example, before and after Allan and Christopher's contributions, in lines 59–60, 80–1 and 90–1); and
- directing individual pupil contributions, for example, 'tell everyone what you think; say I think that …' (lines 170–1).

All of these interventions are intended to facilitate and encourage pupil participation, and many of them are specifically geared to getting pupils to talk to one another, but paradoxically they seem to draw the pupils away from the interactional possibilities afforded by the debate discourse genre. Instead pupils settle back into a more traditional classroom discussion genre in which pupils primarily produce answers for the teacher rather than arguing with one another. And indeed, as noted before, most of the pupil contributions do not directly address the previous speaker's position, with the exception of Natalie, who builds on Ms Lightfoot's idea of bringing the equipment days into the conversation (lines 131–45). This movement between traditional and novel discourse genres is similar to interactional processes observed in Episode 3 (Chapter 6); we recommend that readers consult that chapter for elaboration of the idea of discourse genre.

It appears that genuine controversy in the classroom is generated only by the proposal to require the use of softer balls. Ms Lightfoot, however, shuts down discussion of this issue, initially by declaring it off-topic (lines 51–3), and later by accepting the proposal but then redirecting the conversation away from it (lines 157–65). We might ask why she chooses not to embrace and explore this controversial question? On the face of it, it would seem to make sense to steer the debate to the key point of contention, or at least allow it to progress there naturally. However, it is important to recall that the goal of the debate, at least from the teacher's perspective, is oral preparation for writing a discussion text, and that the discussion text has a certain form (arguments for and against), which may be compromised by developing the issue of hard vs soft balls. Furthermore, bear in mind that the most important context for the class in learning how to write a discussion text is the approaching standardized tests, and not resolution of the actual problems with football playing encountered by pupils on the playground. A written discussion text that started with arguments for and against restriction, but moved on from there to devote most of its space to creative solutions such as softer balls, spray-painted boundaries or establishing a tournament, might be more relevant and helpful for addressing problems at Abbeyford, but would likely also risk being marked down on the tests for not adhering to official genre conventions.

In summary, it appears that the pupils are most engaged, voice their concerns and address one another when the teacher is least involved in the discussion, and *vice versa*. The flip side of this, however, is that the brief spell of heightened involvement at the beginning of the episode, when the discussion really seemed to 'get off the ground' was also the period in which the discussion began to fall apart – by excluding half the class and deviating from the pre-established topic.

How, if at all, might teachers confront this paradox? We explore this question below, after considering another, related episode: the same debate about restrictions on playing football in the Year 6 class introduced in the opening to the chapter.

EPISODE 5: DEBATING FOOTBALL IN MS ANDERTON'S CLASSROOM

Setting the scene

The lesson

The debate in Ms Anderton's classroom was structured differently from in Ms Lightfoot's lesson. In a previous lesson the pupils prepared arguments for and against the motion that 'football [should] be banned from the playground at break and lunch time', and two representatives each were chosen to advocate on behalf of and in opposition to the proposition. At the beginning of the lesson the advocates were seated at the front of the room: two girls in favour and two boys opposed. The rest of the pupils sat in three rows of desks facing them, and Ms Anderton sat on a table at the back of the room. The lesson was composed of five segments:

1. *Introduction* (2 minutes). Ms Anderton reminds the pupils about their preparation of the topic, and elicits from them rules for debating. Among the issues pupils mention are 'do not talk while other people are talking' and 'you don't have to put your hand up' (just 'go for the gap', in Ms Anderton's words). Ms Anderton also emphasizes that the goal of the debate is to produce a balanced discussion of arguments both for and against the proposition. Finally, she checks that everyone has pen and paper ready so that 'if someone says something that you don't agree with you can make notes for the end so that you can discuss it.'
2. *Initial presentations* (5 minutes). First the two girls stand up and present their arguments. While they do so, two of the boys sitting in front of them make thumbs down signs. Among the girls' arguments are that pupils fight over what team they're on, footballs can cause accidents and injuries and money is wasted on first aid equipment to treat injuries and on new footballs (to replace those lost). A few counterpoints are posed, after which Ms Anderton invites the two boys on the 'against' team to present their position. They too stand up and present their arguments, which include pupil enjoyment, interest, fitness and improving their football skills.
3. *Debate* (9 minutes). After establishing that the two boys have finished their presentation, Ms Anderton opens the debate to the floor. The ensuing discussion encompasses a range of topics, including the extent to which the boys allow the girls to join in different games, the amount of space taken up by football, the risk of injuries, the relative advantages of different sports, whether or not football leads to fighting, the attraction of football and who should make space for whom (boys or girls). This discussion is dominated by a series of heated exchanges between the two girls, especially Willow, and the boys. On a number of occasions it deteriorates into a shouting match, leading Ms Anderton to intervene from the back of the room. Part of the debate is recounted in the opening of this chapter, and a large section of it is captured in the episode below.
4. *Conclusion* (3 minutes). Ms Anderton summarizes the arguments from each side and then stages a class vote. The motion is defeated by a vote of 11 to seven: the majority

favour continued football playing without restrictions. Most of this segment is also included in Episode 5 below.

5. *Review of homework on punctuation*(5 minutes). Unrelated to the debate, Ms Anderton moves to the front of the room, distributes pupils' marked homework and reviews the worksheet answers on the overhead projector. The lesson finishes early on account of a special maths activity.

The episode

As in Episode 4, we have chosen to focus on a sequence of the debate (and its conclusion) that captures the debate's dynamics, and the different roles played by the teacher in managing them. Before exploring this episode in detail, we summarize it briefly. As for the preceding chapters, the companion website, www.routledge.com/cw/lefstein includes a video recording and full transcript of this episode. We recommend that readers follow the summary below before watching the video for the first time. For convenience sake, we divide this episode into six segments.

1. 'What on earth made you say a word like that?' (lines 1–35)

At the beginning of the episode, Ms Anderton calls upon Will, who had previously raised his hand. Responding to one of the girls' opening arguments, that football leads to fighting because of disputes over who gets to be on which team, Will points out that 'it doesn't matter what team you're on [since] it's only a game.' Willow agrees with him, but then questions why the boys fight, and then 'why do *you*?' Will protests that he doesn't care if he's on a 'crap team', and is censured by Ms Anderton, who objects to the use of the word 'crap'.

```
1    Ms Anderton:   right Will your point
2    Will:          er I was (.)
3                   I was going to say
4                   that it doesn't matter what team you're on
5                   it's only a game
6                   [it's not like a pro-
7    Sam:           [yeah
8    Will:          it's not like a proper match
9    Willow:        YEAH EXACTLY
10                  SO WHY DO THE BOYS FIGHT OVER WHAT TEAM THEY'RE ON
11   Will:          because they're stupid
12   Willow:        but yeah
13                  SO WHY DO YOU
14                  why do you
15   Will:          I don't
16                  if I- if I go on a crap team
17   Willow:        (xxxxxx)
18   Will:          if I go on a crap team
19                  if we lose
20                  big deal
21   Ms Anderton:   er Will
```

```
22   Willow:         (next time)
23   Ms Anderton:    thank you
24   Willow:         [(next time)
25   Ms Anderton:    [er excuse me
26                   just a minute (1)
27                   what on earth made you say a word like that
28   Will:           sorry
29                   (if you)
30   Ms Anderton:    no Will
31                   w- went off the subject
32                   that's got nothing to do
33                   playing in teams
34                   about the-
35                   motion that we- we're talking about
```

2. Who's moaning? (lines 36–87)

Next, Gareth returns to an issue explored previously, about the popularity of different sports, and – as above in the case of Will – Willow responds personally, pointing out that Gareth doesn't play football anyway. One of the boys – it sounds like Will but we cannot be certain – claims that 'there's enough room for every activity. I don't see why you're moaning.' In response, Sally recounts a time that she and other girls were practicing cheerleading, and the Deputy Head (Ms Anderton) told them to move away from the football pitch 'because the boys moan'. Willow continues the cheerleading topic and uses it to reiterate her point about getting hit by the ball, claiming that the football knocks over the girls while they are playing with pom-poms. This leads to a dispute between Willow and Sam about whether the girls should kick the ball back or not. Ms Anderton intervenes, giving the floor to Anwar.

3. 'A crummy place' (lines 88–114)

Anwar argues that football is the main reason some pupils come to school, and so if it is restricted 'some people might not come to school again because they might think it's a crummy place.' Willow counters that 'if the girls always get hit by the ball, *they* don't want to go to school either', and the discussion deteriorates rapidly into a shouting match.

```
88   Ms Anderton:    right Anwar we haven't heard from you yet
89                   you don't need to put your hands up remember
90                   you just (.)
91                   go for the gap
92   Anwar:          well you should keep football
93                   because well nearly everyone- one plays it-
94                   eve- nearly every boy plays it
95                   yeah
96                   and if you don't keep it
97                   some people might not come to school again
98                   because they might think it's a crummy place
```

```
 99   Ms Anderton: sorry
100                they might not come to school again did you say
101   Anwar:       yeah
102                because they might think it's a crummy place
103   Sally:       yeah but
104   Willow:      YEAH BUT IF YOU THINK THAT
105                IF YOU THINK THAT
106                IF THE GIRLS ALWAYS GET HIT BY THE BALL
107                they don't want to go to school either (.)
108                because they'll always
109                they-
110                [they'll think that the boys (xxxxxxxxxxxxx)
111   Pupil:       [(xxxxxxxxxxxxxx)
112                ((6 seconds; numerous pupils talking at once))
113   Ms Anderton: shh (.)
114                er one at a time please
```

4. 'Girls can't just make space for boys' (lines 115–70)

Gareth suggests that 'if you want more space in the playground, get rid of a different activity' rather than football. Sally asks, 'Why should we play a different activity just so you can play football?', after which Willow, Sam and others talk all at once. When the hubbub settles down, Willow seizes the floor, shouting angrily, 'Girls can't just make space for boys. Boys are not the biggest thing in the world.' This leads to a renewed shouting match, and it takes Ms Anderton a few moments to regain quiet. She then asks if there are any points that haven't yet been raised. Willow bids for the floor and then reiterates her point: 'The world doesn't revolve around boys. The girls can't just make space for the boys.' Again a number of pupils compete for a turn, but Ms Anderton closes the debate.

5. Summarizing the argument (lines 171–98)

Ms Anderton offers a summary of the key arguments raised, first by those in favour of restricting football and then those opposed to the motion.

```
177   Ms Anderton: on the for side (.)
178                we had that children'll (.)
179                fight over football
180                we had about accidents
181                that the ball going over the fence
182                hitting infants
183                and sometimes hitting the children in the playground
184                we had the cost of equipment
185                e::r and that it costs a lot
186                and we're always losing footballs
187                so we kept needing to reple- replenish new (.)
188                equipment
189                on the against side in the argument we had about
190                fitness
191                er we had about the keeping children occupied
192                and we had that the children who played football
193                become better football players
194                so for the team and things that'd be good
```

6. Putting it to a vote (lines 199–226)

Finally, Ms Anderton notes that in the previous day's discussion of the topic more pupils had opposed restrictions than favoured them, and calls for a vote to see if the debate has changed pupils' positions. Seven pupils vote to ban football while 11 pupils vote against the motion. Ms Anderton concludes the debate: 'so, though it was a very good argument on the girls' – or the side for the motion, the motion has now been thrown out.'

Viewing the video recording

We recommend that readers now view the video recording and read the full transcript of this episode. Readers will note that this episode is abridged: we have removed a little over two minutes of interaction in order to save time. Since we anticipate readers viewing and discussing this episode along with the previous episode, we have endeavoured to select relatively brief sequences for both. While viewing, we suggest you consider some or all of the same issues you explored in Episode 4:

- What is happening in this episode? How do you know? What, if anything, stands out as particularly interesting and/or anomalous? How is this clip different from other examples of classroom interaction you've seen and/or experienced?
- What sort of discourse genre (see Chapter 6) are the pupils engaged in? What are its rules and roles?
- How does Ms Anderton position herself – both physically and *vis-à-vis* the content and conduct of the discussion? How, if at all, are changes in her positioning related to changes in pupil participation?
- Finally, what are the key points of agreement and disagreement in discussion? Who is pulling the discussion in which directions, and how?

Analysis: checking pupil passions?

We and the Abbeyford Primary School teachers who viewed this episode (see Box 7.1 for the key points raised by the teachers for this and the previous episode) were immediately struck by how the debate inflamed pupil passions, to the extent that at times pupils seem to almost 'forget' that they're in a school classroom. Indeed, for most of the first half of the episode – until Ms Anderton's summary – the discussion does not resemble conventional classroom discourse. In this analysis, we first describe the key differences between the debate and typical classroom talk, and then discuss possible explanations for these differences.

First, consider the organization of the room. Ms Anderton has vacated the customary teacher space at the front of the room, opting instead to sit on a table in the back left corner. In her place the two debate teams sit on either side of the teacher's desk, facing the rest of the class. This adversarial organization resembles that of a parliamentary debate, or a court of law. Note that though Ms Anderton has vacated centre-stage, she has chosen a strategic spot outside of the main arena of classroom activity, but which is in the direct line of vision of the four principal debaters, and visible to all but six of the other pupils. From this position she can assume both marginal and relatively commanding positions as required.

Box 7.1 Key issues raised by teachers in the reflection meeting

- Pupils were passionate about the discussion

  - That they were allowed to shout at each other and then they came back down again …. That they were that passionate, that they felt they had to get their views across. And that they were all allowed to do it, but then they were all sensible enough to pipe down a bit.
  - So, whether dialogue to be effective, actually needs people to care about the discussion they're engaged in … So, it's about engendering an environment where they actually are passionate about something, and then I think, things work at a different level, perhaps.
  - There was no politeness and no, 'Oh, I can't challenge this person's idea because they're my friend, or they're in the same class as me', it was 'I disagree with them, therefore I'm going to shout them down and challenge them'

- Pupils gave reasoned responses and backed up their views with evidence

  - I liked the fact that, in [Episode 4], all of their responses were quite reasoned, they were able to sort of back their answer up straight away, without being prompted, so there was no, 'why do you think that?' going on.

- Pupils were willing and able to challenge each other

  - In [Episode 4], it was really good that they were really comfortable with challenging each other's ideas.
  - I thought, in [Episode 5], although they were very open to challenging each other, you couldn't tell from the extract whether or not they were also open to accepting other people's points of views, or whether or not they could develop their own thinking, having heard someone else's point of view.

- Pupils were able to chain responses together

  - In [Episode 4], the children actually went through and said, 'oh, like so-and-so said.' I'd like to know how they know that, is it something that you taught or did they just pick it up?

- Momentum of the debates continued with minimal teacher involvement

  - They actually managed to keep the debate going [without teacher input]… they actually carried the argument on and gave both points of view, without you having to say, 'no, you put your point of view'.
  - How to make sure that the focus doesn't come back to you, as a teacher, all the time … the children are very happy just to throw ideas across the room without it coming back to the teacher.

- Minimal input from quieter pupils

  - How do you really get children that don't speak involved, how can you do it? Some people don't like speaking at all. Can you make them?

Second, consider the patterns of classroom communication:

- Pupils address one another directly, rather than addressing the teacher or talking with one another indirectly, via the teacher. This orientation is evident in the physical positioning of the pupils, who face one another. Interestingly, Sam and Kieran tend to face Willow and Sally, while the two girls tend to face the pupil audience; in so doing, the girls adopt the position expected in a formal debate (speaking to the audience they are trying to persuade), while the boys adopt a position more common in an informal argument, in which one's opponent is also one's audience. That pupils are oriented toward addressing one another is also evident in the substance of their talk, which either builds upon or counters the ideas of the previous speaker (see for example how Will and Willow respond to one another in lines 2–20, or how Sally and Willow respond to Anwar, Gareth and Sam in lines 103–10 and 125–41).[7]

- Pupils' talk frequently overlaps, and they allocate turns at talk by selecting one another as next speaker or by 'going for the gap' as Ms Anderton instructed (or forcibly 'creating' a gap), rather than quietly raising a hand to bid for a turn and waiting for the teacher to allocate the floor. The only exception to this observation is that Ms Anderton nominates the next speaker after each of her interventions to restore order (see her selections of Gareth, Anwar, Gareth and Willow in lines 36, 88, 121, and 164 respectively).

- The tenor of the talk is excited, passionate and even angry at times, rather than the more restrained, 'emotionally flat' talk that is so typical in classroom discussions.[8] This is particularly apparent in Willow's outbursts (lines 104–10, 132–3, 165–7), but also to a certain extent in Will's references to 'stupid' boys and 'crap' teams (lines 11–18), in Anwar's description of school as a crummy place, in Philip's pantomimed 'shooting' of Willow (lines 169–70) and in the pupil cheering when the outcome of the vote is announced (line 218). In some of these cases pupils act as if they have forgotten that they're in a school lesson rather than in a more informal setting. This is evident in the way the girls and boys taunt one another, Will's use of the proscribed word 'crap', and even in Sally's reference to 'Deputy' even though the Deputy Head, in her role as the class's literacy teacher, is in the room with them. Sally catches herself and self-corrects (lines 61–3).

- Talk ranges freely over a broad range of topics, introduced and developed by the pupils, rather than narrowly focused on the topic as defined by the teacher. For example, consider the various topics that engage Willow: why does Will allegedly fight if he's not happy with his football team (lines 13–14); Gareth doesn't play football anyway (line 53); the girls return the football when it's kicked at their feet (lines 79–81); and the world doesn't revolve around boys (lines 133, 137). The only occasion in which Ms Anderton criticizes a pupil for going off topic is her censure of Will (lines 31–5), but her response seems primarily motivated by his use of the word 'crap' and not by the topic of choosing teams, which had been introduced earlier.

The cumulative effect of these differences between the communicative patterns in the episode and in usual literacy lessons is that, in many respects and for much of the time, conventional teacher and pupil roles are inverted. Pupils dominate the floor, controlling the topic and allocation of turns, while the teacher sits passively in the back of the room and takes notes. Then, in the latter part of the episode, the teacher summarizes what pupils have said and the pupils express by means of a vote their judgment of what should be done. Note that this is the exact opposite of the common pattern in which pupils listen to the teacher, take notes and summarize what she has said, and the teacher judges which answer is correct. This inversion is not consistent throughout the episode as, like Ms Lightfoot in Episode 4, Ms Anderton steps back into a more conventional teacher role when the pupil-led discussion begins to disintegrate.

How can we explain these radical shifts in classroom communication and roles? The most obvious factor is that Ms Anderton declared the activity to be a debate, and assigned pupils to 'for' and 'against' teams, positioned at the front of the room. The adversarial, competitive nature of the debate can be at least partially attributed to the gender-based identities of the teams ('the boys' and 'the girls'), which coincided with tensions between boys and girls on the playground. The relevance of the topic was further intensified by Ms Anderton's role as Deputy Head of the school, which made her a particularly meaningful audience for the discussion, someone with the authority to actually restrict football playing. Advance preparation of arguments likely assisted the pupils in realizing their roles as competent debaters. Finally, Ms Anderton's positioning at the back of the room made space for the pupils to control the debate.

The pupils' capacity to manage the debate was limited, however, and – like Ms Lightfoot in Episode 4 – Ms Anderton repeatedly intervened to check excesses such as pupils talking over one another or use of inappropriate language. In many ways, the debate's dynamic was very similar to that discussed in Episode 4: by adopting a marginal position the teacher encouraged and facilitated greater pupil involvement and control, but heightened pupil engagement threatened to pull the debate apart, leading in turn to greater teacher involvement and control. Alongside these similarities, there were some important differences, which we discuss in the next section, along with a more general discussion of organizing and orchestrating classroom debates.

Organizing and orchestrating classroom debates

The organization and orchestration of classroom debates is a useful tool for one's pedagogical repertoire. The two episodes have shown that there is more than one way to go about conducting this activity, and have also uncovered some central problems and dilemmas teachers may encounter.

An advantage of debating is that it centres teaching and learning around disagreement, and places pupils in the position of presenting and defending their ideas. When done well, the competitive nature of this adversarial activity promotes pupil engagement. These issues of pupil engagement and quality of argumentation were cited by the Abbeyford Primary teachers as key advantages of the activity when discussing the two episodes (see Box 7.1). In particular, teachers welcomed pupil passion as an indication of the sort of breakthrough to authentic participation valued in dialogic pedagogy: pupils cared about the discussion, 'felt they had to get their views across', and did not shy away from disagreement.

However, teachers expressed concern about the fervour of some pupils' participation, and the competitive nature of the debate, questioning whether pupils' passion – and raised voices – interfered with their capacity to be open to others' viewpoints. Hyper-engagement in the debate also threatened to tear it apart, and this dynamic presents dilemmas for the teacher, since interventions to rein in the debate can also stifle pupil participation.

The two debates developed in different ways, in part as a result of the different strategies and roles the two teachers employed in setting up and orchestrating the debate. While the debate in Ms Lightfoot's classroom was relatively calm, passions ran high in Ms Anderton's classroom. To what can we attribute these differences? Key factors include:

- *Debate teams*: Ms Anderton created clearly demarcated teams advocating for and against the motion. Ms Lightfoot let the discussion develop fluidly, without assigning roles. This issue was particularly significant given the gender composition of the two teams ('the girls' vs 'the boys') and the way they assumed the roles of representing their gender on a topic of tension between the boys and girls in the school.

- *Physical organization of classroom*: Ms Anderton staged a confrontation between the two teams by setting them opposite one another at the front of the room; Ms Lightfoot organized her class into a non-hierarchical circle (with some pupils caught in the middle).
- *Sequencing*: The debate in Ms Anderton's classroom began with opening speeches for and against the motion, and proceeded from there to questions, answers and counter-arguments. The debate in Ms Lightfoot's classroom was more loosely structured.
- *Teacher roles*: Ms Lightfoot stayed completely outside the arena initially, and moved in to restore order when the debate began to fall apart. After that intervention, she maintained relatively tight control over the discussion, including orchestration of turn-taking, helping pupils articulate their positions and inserting new ideas into the discussion (such as the issue of equipment days). Ms Anderton positioned herself on the edges of her class's debate, and moved in and out of active involvement as she saw fit. She intervened primarily on points of order, leaving the content of the debate almost entirely to the pupils.

As noted above, each of these different tactics had its advantages and trade-offs. The key advantage of the more minimalist teacher role was that it allowed passions (and topic) to run free. But on the other hand, how productive is such competitive hyper-engagement for clear thinking about (both sides of) the issue, for learning how to discuss controversial issues, and for subsequently writing a balanced discussion text? Moreover, what are the social ramifications of accentuating the classroom gender divide? By tightly steering the debate, the more interventionist teacher role mitigated the risk of pupils getting swept away in the competitive fervour, and focused the debate on the sort of issues that were needed for the subsequent writing task. But it also put a damper on pupil participation (relative to participation patterns prior to Ms Lightfoot's shift in positioning and role). How should teachers negotiate this dilemma? Is there a 'best practice' for managing pupil debates? The question of how to intervene – in what circumstances and in what ways – requires individual judgement about the particular conditions of the case, including pupils' prior experiences and needs, social dynamics, pupil and teacher capacities, topic and learning goals.

Nevertheless, though this dilemma will be present to a certain extent in all pupil-led discussions, careful consideration of the debate's organization, preparation and orchestration can at least partially obviate the need for teacher intervention. In this regard, a few lessons can be drawn from the two episodes:

1. *Ground rules.* Some of the trouble arose in the debates from pupil uncertainty about the rules governing participation in the debates. What roles will be performed, and by whom? Who selects the speakers? When are questions and counter-arguments allowed? What about interruptions? What are the boundaries of the topic? What is the purpose? How will success be measured? In both cases, the class spent a few minutes reviewing expectations, but these discussions left most of the key issues about who is allowed to talk about what, how and when unanswered. Ms Anderton's reticence to chair the debate and allocate turns at talk is entirely understandable, but 'go for the gap' is a recipe for interactional trouble, especially given the emotionally charged nature of the topic. For this reason, competitive debates are typically tightly structured, with a preordained schedule of speakers and time limits. These structures also have their disadvantages of course, as they require participants to give uninterrupted speeches and thereby stifle the free exchange of ideas. Another possibility is to appoint a pupil chair, tasked with

managing the floor, and thereby remove the teacher from her conventional position as classroom communication hub. This solution will only be as successful as the selected chair's capacity to manage their peers assertively and fairly.

2.   *Framing the debate.* Discourse genres are governed by both formal rules and informal norms. We should not assume that pupils will instinctively understand the expectations of a new discourse genre, or know how to participate effectively in it. One way of addressing this problem is to be explicit about the activity's structure and ground rules. Another way of facilitating their understanding is to use a more familiar model or metaphor as a way of framing the unfamiliar discourse genre. For example, a parliamentary debate, or court of law, may be more familiar to them than simply a 'debate', and teachers could show them televized examples or dramatizations. Such familiarity may facilitate intuitive understanding of the informal rules and expectations (much like the *X Factor* model shaped pupil participation in Episode 3). Such 'imported' discourse genres can also pose problems; see the discussion in Chapter 6.

3.   *Physical organization.* Both teachers changed the physical organization of their respective classrooms prior to the debate. This is a good way to impress upon participants that 'we're doing something different now.' We have noted how in both debates the organization of the room shaped opportunities for pupil participation and control, direct pupil communication among themselves and teacher intervention. Likewise, we argued, the adversarial arrangement of the two teams in Ms Anderton's classroom contributed to their direct confrontation of one another. This arrangement poses both advantages and problems. On the one hand, it facilitates direct communication between the pupils, accentuates the division between the two sides, and provides the key advocates with a 'stage' upon which to perform for the rest of the classroom audience. On the other hand, the clear demarcation of competing teams – especially given the way this constructed (and exacerbated) the gender divide – also led to some of the debate's less helpful confrontations.

4.   *Topic selection.* Part of the success of the debates in engaging the pupils was rooted in the selection of a controversial topic, which divided the pupils, was of real concern to them, and could lead to meaningful outcomes (changing school policy with regard to football on the playground). However, the topic also posed troubles. In Ms Anderton's classroom the issue aggravated the classroom gender divide, leading to an explosive discussion of gender relations in the school and classroom, under conditions that were not conducive to dealing with the problems that emerged. We can learn from this that it's not sufficient to find a topic that is open for the particular group of pupils, we also need to consider how it divides them, and what the implications might be for the conduct of the debate. This line of thinking can facilitate allocation of pupils in ways that either minimize or maximize social tensions. For example, imagine how the debate might have unfolded if Willow had captained the 'boys' side', and consider both the advantages and disadvantages of such a decision.

5.   *Advance pupil preparation.* One of the key differences between the two classes was that Ms Anderton's pupils had an opportunity (in a previous lesson) to think about the topic and prepare their arguments in small groups, in writing. Such advance preparation likely contributed to their relative fluency in presenting their arguments, and also to their commitment to their respective positions.

6.   *Patience.* Finally, it's important to note that these two debates represent a first foray into this unfamiliar discourse genre. Any new form of activity is expected to initially

create uncertainty and trouble (demanding intervention), but over time pupils will become accustomed to it and the teacher will not need to be as actively involved in orchestrating the interaction. Teachers and pupils need time to grow into the new roles afforded them by debating, and therefore the potential of the activity should not be assessed on the basis of its first trial.

Questions for further discussion

- How should classroom debates be resolved? Both teachers conducted votes (one public and the other blinded)? Which type of vote is most appropriate? What are the advantages and/or disadvantages of voting? What other means of resolution can you think of? And what are their relative strengths and limitations?
- Consider your own classroom(s): How would you organize them for a debate? How would you organize the pupils? Where would you position them? What would your role be, as teacher? And where would you position yourself?
- To what extent are the paradoxes of teacher involvement and pupil engagement discussed in the context of debating relevant to other classroom activities and forms of talk?
- What are the different ways of intervening when the debate gets out of hand and/or off-topic? Pick a critical moment in one of the transcripts and discuss different possible courses of action that were available to the teacher: What are their advantages and problems? What would you recommend doing?
- What do you think about the overlap between gender divisions and division into debate teams in Ms Anderton's class? How might you have dealt with this differently (if at all)?
- One of the teachers that viewed the incident expressed concern about the limited participation of quieter pupils in the debates: 'How do you really get children that don't speak involved? How can you do it? Some people don't like speaking at all. Can you make them?'

COMMENTARY

DEVELOPING SPEAKING SKILLS IN THE SHADOW OF WRITTEN EXAMINATIONS: A HEAD TEACHER'S PERSPECTIVE BY JEFF BARRETT

So why would a school submit itself to this kind of scrutiny and extra workload? There were two main reasons – at least as far as the leadership of the school was concerned. First, it was felt that practice should be built on proper research – we wanted to base our efforts on something that was shown to really work when developing children educationally. Second, as a school serving a working class area, we felt that lack of oracy was one of the factors holding our pupils back once they were competing in the job market with pupils from more privileged backgrounds. So the aim was to raise confidence in public speaking and develop an ability to sell themselves. The clips featured in this section show, I think, that this was beginning to develop, at least for some pupils.

An interesting factor in watching these clips concerns power, power in the sense of teacher authority and in the sense of peer-to-peer interaction. Teachers can control pupils in a classroom through the kinds of work that they set. The notion of a dialogic approach is, therefore, fraught with possibilities for a session going out of control – there is no safety net here. A teacher must have the self confidence to be sure that they can restore order, in other words regain power, whenever they need to, once they have chosen to give it up. These approaches are not for the inexperienced nor the faint-hearted. It also surprised and pleased me that rarely did a child dominate these sessions through force of personality or their place in the group pecking order.

In the hands of an experienced and skilled practitioner pupils can be developed. Both of these groups contained pupils whose first language was not English – they still contributed as did some other, native, pupils who were not high achievers academically. The sadness is that the spectre that is SATs curtailed the opportunity to take this work as far as it could have gone – given time and an agenda that really thought that every child mattered.

Year 6 SATs are very low status for pupils – a child who misses the tests through illness suffers not one iota – but have become, through Government action, extremely high status for schools. So much so that these days a head teacher can be dismissed if their school fails to meet 'floor targets'. Schools, therefore, have to take them seriously – and this can mean an extreme narrowing of the primary curriculum, particularly in the last two years and especially in Year 6. The SATs are not an educational tool – no one learnt anything by doing one – but are an assessment tool. Thus good teachers can raise levels by focusing on narrow content and examination technique. Oracy, whilst of itself valuable, plays no part in SATs. During the time of the research project it was Reading, Writing, Spelling, written and mental Mathematics and Science that counted.

So it was that SATs hindered the development of the pupils, and for the School it was a balancing act between activities considered worthwhile educationally and giving enough time for cramming. As a school leader it was negotiated with what I called the 'Old Lags' – Year 6 teachers with a proven track record – who knew what needed to be done and who had to be left to get on with it. With SATs the tail definitely wagged the dog – and to no real purpose. The first thing our secondary colleagues did in September was test the pupils again to give themselves a baseline. Giving the pupils six more months to develop themselves through meaningful activities would have been so much better – but we all had mortgages to pay!

Jeff Barrett worked in five schools during 31 years in primary education, 14 of them as head teacher. He served as Head Teacher of Abbeyford Primary School while the lessons appearing in this book were recorded, and participated in all the workshops in which the teachers and researchers analysed video-recorded episodes.

COMMENTARY

WHAT ROLE IS THERE FOR ORGANIZED DEBATE IN A LITERACY LESSON? BY LUCY HENNING

The most striking thing for me in these debates was how engaged many of the pupils were. The theme of playground football was clearly an issue of immediate and considerable relevance for many of them and, particularly in the class where the school's deputy was the literacy teacher, appeared to provide a forum for airing some deeply held views.

In the second video Will, Willow, Anwar and Sally used language and expressed viewpoints that appeared to spring from their own worlds and this perhaps caused a cross over of language from the playground to the classroom, especially when Will talked about 'crap teams' and Anwar 'crummy schools'. I thought it was significant that Willow and Sally appeared to perceive that the school placed boys' needs over girls', particularly when Sally described her cheerleading group being moved on by the deputy to prevent the boys from moaning at lines 57–66 and when Willow angrily said 'boys are not the biggest thing in the world.'

I didn't feel that there was a threat of a breakdown in order – the children quickly reverted to more orderly debate when supported by their teacher, for example when Ms Anderton summarized the main points at line 171. I felt that it would support the children in the future to encourage them to manage the debate for themselves, establishing their own ground rules and electing their own chair to enforce them. Discussion of this first debate on school football could be used as a starting point for this work, the children could reflect on their own practice and consider how it could be improved, not just in terms of managing themselves to avoid overheating, but also to present their points more clearly and strengthen their arguments. The use of video might be helpful here.

The high level of importance of this issue for the pupils in the second video also suggests to me that debating activities on such crucial issues for the children might best be separated from writing activities. If the debate were a speaking and listening activity in itself a concluding vote may not have been necessary, and the class and their teacher might have had the chance to explore some of the unexpected issues raised and even think about asking the school's management team to consider some of the children's concerns and suggestions. The teachers' responses seemed constrained by the need to have appropriate content for writing as when Ms Anderton summarized 'for' and 'against' points which were useful for writing but did not seem to include Sally and Willow's points about the relative importance of boys' and girls' activities. It may be that if the purpose of a debate is to support writing development a less emotive topic might allow for a considered approach, whilst if the debate is on an issue of great importance to the pupils it may work better as an activity in itself which has the potential for having a genuine impact on school life.

Lucy Henning has been a Primary National Strategies literacy consultant for two West London LEAs. She taught across the primary age range for 14 years and is currently a lecturer in Primary English at St. Mary's University College, Twickenham. She is currently conducting PhD research on young children's early encounters with formal literacy teaching at King's College London.

COMMENTARY

CONSTRAINTS AND OPPORTUNITIES
BY JAYNE WHITE

It seems unsurprising to me that the pupils in both classrooms would engage passionately with a topic that was clearly of great significance to their daily experience. As such their internally persuasive discourses (Bakhtin 1981, see Chapter 2) were unleashed from the outset, setting the scene for a potentially dialogic experience. However, the extent to which either episode realises its dialogic potential is frustrated by a host of factors. These might be best explained by the particular type of 'pedagogical chronotope', in which the learning takes place, including: the set-up of the room, with desks acting as a potential barrier to participation; the body language of the teachers, crossing arms and maintaining a higher position than the students by sitting on a desk;[9] and seating structures which appear to privilege those in the front or middle.[10] The selected genre of 'debate' has the potential to sponsor 'lively and interesting disputes' (Bakhtin 2004: 22), but seeks resolution in the majority vote, i.e. the voice of one group over another. In this locale emphasis turns away from the dialogic aspects of the experience, towards a set of agreed outcomes.

The experience might be considered monologic from the outset because the teacher has already established the agenda of 'oral preparation for writing a discussion text'. This is a contentious point much debated within the dialogic pedagogy community: To what extent should the teacher drive (author) the agenda and at what cost to whom? Here, the teacher appears absent from the 'debate' but is nevertheless taking a discursive position (as a female, person of authority, mediator, etc). When the students tried to seek solution (as opposed to argument) – as in the case of the soft ball dialogue – teacher orientation towards established goals was evident and silenced alternative points of view. Coupled with the gendered alliances that took place, some students were thwarted in their attempts to solve what they saw as a very authentic problem (as opposed to generating and responding to arguments). As an alternative, perhaps the teachers might consider inviting learners to take on oppositional positions to those they were aligned? Such an approach gives rise to alternative perspectives that are so important to dialogic pedagogy. They may also play a very important role in supporting students to think outside of their own ideologic position – as boys or girls/players or non-players in this case – through engagement with other points of view.

In my analysis neither Ms Anderton's democratic summary of the debate nor Ms Lightfoot's constant maintenance of the dialogue fully equip them to recognise students who had not had the opportunity to express their ideas in the competitive climate of the debate. A visual analysis in both settings reveals unequal participation. The same 'white' learners dominate the verbal discussion. Based on Wegerif's (2013) suggestion that it is often the (initially) silent learner who proffers important insights, how might these classrooms create spaces for silence as well as talk (and perhaps even passionate shouting) – since both are potentially dialogic? How might teachers think differently about their role(s) in promoting 'lively disputes' while supporting the agency of all?

Jayne White is Senior Lecturer in the Faculty Education at University of Waikato, New Zealand. Her recent co-edited books include Bakhtinian Pedagogy: Opportunities and challenges for research, policy and practice in education across the globe *(Peter Lang, 2011) and* Educational Research with Our Youngest: Voices of Infants and Toddlers *(Springer, 2011)*.

Notes

1 The guidance is Barking and Dagenham Primary English Project (2002). Note that the teachers took 'dialogic teaching' to mean primarily highly interactive oral activity. See Chapter 2 for a review of approaches to dialogue.

2 Note that we are representing the teachers' views here. As we clarify in Chapter 2, according to our own view, dialogic pedagogy involves interplay of voices, thinking together, developing a critical stance toward knowledge and more. Such activities can be developed in many different forms of talk, and with regard to many different forms of text.

3 Openness of the question, defined as actual disagreement between pupils, is a precondition for authentic discussion. Imagine, for example, if we had conducted a debate about whether smoking is bad for you (the other topic recommended in the local authority guidance): defending smoking is not a legitimate position within the school setting, and as such the debate would likely not take off. The other two criteria – charged question and real audience – are related to heightening pupil engagement and making the event meaningful. 'Open' and 'charged' are two of the six characteristics of a 'fertile question'. The other four characteristics are rich, undermining, practical and connected (see Harpaz and Lefstein, 2000).

4 Barking and Dagenham Primary English Project (2002: 102).

5 Throughout the episode Ms Lightfoot attends to some business taking place outside of the classroom, including twice sending pupils out of the room – once to deliver a note for her, and the second time to go to an alternative English lesson. Also visible in the recording is one of the researchers, sitting with the pupils in the upper right corner of the video frame. (The other researcher is behind the camera.)

6 It's worth reflecting on how busy Ms Lightfoot is, attending to matters beyond the lesson, and how seamlessly she manages to conduct these affairs without disrupting the lesson.

7 This may seem obvious and natural: after all, a basic tenet of Conversation Analysis is that speakers orient and respond to the ideas of the preceding speaker (see, for example, Heritage 2005). However, classroom talk is often much more fragmentary, with pupils responding to one another primarily via the teacher, and teachers proceeding through a preordained progression of topics rather than responding to pupil utterances that seek to move the conversation in a different direction.

8 John Goodlad (1984) characterized classrooms as 'emotionally flat' in a major survey of teaching and learning in US schools.

9 Interestingly this would never occur in New Zealand, where sitting on a table is seen as culturally inappropriate.

10 Matusov (2009) describes a pedagogical chronotope, as a combination of context, practice and assigned value within and between learning communities. See also White (in press).

Chapter 8

Dialogue, ability and pupil identities

This chapter is about a predicament facing teachers at Abbeyford Primary as they sought to enact dialogic teaching and learning in their classrooms. On the one hand, dialogic pedagogy rests on the assumption that children learn best through participation in rich and challenging classroom discourse, and therefore requires that all pupils be encouraged to participate in such activity. On the other hand, English primary education is dominated by the idea that pupils have inherent, stable, context-independent abilities – e.g. 'bright' and 'intelligent' versus 'low ability' and 'inarticulate' – and only the former are considered capable of participating productively in dialogue. In this chapter we explore how teachers and pupils manage this conflict in practice, and consider the implications this has for levels and patterns of pupil participation and for pupils' evolving identities.

EPISODE 6: 'WHAT DOES FEAR MEAN?'

We begin by introducing the SATs revision lesson in Ms Alexander's Year 6 classroom upon which this chapter is based. We then go into more detail about the tension between dialogic pedagogy's egalitarian ideal and the teachers' views about pupil ability and participation. Next we present our analysis of a six-minute excerpt from Ms Alexander's lesson in which pupils debate competing interpretations of a poem. We focus in particular on who participates, when, in what way and with what consequences for pupil identities and opportunities for learning. We conclude the chapter by drawing out the pedagogical significance of this analysis, including: the issue of pupil pseudo-participation (and even pseudo-*non*participation); the relationship between discourses about pupils and instructional practices; the importance of identity to learning; and the impact of high-stakes testing on classroom dynamics. We end with four commentaries, one from Pie Corbett, whose poem is being discussed in the focal extract, and three from Education researchers from England, Canada and the United States.

Setting the scene

The lesson

The lesson from which our focal episode is drawn took place in Ms Alexander's Year 6 classroom at the end of April 2009, in the second week of a concentrated three-week block of revision for the standardized assessment task (SATs) tests, which the pupils were to sit in the week beginning 11 May 2009. The Year 6 classes at Abbeyford had been working towards these tests since January, but following the April Easter break, they had redoubled their efforts, making the most of the remaining time by intensively recapping the areas covered in the previous four months. The focus for this week was on reading comprehension, and in the lesson prior to our focal episode, attention had turned specifically to poetry. The introduction of poetry had been met with audible dissatisfaction from the pupils – there were multiple groans and exclamations of 'Oh no' – but by the end of this second lesson in this series (our focal lesson), pupils were beginning to warm up to this area of study. The lesson can be broken down into the following five sections:

1. *Recap* (9 minutes). Ms Alexander recaps the previous lesson, in which the class had discussed the four key categories of skills that pupils must display when answering SATs questions on reading comprehension: Deduce ('draw conclusions from your reading'), Infer ('go beyond what is in the text to draw conclusions based on your life experiences'), Evaluate ('decide how effective the writing is and comment on your own personal response to it') and Justify ('use parts of the text to back up what you are saying'). One of the pupils says that she finds it difficult to answer questions which ask 'why the author has done something'. She refers to a specific example from a previous reading comprehension test, which had asked pupils to explain why the author had used a question mark at the end of the poem's title. Ms Alexander walks through a possible answer to this question, explaining 'this is a technique, something the author has done for a reason, and all the question is asking you is what's the reason he's done that.'

2. *Introduction of new poem and annotation task* (10 minutes). Ms Alexander gives the pupils a new poem, *Owl* by Pie Corbett (reproduced in Box 8.1). They spend time working individually to read, analyse and annotate the poem (in order to simulate the SATs tests). In particular, Ms Alexander instructs the pupils to think about 'a certain technique that the author has used' in addition to structure, layout and the atmosphere the poem creates.

3. *Whole-class discussion of the poem* (16 minutes). Ms Alexander asks the pupils for their first impressions of the poem. One pupil replies that she didn't like it because she couldn't understand it, and several others agree. Ms Alexander guides the pupils through the poem, and by the end of the discussion most are engaged by the challenge of deciphering the poem's metaphors.

4. *Pair work on possible SATs questions* (6 minutes). Pupils are tasked with working in pairs to come up with possible SATs questions related to the poem. Each pair must devise a one mark question and a three mark question.

5. *Final plenary* (4 minutes). Each group shares the questions they have devised with the rest of the class. Ms Alexander brings the session to a close by telling the pupils that they have worked very well today.

The episode

In this chapter we examine in more detail a part of the whole-class discussion (Section 3), in which teacher and pupils work together to better understand the poem. In particular, we focus on a six-minute segment devoted to exploration of the final three lines of the poem. Before exploring this episode in detail, we summarize it briefly. As for the preceding chapters, the accompanying companion website includes a video recording and full transcript of this episode. The transcript is more detailed than the others presented in this

Box 8.1

Owl
Owl
Was darker
Than ebony.
Flew through the night,
Eyes like amber searchlights,
Rested on a post,
Feathers wind-ruffled.
Stood stump still,
Talons ready to seize
And squeeze

Owl
Was death
That swamped the fields,
For it flew through the dark
That tightened its knot,
That bandaged the hills
In a blindfold of fear.
Owl flew – who – who – who

book because it includes a number of references to non-verbal actions, such as the raising and lowering of pupils' hands and the direction of pupils' gaze. This kind of information is important to our analysis, because the topic that we have chosen to pursue in the chapter – patterns of participation and non-participation – requires that we investigate a broad range of behaviours, not just speech.[1] It would be impossible, of course, to include information on all actions (gestures, facial expressions, gaze etc.) for all pupils. Inevitably the transcript is still only a partial representation, and while it does detail all visible pupils' bids for a turn to talk (via the raising and lowering of hands), it is selective in terms of the other behaviours it represents and is thus not a substitute for close viewing of the video clip.

We recommend that readers follow the summary below before watching the video for the first time. The episode can be roughly broken up into four main stages:

1. 'What do we think about the poem?' (lines 1–216)

Ms Alexander begins the discussion by asking pupils what they think about the poem: 'Do you like it? Do you not like it?'. Around five pupils raise their hands to speak and Ms Alexander calls first upon Elsa, who replies that she didn't like the poem because she couldn't understand it. Several pupils agree. Ms Alexander probes Elsa's response, trying to establish what meaning(s) Elsa *did* get from the poem. This line of discussion is interrupted temporarily by Aaron, who points out that the poem 'repeats stuff' (this is not included in the video clip– rather is marked as a passing of time between lines 42 and 43 of the transcript), but is picked up again when Charlotte tells the class that she 'understood it all apart from two lines', which are 'that bandaged the hills / in a blindfold of fear'. Ms Alexander encourages the pupils to 'link up those two lines to the rest [of the poem] and try and make it match up' and tries to facilitate their understanding by considering what words such as 'bandaged' and 'blindfold' mean outside of the poem. The class then move on to explore the meaning of the metaphor: What is it that is acting as a bandage or blindfold? The discussion is disrupted temporarily by an off-the-cuff comment from one pupil, Ash:

```
115    Ms Alexander:    okay
116                     so basically that part there is saying that
117                     the hills are covered with something
118                     so that you can't see
119                     you're in a blindfold
120                     you can't see
121    Ash:            trees ((looks up at teacher and maintains gaze))
122    Ms Alexander:    so what is it that is covering
123                     is it tr-
124                     does it mention trees
125                     does it mention anything to do with trees Ash
126    Ash:            no but it hasn't mentioned anything to do with
127                     the thing that [covered xxxx
128    Ms Alexander:                  [ah it has
129    Ash:            has it
130    Ms Alexander:    it has
131                     look further up
```

Following Ash's lead, other pupils make guesses about what might be covering the hills. Some answers are grounded in the poem (e.g. 'feathers', lines 141, 145–6), and as such are more plausible than other guesses (e.g. 'swamps' on lines 158, 162). Eventually Daren offers the answer Ms Alexander is looking for: 'the dark' (lines 168, 170, 174).

2. 'What does fear mean though?' (lines 217–51)

Having established that the dark is closing in on the hills, Daren is still confused. He asks a question, which is met initially by derision from his fellow pupils, but which is taken up by Ms Alexander:

```
216    Daren:          what does fear mean though
217    Aaron?          (you actually xxxx)
218    Ash:            ((smiles to himself))
219    Ms Alexander:    [what does fear-
220    Victor:         [((puts his hand down))
221    Aaron:          ((puts hand up))
222    Maisy:          oh my God
223    Daren:          [I know what it means
224    Aaron:          [(xxxxxxxx) sca::red
225    Daren:          I know what it means but (.)
```

226		why'd they use that
227	Aaron:	[because it's like (xxxx)
228	Ms Alexander:	[why use that
229		because it's linked to the rest-
230		that's- that's the whole point
231		because it's linked to the rest of the poem
232	Daren:	[but fear
233	Charlotte:	[((puts hand up))
234	Daren:	who's (.) scared

3. 'A very clever technique' (lines 252–378)

Ms Alexander encourages the class to think about Daren's question: who is scared? To help them answer this question, she directs their attention to the last line of the poem, 'Owl flew– who – who – who'. She explains that this is a clever technique that the author has used and asks Hayden if he can explain what it might mean. Ms Alexander tries to help Hayden by appealing to his interests outside of school (that his family keep pet owls), and gives him space to formulate his thoughts by quieting other pupils, but he declines to answer.

268	Ms Alexander:	Hayden do you have any idea
269		((several pupils turn to face Hayden, including Charlotte, Daren, Aaron, Mark and Elsa))
270	Ms Alexander:	what that might mean
271		in any way
272		[anything
273	Aaron:	[Miss I know
274	Ms Alexander:	anything basic
275		shshsh ((to Aaron))
276	Aaron:	because it (don't)
277	Ms Alexander:	you like owls
278		[you're into animals
279	Charlotte:	[((waving her raised arm energetically))
280	Hayden	(yeah)
281	Ms Alexander:	so what might it mean
282		owl flew [who who who
283	Ash:	[(in an animal world) ((looks up and turns around to sing directly at Hayden))
284	Aaron:	because it (don't tell you xxxx)
285	Hayden:	[((smiles at Ash))
286	Ms Alexander:	[oh are you Hayden ((directed at Aaron))
287	Ash:	((turns again to sing at Hayden))
288	Ms Alexander:	give Hayden a chance
289	Hayden:	((puts head down))
290	Ash:	it wasn't me ((looks at Hayden and raises his eyebrows in conspiratorial manner))
291	Hayden & Ash:	((laughing))
292	Ms Alexander:	nothing
293		you have no idea
294	Hayden:	no

Ms Alexander then turns to Daren to give the correct answer: 'noise the owl's making' (line 303). She positively evaluates this answer and begins to elaborate – 'good ... doesn't it sound like (.) the noise an owl makes' – but Daren interrupts her by requesting confirmation from Hayden: 'Hayden what does it sound like?'. Daren then uses Hayden's response to challenge the teacher: 'Hayden says no' (lines 324, 326). Ms Alexander resists this challenge and encourages the class to link up their new understanding of the final line of the poem with their earlier discussion of fear. Charlotte explains that 'what's fearing is like the food that the owl wants and then ... when the owl's flying through the air he's making the noises'. Ms Alexander summarizes by explaining that this final line could be a question – one that Daren had asked earlier: Who is scared? Who is next?

Viewing the video recording

We recommend that readers now view the video recording and read the full transcript of this episode. While viewing for the first time, think about what (if anything) stands out as particularly interesting. You might like to consider the following questions:

- What is happening in this episode? How do you know? How is this clip similar to or different from other examples of poetry teaching and/or revision for high-stakes tests that you've seen and/or experienced?
- Which pupils participate most actively in this part of the lesson? Are there any pupils who do not participate at all?
- Do pupils seem engaged in this lesson? Which pupils appear particularly interested or disinterested? What is it that signals their interest/disinterest?
- What might explain pupils' relative engagement/disengagement with this lesson?

Now watch the video again, focusing this time on the pupils highlighted in Figure 8.1. Consider the different ways in which these pupils participate in the lesson and how the teacher responds to them:

- Do these pupils frequently raise their hands to bid for attention? Do they answer the teacher's questions? Or, do they participate in other (perhaps less conventional) ways?
- Do you recognize these individuals as being certain 'types' of pupil? How are they similar to or different from pupils in your own classrooms?
- What kinds of identities are these pupils projecting? How are they being identified by others?

As indicated by the final two questions, we see the issue of who participates and in what ways as being consequential for pupil identities; thus before we proceed, we briefly set out our approach to identity. By identity we mean the way an individual is viewed by themselves and others (for example, 'class clown', 'nerd', 'bright pupil'). Identity emerges in interactive processes and develops over time, rather than reflecting a fixed and stable property of an individual, located deep in the psyche. In the classroom context this means that pupils' identities are co-constructed as they interact with other people; they are a product of the pupils' own behaviour and the ways in which they are identified by their teachers and peers.[2]

Figure 8.1 Ms Alexander's Year 6 Class. Pupils central to our analysis are numbered: Jamie (1), Hayden (2) Ash (3) and Victor (4).

Analysis: ability, identity and whole-class participation

Dialogic pedagogy rests on the assumption that children learn best through participation in rich and challenging classroom discourse, and therefore requires that all pupils be encouraged to participate in such activity. All of the teachers taking part in the professional development programme embraced dialogue's egalitarian ideal in theory – this ideal sits very well within the wider school ideology of inclusion – but they often questioned to what extent it can be achieved in practice. For example, one of the teachers told us in an interview at the end of the study:

> I think dialogic [pedagogy] doesn't help children who find it difficult to vocalize. It doesn't help those children who are shy or intimidated or, you know, feel less confident. So, if they have low self-confidence, I think it really hinders them, because they feel either – they might feel either pushed out or unable to speak because they're scared of the other children challenging their idea, and that knocks their confidence even more.

Comments like this one often cropped up in the reflection meetings, where they prompted further discussion around the thorny issue of whole-class participation. Some teachers wondered how far they should reasonably push reticent pupils, especially given their responsibility for pupils' social, as well as academic, well-being. Shouldn't those who feel nervous about airing their opinions in front of a large group have the right to follow the discussion silently?

We began to explore with the teachers possible reasons behind some pupils' reluctance to speak, and found that in addition to the idea that some pupils are just too shy or lacking in confidence, many teachers also felt that some pupils lacked the relevant capabilities to participate in certain types of discussion. For example, the following comments came up in the reflection workshops and interviews:

> Well, it depends on the ability of the children. You've got two children who are quite bright and articulate, but you've got a lot of the class that are not. And asking them to take over, you wouldn't get the same sort of dialogic [teaching and learning] going on.
> (Teacher workshop discussion, 23 February 2009)

> I do think it works better for the middle and above, and you can see that from the details in the answers.
> (Teacher workshop discussion, 1 June 2009)

> The conversation skills that [the low ability pupils] need are just so far out of their rein.
> (Teacher workshop discussion, 23 February 2009)

> I think they're all capable. I think there are some that are obviously, you know, lower achievers, and I wouldn't expect certain things from them – not that I tell them that – but I try to keep my expectations realistic.
> (Teacher interview, 30 June 2009)

These comments – and the discussions from which they are excerpted – capture the conflicting perspectives shaping these teachers' work. On the one hand, the school and local authority has embraced dialogic pedagogy, with its emphasis on inclusion, voice and empowerment – in short, the idea that all pupils should be given equal opportunity to participate in classroom discourse. On the other hand, in the teachers' comments we can hear echoes of a widespread understanding of pupil ability as being relatively stable over time[3], and the idea that 'low ability' pupils lack the linguistic and cognitive resources to participate in and benefit from cognitively challenging, dialogic teaching and learning.

Related to the issue of whole-class participation were anxieties about managing levels of pupil engagement and interest: If significant time and space is devoted to developing the less confident or lower achieving pupils' voices, what happens to the other pupils in the class? How much time should be given to pupils who appear to be having difficulty – for whatever reasons – in formulating a response to a question when other pupils in the class are keen to respond and/or are becoming frustrated? How can teachers maintain pupils' interest and enthusiasm? This issue was particularly meaningful for the Year 6 teachers, who were tasked with preparing their pupils for the SATs tests. One teacher said about her SATs revision lessons:

> The enthusiasm's not there, and when that's not there, the answers are not great, you know, their thinking's not great. So, it's kind of getting that enthusiasm into them, is difficult.

The changes in pupil interest and classroom dynamics noticed by teachers in the run up to the SATs were also observed by us, and by an external visitor to the school.[4] Two months before Ms Alexander's SATs revision lesson on poetry, we visited her classroom with Ray McDermott, Professor of Education at Stanford University. In a later research seminar, Ray served as discussant for a presentation we gave on the six-minute clip which forms the focus of this chapter. Among his comments he noted:

> I've been to this classroom – with Adam and Julia – and I love this teacher. I was amazed when I was there how much on the one hand she was in control of everything but on the other hand she didn't have to put a lot of work into control. And the kids seemed to have considerable freedom. At the same time, I couldn't find many people who were not paying attention to the task. I remember that even when she went to whole-class teaching, the discussion kept a nice pace, but here [in the video clip] it seems like she's working a little bit harder to get everything synchronized, to get everyone involved.

We were interested in the episode presented in this chapter because it highlights several of the issues outlined above, including why the teacher had to work 'a little bit harder ... to get everyone involved'. Specifically, it raised for us the following questions:

- How can whole-class participation be managed in relation to anxieties regarding differences in levels of pupil ability and confidence; unruly classes; pupil disinterest; and the constraints imposed by high-stakes testing and the requirement to cover the curriculum in a limited period of time?
- Can all pupils participate productively in whole-class dialogue? How can and should dialogic pedagogy be adapted to facilitate the participation and learning of less confident, talkative and/or academically gifted pupils? How can teachers manage the competing demands to draw such pupils into whole-class discussion while also protecting them from embarrassment or loss of self-esteem?
- Finally, and importantly, how does all of the above impact on pupils' own beliefs about their abilities, their attitudes to participating in classroom discussion and their identities and relationships with peers?

We address these issues in the following discussion, beginning with whole-class participation.

Whole-class participation

Hands up or down?

Pupils usually signal that they want to contribute to whole-class discussion by raising their hand, after which they wait to be nominated by the teacher. Pupils such as Elsa, Charlotte and Adin follow this protocol in the focal episode. Other pupils keep their hands (and often their heads) down, but this does not entirely eliminate their chances of being called upon; in fact those who consistently refuse to volunteer answers may find themselves regularly drawn into class discussion by a teacher keen to ensure that *all* pupils are participating in – and paying attention to – classroom activities.

There are three examples in the episode in which Ms Alexander addresses pupils who have not indicated that they want to speak either by raising their hand or shouting out.[5] The most marked example is on line 286, when Ms Alexander calls upon Hayden (Pupil 2 in Figure 8.1). The scene begins a little earlier, on line 251, when Ms Alexander addresses a question to the whole class using the informal 'guys' (the informality designed perhaps to create a more relaxed environment for pupils to offer their initial thoughts). In elaborating her question, she points out that the poet has used 'a technique' (line 258), 'a very clever technique' (line 260, repeated line 263). This is an important point because the SATs are likely to test pupils' knowledge of authorial techniques (which is why Ms Alexander had instructed the children to look out for 'a certain technique that the author has used' at the start of the lesson). Aaron indicates that he knows what this technique is on line 261, attempts to answer unofficially on line 266 and reiterates his claim to knowledge on line 267. Charlotte signals that she too is keen to answer by raising her arm (line 259), then rapidly tapping the desk with her hands (line 262), before raising her arm again, waving it around and stamping her feet for added emphasis (line 265). Rather than call on either Aaron or Charlotte, however, Ms Alexander redirects her original question to Hayden, who did not raise his hand (on line 268). In line with the ideology of inclusion, teachers try to encourage *all* pupils to participate in class discussion, rather than just call on the few who are consistently keen to respond; so Ms Alexander's utterance on line 268 does not stand out as particularly unusual. Moreover, we must remember that Ms Alexander has detailed knowledge of the pupils in this class. Whereas the episode presented here allows us to glimpse just six minutes of classroom life, Ms Alexander had spent over 500 hours with these pupils by this point in the school year. She explained to us that certain pupils had the capacity to completely change whole-class dynamics, sometimes for the better, but often for the worse if they persistently interrupted other pupils. She was keen to ensure that these dominant individuals did not prohibit contributions from other, more hesitant, pupils. At this point, then, Hayden is identified as someone who is perhaps reluctant to participate in classroom discussion.

Ms Alexander's 'any idea' (line 268) suggests that she would be happy for Hayden to have a guess. 'Any idea' then becomes 'any way' (line 271) and 'anything' (line 272) before giving way to 'anything *basic*' (line 274). Hayden is thus perhaps being identified not just as a reluctant participant but also as one whose academic abilities are at the 'basic' level (we return to this point below). Ms Alexander gives Hayden the space to formulate his answer by quieting other pupils (on lines 275, 286, 288). In doing so, she signals that this interaction is not about getting quickly to the right answer; it's about creating space for a different pupil's voice to be heard. After 20 seconds, however, Hayden still does not answer, and the possibilities inherent in the 'any'/'anything' of lines 271–4 become 'no' (line 294) and 'nothing' (line 292).

The remaining two examples in which Ms Alexander addresses individuals who have not volunteered to speak both involve the same pupil, Jamie (Pupil 1 in Figure 8.1). Ms Alexander calls upon Jamie for the first time on line 138, in order to elicit a response to the question of exactly what is 'covering the hills'. Jamie responds by shaking her head. Ms Alexander gives her another chance on line 140, 'no?', before moving on and telling the class 'come on, you're very quiet today ... come on guys' (line 142). This comment reveals Ms Alexander's concern with the issue of whole-class participation. Not all of the pupils are being quiet – if anything the discussion is becoming more animated – but some pupils are not participating to the same extent as others, if at all. Just under a minute later, Ms Alexander calls on Jamie again, coaxing her gently with 'go on have a go' (line 193). Ms Alexander doesn't use Jamie's name here, but there's good reason to believe that her utterance is addressed to this pupil. Unfortunately the camera does not capture the teacher's gaze, but it's clear from the video that Charlotte is responding to something on line 192, when she puts her hand down and turns to face Jamie, and it seems reasonable to suggest that she's responding here to the teacher. Perhaps Charlotte is mirroring Ms Alexander's gaze, and/or received a subtle 'hands down' signal from her. Again, Jamie declines to answer and Ms Alexander moves on without exerting any further pressure.

Although it seems at first that Ms Alexander calls upon Jamie at random, closer scrutiny of the video record shows that she is in fact responding to signals that Jamie may have something to say. Jamie had raised her hand, albeit fleetingly, on line 133. It's not clear whether this movement began as a bid for attention that then morphed into something more like the stretching of a cramped arm, or whether it was never meant to signal a bid for attention at all, but Ms Alexander seems to have picked up on the smallest possibility that Jamie may have something to contribute (that Ms Alexander is also confused by Jamie's intentions may be signalled by her questioning intonation on line 138, 'Jamie?'). Similarly, on line 190 Jamie moves her hand forward on the desk as if about to bid for a turn to speak but then quickly brings it back. Again, it seems that Ms Alexander picks up on this movement on line 193 when she encourages Jamie with 'go on have a go'. Ms Alexander may be particularly sensitive to Jamie's positioning because she had identified this pupil as someone who is shy and rarely speaks in class (even though she does very well in her written work). When invited to talk about her class in general terms, Ms Alexander told us:

> I've got a few quiet, very quiet, girls, who don't want to talk … And I've got particu-larly two girls that are extremely shy, and they won't – they just don't want to talk. But I've been encouraging them, they're coming for parents' evening, and I've said, you know, to get that A, you know participation is kind of needed. Even if it's wrong, even if the answer's wrong, I don't care, it's just talk, just say something. And then I can see what your thought processes are and then you can see, as well, what you're getting wrong, because then at least you're engaged.
>
> (Interview, 5 December 2008)

Ms Alexander was clearly sensitive to the needs of these girls, and this may explain why she was so keen to involve Jamie in the discussion, to get her to 'have a go' and at least say something, 'even if it's wrong'.

Just as pupils who do not volunteer may be called upon by the teacher to speak, so too, some pupils who regularly raise their hands to bid for attention may find that they are not called upon at all. We've already seen one example of this with Aaron. He speaks on a number of occasions in the focal episode but his contributions are never directly elicited from Ms Alexander. One reason for this is that his overexuberance has disrupted lessons in the past. A potentially more interesting, or at least less obvious, case is Victor (Pupil 4 in Figure 8.1). Victor, who seems to be quietly following the discussion, raises his hand three times in this six-minute clip, but is not selected to speak. The reason behind this becomes clear if we look at exactly when Victor raises his arm and when he lowers it.

Victor raises his hand confidently on line 178, but the timing is a little odd as no question has been posed at this point; in fact, the question that had been preoccupying the class for the last minute had just been answered by Daren (line 173) and confirmed as correct by Ms Alexander (line 174). Victor keeps his hand raised while Ms Alexander elaborates Daren's answer (lines 179–84), but when she asks a follow-up question, 'So the dark is tightening its knot. What does that mean? (lines 184–5), Victor casually lowers his hand (line 186). He raises his hand again on line 203, and again, this action comes immediately after another student (this time Ash) has given a correct answer (lines 197–8), which has been confirmed by Ms Alexander (lines 199–201). Again, the hand stays up until another question is posed, first by Daren (line 216) and then by Ms Alexander (line 219), at which point Victor brings his arm back to the table. It seems then that Victor is rather adept at bidding for a turn at the precise moment in which the chances of being called upon are rather slim. Similar acts of pseudo-participation have been documented by other researchers; for example, Ray McDermott and Henry Tylbor famously showed how a young girl in a reading group 'seemed to be doing much work to arrange *not getting a turn*' in order to avoid getting caught out not being able to read.[6] Victor clearly raises his hand on a number of occasions and appears to be keen to contribute, but he times this non-verbal signal so that there's little chance that he will actually be called upon. As a result, he is (ironically) much less likely to be drawn into the discussion than pupils like Hayden and Jamie who try to avoid drawing attention to themselves. It is possible that Jamie may have been trying to do something similar to Victor with her own arm movements, but if that's the case, it seems that her gestures were not as exquisitely timed as Victor's.

Active disinterest or concealed engagement?

The above accounts of Victor and Jamie's actions show that once we move our analyses beyond an exclusive focus on what is said and instead incorporate a 'multimodal' perspective (in which language is just one amongst a number of different modes of communication, including body positioning, gesture and gaze), new perspectives on classroom participation open up. This point is further reinforced if we turn our attention to another key participant in the episode, Ash (Pupil 3 in Figure 8.1). Ash is sitting at the front of the classroom, directly facing the camera, and thus it is impossible to overlook him when watching the video clip, especially as he is very active both verbally and non-verbally. He does not raise his hand to speak at any point in the episode, but he does contribute to the interaction several times by calling out. This behaviour is sometimes accepted by the teacher (as when he responds with the right answer on lines 197–8) but is at other times reprimanded (e.g. lines 124–15, line 333).

Overall, it is fair to say that Ash is 'acting up' in this lesson, which was not unusual for him (based on our observations of other lessons in this classroom and concerns expressed by Ms Alexander). Ash seems to go out of his way to demonstrate his lack of interest in the lesson. His default position throughout the episode is head down, often fiddling with a piece of paper or something under his desk. When he does look up it's often to make inappropriate gestures or noises. For example, during Ms Alexander's turn on lines 58 to 62, Ash stretches out his arms then crosses them, looks to his left, and makes a circling motion with one hand while making a funny noise. He makes side comments or sings to other pupils (for example, lines 283, 287), performs for the camera (for example, lines 202), and even throws bits of paper at Charlotte during her explanation at the end of the episode. When we view the video focusing only on Ash, however, we see that despite his obvious and active *dis*interest in this lesson, there are signs that he is still very much tuned in to the discussion. During Charlotte's turn on lines 48–9, for example, he leans forward and moves towards Charlotte in order to look at her poem. When Ms Alexander asks a question on lines 77–8, Ash glances up at her. When she presents an explanation on lines 116–20, pointing out to the class 'so basically that part there is saying that the hills are covered with something' (she is highlighting the relevant part of the poem, which is displayed on the whiteboard), Ash looks up at the whiteboard indicating that he is listening and responding to the teacher's directions. The answer he subsequently offers, 'trees', is not correct (as we see from Ms Alexander's response to it in lines 124–5), but it does indicate that he's listening (in the world outside of the poem trees do cover hills). His continuing interaction on the issue with Ms Alexander on lines 124–31 is rather antagonistic, but again, when the teacher directs Ash and the rest of the class to 'look further up' (line 131) Ash leans back and cranes his head slightly in order to see the whiteboard. Likewise, his contribution on line 197 ('getting *darker*') is not entirely cooperative – his intonation appears sarcastic and suggests that the answer is overly obviously – but he follows this up immediately with 'closing in' and is praised for arriving at the right answer (lines 204–6). Even the strange arm movement described above (during lines 58 to 62) makes sense when we match it up with the ongoing class discussion, which at that point was about bandages and what they're used for – Ash's elaborate circling motion seems to demonstrate the wrapping of a bandage.

While Victor appears to be enacting a form of pseudo-participation in this episode, Ash is doing the opposite, a kind of pseudo-*non*participation. We consider some reasons for this in the next section, after first addressing the relationship between teacher expectations, pupil identities and learning.

Pupil ability and identity

The teachers' comments quoted above, together with our informal conversations with them, suggest that the teachers at Abbeyford had different expectations for pupils based upon their position in the class hierarchy. Teachers might not directly vocalize expectations to pupils (as demonstrated in the final quote), but such expectations are nonetheless communicated through teacher–pupil interactions in the classroom. Educational researchers and practitioners have noticed that teachers very often vary their pedagogical techniques in order to ensure that lower as well as higher achieving pupils are included within whole-class discussions. For example, teachers tend to pose cognitively challenging questions to pupils perceived as higher achievers and less challenging questions to pupils perceived as academically weaker.[7] In doing so, they implicitly communicate low expectations to those pupils identified as less able, and this may impact negatively on pupils' effort and motivation.[8] In a number of cases, researchers have found that the popular method of posing less demanding questions to weaker pupils backfires with the effects that:

(a) pupils already perceived as underachievers are less likely to participate in whole-class discussion;[9]
(b) when they do participate they are more likely to engage in 'unproductive' interactions with the teacher (that is, interactions in which the pupil plays a relatively passive role, offering at most monosyllabic contributions), and thus miss out on the dialogic exchanges that have been shown to facilitate learning and development;[10] and
(c) unproductive interactions can impact negatively on the pupil's identity (as perceived by themselves and others), which in turn impacts negatively on their learning.[11]

Processes (a) and (b) appear to be at play in Ms Alexander's interactions with Hayden: Hayden is not keen to participate in the discussion and when directly asked to participate he gives just two single-word responses (lines 280 and 294).[12] It is more difficult to draw inferences around the processes described in (c), however, especially as the focal episode is not a typical example of differentiated teaching. In this example Ms Alexander does more than simply modify her question. She also draws upon her knowledge of Hayden's interests outside of school (that his family keep pet owls) to personalize the question and to help Hayden access the information relevant to answering it. This helps us to better understand why Ms Alexander chose to ignore Aaron's and Charlotte's bids for attention, focusing instead on a pupil who did not raise his hand, when in other situations she accepts their bids: Hayden has a special interest in owls, and therefore has something to contribute to the lesson at this point. Ms Alexander is thus not necessarily (or not only) identifying Hayden as a weaker pupil; she is potentially positioning him more favourably, as an expert, or at least as someone who has interest in and extracurricular knowledge of the relevant topic.

A second complication is the role that other pupils play in managing Hayden's contributions to the lesson. When Ms Alexander suggests that 'who who who' sounds like the noise an owl makes (line 314), Daren makes an appeal to Hayden's superior knowledge of owls: 'Hayden, what does it sound like' (lines 316–19). In this moment, knowledge of an extra-curricular topic becomes salient – unlike the other pupils, Hayden has first-hand knowledge of owls. Daren then uses Hayden's knowledge to challenge the teacher, 'Hayden says no' (lines 324, 326). In doing so, Daren positions Hayden as a knowledgeable animal enthusiast (though Hayden is still positioned interactionally as someone who needs others' support to participate in group discussion). We can speculate about Daren's motivations here: Does he genuinely defer to Hayden's superior knowledge on this topic? Or is he just seizing the opportunity to challenge the teacher and/or show off? But whatever his reasons, the effect is that Hayden's voice is drawn back into the discussion and his role as an important member of this classroom community is reasserted.

This example illustrates the important role of the peer group in constructing pupil identities in the classroom and in ensuring equal participation for all class members, regardless of confidence or ability. In this case, it seems that Daren took Ms Alexander's lead in appealing to Hayden's out-of-school knowledge. It is also important to note that this kind of pupil intervention would likely not be possible in all classrooms – a particular kind of environment has been fostered in this classroom, one in which pupils feel comfortable and confident to speak up in order to challenge received knowledge or to ask their own questions (notice that Daren had raised the questions that brought about this particular strand of the discussion in the first place, on lines 216, 226 and 234).

Other types of peer-group interaction may have a more negative effect on pupil identity and learning. Consider, for example, the impact of Ash's behaviour. Ash's oppositional behaviour (described above) may signal his desire to construct a 'cool' anti-school identity – a point noted by many educational researchers and practitioners (including Ms Alexander) with regards to boys in the classroom, especially as they approach adolescence.[13] Ms Alexander told us:

> I would say 40 per cent of my class can be difficult, and, you know, they can be- they struggle with behaving well, because I think they see it as, you know, 'if I behave well, I'm going to be classed as a geek, I'm going to be classed as a nerd', you know.
>
> (From Interview, 5 December 2008)

Openly participating in school activities would threaten Ash's identity as a 'cool' and 'rebellious' male, hence his exaggerated disobedience. As noted above, however, Ash manages to maintain the persona of 'misbehaving boy' while also paying attention to the lesson. As a result, he is able to do well at school. We might ask, though, what influence his behaviour has on other pupils, and in relation to this episode, specifically Hayden?

When Ms Alexander asks Hayden 'so what might it mean, owl flew who who who?' (lines 281–2), Ash moves around to face Hayden and sings to him. The teacher turns her attention away from Hayden momentarily in order to reprimand Aaron, who is sitting on the other side of the room (line 286), at which point Hayden responds to Ash with a half laugh and a smile. When the teacher's attention turns back to him, Hayden puts his head down (line 289), but Ash gets Hayden's interest again by turning to him and saying 'it wasn't me' and raising his eyebrows in a conspiratorial fashion. Both boys now laugh together, presumably to signal their shared stance against the teacher's authority. It's at this point that Ms Alexander gives Hayden one last chance to answer the question, 'nothing, you have no idea?' (lines 292–3), and Hayden responds with a firm 'no' (line 294). Hayden takes on the role of uncooperative participant here, but there exists the possibility that he does so, at least in part, to identify with Ash and project a rebellious, masculine identity. Children often look to their peers for ideas about how to behave in a given situation, and more widely for direction on the kinds of attitudes they should have towards teachers, learning and schooling. Ash's interactions with Hayden are tangential to the centre-stage classroom learning, but they serve to co-construct a particular attitude towards that learning. Hayden's refusal to answer appears to be influenced by this co-constructed attitude. What is seen by the teacher at the front of the class, however, is simply an uncooperative pupil. It is easy to imagine how this identity might thicken, across a chain of similar events during the school year, into a more enduring impression of Hayden as a pupil who just 'can't be bothered'.[14]

Conclusion

Like most teachers, Ms Alexander is keen to ensure that all pupils in her class have the opportunity to participate in class discussion. In keeping with this aim, she calls upon pupils like Hayden and Jamie, who have not volunteered answers. She does not make these selections at random, however. In the case of Hayden, she takes the opportunity to capitalize on his out-of-school knowledge, and in the case of Jamie, she responds to subtle visual signals that this pupil appears to have something to say. She does this while also watching other students for signs of understanding or inattention, responding to misbehaviour, formulating her next move, and ensuring the logical development of the lesson. As noted in Chapter 1, teaching is a complex practice in part because of the enormous demands practice places on teacher's attention: there's a lot going on in the classroom both verbally and visually. The above analysis highlights, in particular, the importance of non-verbal cues, including those that might indicate pseudo-participation (or even pseudo-*non*participation, as in the case of Ash).

We should make clear that we are not suggesting that teachers should add to the already difficult task of managing whole-class discussion the requirement to systematically monitor all pupils' non-verbal as well as verbal behaviour. What we *are* suggesting is that by engaging in the kinds of video-based reflection we advocate in this book, teachers might notice aspects of pupil behaviour and classroom organization that are usually hidden from view. When a teacher reflects upon video-recorded episodes from her own classroom, she is able to slow down the action, focusing more on the contexts surrounding pupils' behaviour than on the traits displayed by individual pupils already identified as disruptive, shy, low ability and so on.

This teacher may notice, for example, that someone who seems uncooperative (like Hayden) is actually preoccupied with social and relational issues. She may find that someone who appears disengaged and disruptive (like Ash) is really following the flow of the lesson; and conversely, that someone who does not normally command her attention in class (like Victor in the focal episode) may be falling behind. This noticing might challenge accepted beliefs. For example conventional wisdom tells us that being a good student means being quiet and attentive, raising a hand to bid for attention, only speaking when spoken to and so on. Victor does all of these things, yet he does not contribute to the lesson or demonstrate an understanding of the poem. Ash does the opposite, yet he manages to keep pace with the discussion.

Challenging perceptions and prevailing orthodoxies can have important consequences for teaching and learning because the way we think and talk about pupils influences our instructional practices. Ms Alexander's subtle coaxing of Jamie was quite different to the approach she adopted with Hayden because her actions were influenced by prior experience and knowledge of these pupils – including that Jamie is shy and does not like speaking in front of the whole class – as well as her ideas about how best to interact with pupils who are shy or less academic. These ideas reflect more widely circulating discourses about pupils (for example, that pupil ability is stable, that only certain types of pupil can contribute productively to class discussions and so on). Pedagogy includes discourses about pupils – their abilities, motivations, in short, what kind of people they are – and these discourses influence teacher practices in the classroom.[15]

In turn, our analysis suggests that these discourses and associated practices have implications for social identification, that is, for the way pupils are identified by themselves and others. For example, teachers who believe that everyone should participate in classroom discussion but that only certain types of pupil are able to handle cognitive challenge are likely to direct demanding questions only to those pupils perceived as high ability and easy questions to those pupils perceived as low ability. In this way, individuals are positioned as certain types of pupil: 'bright' and 'clever' versus 'low ability' and 'inarticulate'. Pupils who are consistently positioned as academically weak may become discouraged by low expectations, switch off from learning (replacing active participation with a passive shrug or one-word response), and thus continue to fulfil the identity of low achiever attributed to them. The critical importance of identity for learning is increasingly recognized in learning theory and in studies of classroom practice.[16] In short, pupils who are identified (and come to identify themselves) as competent and productive members of the classroom community are likely to experience learning and participation in classroom activities as much easier and generative than pupils who have been identified as incompetent or otherwise problematic. If pupils come to see their own ability as fixed and accept the identity of low achiever, they may decide that making an effort and striving to do better are pointless.

We should emphasize, however, that there is no simple, linear connection between pedagogic beliefs, teaching practices, pupil identity and learning. Further, the teacher is not necessarily at the centre of this complex process. Classroom interaction (like all interaction) is co-constructed. The actions of one participant limit the range of possible actions available to others, and every action has consequences. For example, Aaron's overexuberance during Ms Alexander's interaction with Hayden (especially on line 284), constrains the range of actions available to Ms Alexander at that moment. She can either allow Aaron to give away the answer (and thus miss out on the opportunity to involve Hayden in class discussion) or she can reprimand Aaron for shouting out. She selects the second option, turning her attention momentarily away from Hayden. In the absence of Ms Alexander's gaze, Ash and Hayden collude in silent opposition to the teacher. The result is that Hayden is positioned as 'unco-operative pupil' or 'pupil lacking the ability to answer a basic question', but these identities are co-constructed through the actions of Aaron, Ash and Hayden, as well as Ms Alexander. Later Daren plays a key role in positioning Hayden more favourably.

Teaching through dialogic pedagogy further complicates this relationship between peda-gogic beliefs, teaching practices and pupil identities. On the one hand, dialogue calls for an inclusive, egalitarian, caring and non-competitive environment, but on the other hand emphasizes oral discourse, full participation and cognitive challenge, which together can be threatening for pupils lacking in confidence or perceived as lower achievers. This problem has received little attention in discussions of dialogic pedagogy, yet our work suggests that it is a key factor shaping the enactment of dialogic pedagogy, and one that advocates of such pedagogy need to actively confront in their work in English schools (and, likely, elsewhere as well).

The tension between the inclusivity of dialogic pedagogy and the perceived inability of some pupils to participate in challenging classroom discourse emerged as a central issue for teachers participating in the project. The teachers were clear about the importance of dialogue for learning, as is evident in Ms Alexander's commitment to developing pupils' thinking through their talk: 'Even if it's wrong, even if the answer's wrong, I don't care, it's just talk, just say something. And then I can see what your thought processes are' (Interview, 5 December 2008, quoted in full on page 145). But if all pupils are to benefit from dialogue it is important to raise expectations about what academically weaker pupils can achieve and to push *all* pupils (not just the academically gifted) to challenge themselves. If we start from the assumption that some pupils cannot handle difficult ideas and keep everything basic for them, we may be preventing them from developing their capabilities.[17]

Finally, cutting across this discussion of whole-class participation, ability and identity is the issue of high-stakes testing. First, SATs revision intensifies the demands on both teachers and pupils, and more than any other aspect of primary schooling, highlights differences in pupils' levels of ability and school knowledge. Ray McDermott has written that classrooms 'can be so well organized for putting the spotlight on those who are doing less well than the others that hiding becomes a sensible strategy for all of the kids some of the time and for some of the kids all of the time'.[18] The SATs intensify this spotlight, such that there is even more reason in SATs revision lessons than in other types of lesson for pupils like Hayden, Victor and Jamie to adopt a 'hiding' strategy. Second, the sense of hierarchy and competi-tion that the SATs engender was palpable at Abbeyford Primary. In a class discussion on whether secondary schools should be streamed for ability, Aaron (who was *for* streaming) made the following comments:

> Say you- in your SATs, and in your whole life, you were like doing level threes and everything, you're not going to make them a good job because you're not- they're not capable. If they're not capable you can't just say, oh sorry I feel sorry for them oh sorry we'll give you the job just because we feel sorry for you, and they'll do- they'll do the job wrong. You'll get someone who's clever, done their work, and give them a good job, and the other people, if they ain't clever then they ain't clever.

Little wonder, then, that he was keen to make his mark in SATs revision lessons by shouting out the answers to prove he's got level 5 ability. Finally, as the Year 6 teachers at Abbeyford have noted, it is very difficult to spark pupils' interest and enthusiasm during SATs revision, and when that's not there 'the answers are not great … their thinking's not great'. It is perhaps during SATs revision lessons that pupils like Ash are most likely to look for other ways to occupy themselves. It seems to us no coincidence, then, that Ray McDermott's experience of this Year 6 lesson, recorded just before the testing period, was slightly different to his experience of the lesson he observed earlier in the term.

Issues for further discussion

Following analysis of the episode, readers might want to consider the following issues:

- What do you think of our analysis? What points resonate with your own interpretations of what's happening? What points seem problematic to you?
- How, if at all, can dialogic pedagogy be reconciled with preparation for SATs tests – with their emphases on finding the correct answer, and encouragement of a high-stakes, competitive classroom culture?
- Several of the pupils in the focal episode become enthusiastic about exploring the poem's metaphors, but at the point at which the discussion really takes off, pupils start to shout out and there's a risk that the interaction will break down (e.g. Ms Alexander has to tell pupils to 'Be sensible' on line 163). What strategies can be used to maintain productive and open dialogue but avoid disorder in the classroom?
- Are there ways in which apparently disruptive pupils (like Ash) or overly exuberant pupils (like Aaron) can become a resource in the classroom, made to act with rather than against the teacher?
- What kind of classroom environment encourages reluctant or shy pupils to contribute? How can we create such an environment?
- What kind of categories and terms do we use to identify our pupils? What are they based upon?

COMMENTARY

WHAT THE DISCUSSION OF 'THE OWL' MADE ME WONDER
BY PIE CORBETT

Every time someone reads a poem, it becomes whatever they create.

Watching the video, I wondered whether the SATs testing of a poet's 'authorial intent' might be unhelpful. Writing poetry is not always an explicit, intellectual process but rather an intuitive act of creation – ideas, patterns, rhythms and images spring into the mind, as if from nowhere. So, I am unsure whether digging away at the 'meaning' and trying to 'understand' or 'explain' a poem is all that helpful. Is there one fixed meaning? How would you explain a Dali painting? Poems are not sums.

A poem is an experience. What sorts of activities might help a child become familiar with a poem – especially for city children reading about an owl? Perhaps – look at an owl in flight at dusk as it glides over a field (a YouTube clip might help). Use pen and ink to draw an owl. Ask groups to work together on a performance – use an ominous drum beat as the children experiment by varying pace, volume and expression. Grow the poem in the mind, body, ear and eye.

Ash is probably right when he suggests that the hills are bandaged by a line of 'trees'. They may also be bandaged by darkness, by the owl gliding, by the fear that darkness and the owl bring. Perhaps, when we are talking about a poem, 'all ideas are accepted' (not necessarily 'right' but taken on board for consideration and development). Sometimes ideas might take us up a side-alley but that is fine. Ideas can be tested out, developed or abandoned.

For there to be a fruitful discussion, the right atmosphere is needed. You cannot share ideas, building or challenging others' thinking, without certain conditions. Watching the video, I wondered whether it helped to be in rows? More questions arose for me – how do we develop the skills of listening to each other, valuing contributions and reflecting on what has been said before forming new understandings. In my own teaching, I found Aidan Chambers' wonderful book *Tell Me* (Thimble Press) invaluable. It explores 'Book Talk' – how to help children talk about literature.

I find that sometimes those who have been labelled as 'low ability' contribute the most insightful thinking – being less bound by clichéd ideas. How can you label a child's response to a poem? You see years ago, I was on the 'slow' table. That label still haunts me (like the owl). It was why I went into teaching. I may have been a 'low achiever' but whoever decided I had little ability was wrong. Consequently, I didn't 'try'. Consequently, I 'failed'. It was a self-fulfilling prophecy. Yet this still happens. Why not ask hard questions of everyone? Then accept their thinking … value their thoughts … value 'trying' … and then encourage the thinking of others, so that understanding may deepen collectively.

PS '*Who Who Who*' – is the moment when the reader becomes the owl and the poem takes flight.

Pie Corbett, educator and author, has written extensively on teaching creative writing, worked as a teacher, head teacher and inspector. Currently, Pie continues to develop 'talk for writing' through teacher-research and development projects across the country. He is also a poet and storyteller. His poem, The Owl, *is the focus of class discussion in the episode.*

COMMENTARY

'TIGHTENING THE KNOT?': FEAR, POETRY AND TESTING BY MELANIE COOKE

I am a teacher of adults so it was interesting that my response to this excerpt was one of heart-sinking familiarity; not at the considerable achievements of Ms Alexander, who, despite their groans, manages to engage almost all the children in a discussion about a *poem*, but at the stranglehold (the blindfold of fear?) that relentless testing has on teaching and learning, and its impact on any prolonged, deep engagement with knowledge – especially when that knowledge is difficult, challenging or new.

I agree with the authors that the excerpt cannot be understood unless test preparation is taken into account, and that this is why Ms Alexander seems to be working *so* hard to get all the kids involved. The urgency that they get the right answers and reach the correct interpretation quickly and efficiently is absolutely palpable. For me, this excerpt reveals a striking contradiction between test preparation and what interpreting *poetry* requires, i.e. time to read, absorb, reflect and allow the sometimes strange language to work in one's mind. For the same reason, whole class 'dialogic' teaching – although undoubtedly good for learning – needs to come at a point in which the children are actually ready to contribute meaningfully after deeper engagement with the text, thereby liberating the teacher or the confident pupils from having to do all the work. This might mean a much longer period of quiet study than the ten minutes allotted in this lesson and providing prompts and suggestions which allow pupils to come first to their own understandings. Only after this stage does it seem feasible to ask them to combine their interpretations and come to some kind of consensus about the interpretation acceptable to writers of the SATs test.

So, in a classroom where there was no test and no rush to get the 'right' interpretation pupils might: talk, write about or even draw their own thoughts about owls, fear, the dark and the countryside; compare their words and phrases to each others' and the poet's; share their own knowledge of owls without it having to be 'correct' or poetic; read the poem aloud and so on. And, importantly, in the process of coming to a consensus about the best interpretation of this poem, the children could be invited to talk *critically* about it: Is there really an easy interpretation of phrases such as 'bandaged the hills' which can be just 'found' in the text? Are the metaphors indeed good ones? (I personally am doubtful about some of them). And how can we say whether an interpretation is 'sensible' or far-fetched? Finally, for me a dialogic classroom means checking in with children about the pedagogy itself: Why do they groan when asked to do poetry? How do they feel when asked to discuss something publicly they feel they have only a partial understanding of? Do they think poetry is amenable to testing? And do they themselves have any alternative suggestions for how poetry – and other genres and topics – might be approached in their classrooms?

Melanie Cooke has worked as a teacher in adult and further education in the field of English for Speakers of Other Languages (ESOL) and is now a researcher and lecturer in the Centre for Language, Discourse and Communication, King's College London. She is currently working on a PhD on ESOL and citizenship and is co-author (with James Simpson) of ESOL: A Critical Guide'.

COMMENTARY

ON PRACTICE, ON PURPOSE
BY JENNIFER A. VADEBONCOEUR AND LOUAI RAHAL

Creating the conditions for a dialogue that includes the participation of all pupils is a challenge that every educator is likely to face. A commitment to dialogic teaching requires *practice* as both teachers and pupils learn to participate differently to ensure the inclusion of all voices in a whole-class dialogue. In addition, the *purpose* of the dialogue comes center stage.

One way for both teacher and pupils to practice participating in dialogue is by preceding whole-class dialogue with discussions in pairs. Checking in with each pair individually lets pupils know that they have valuable perspectives, experiences and expertise to share. In addition, as the teacher inquires into the ideas of the pair, she may learn from pupils how they feel about sharing their views, as well as what they would like and are prepared to contribute.

Sometimes, pupils may ask a teacher to allow them to self-identify as having a contribution through raised hands, rather than being called upon. This gives pupils an opportunity to decide how they would like to participate in a given discussion, while ensuring that they know that contributions are valued. Under these circumstances, a teacher may be able to bring pupils' voices into the dialogue by 're-voicing' their ideas in their own utterances.

The idea that a person's voice may be incorporated in a dialogue through the utterances of others surfaces from Bakhtin's (1981) theory of communication. For example, a teacher may share pupils' voices by re-voicing the themes that emerged from their earlier work in pairs. In this way, pupils' voices may be present in a dialogue even when they are silent. Potentially, when pupils hear their dialogue re-voiced – as thinking worthy of consideration – they may be more inclined to step into future dialogues as vocal participants.

In addition, however, it is also vital to build a classroom culture where pupils' contributions are both an expected and supported norm for everyone. Teachers can encourage pupils' participation by assuring them that there may not be one 'right' answer, and/or that 'wrong' answers are as welcome as 'right' answers; however, the implicit rules of collective dialogue are not created by teachers alone. Peers also shape, in part, what is taken to be appropriate participation in whole-class dialogues, as does the purpose of the dialogue. Thus, the difficulty of the dialogue at the heart of this chapter may have less to do with the teacher's and students' abilities and more to do with its purpose: as preparation for a testing situation that is not open and generative, but rather about 'getting it right'.

Dialogic teaching requires a continuous and cumulative effort of every member of the classroom community. When a teacher communicates the value of participation and dialogue, and peers come to see what each pupil shares as contributing to their work together, dialogue is embraced as a joint practice of learning and teaching. Dialogue, however, is likely to be limited if its purpose is to prepare pupils to complete narrowly defined standardized assessments.

Jennifer A. Vadeboncoeur is Associate Professor, in Human Development Learning and Culture at the University of British Columbia.

Louai Rahal is a PhD student in the Human Development, Learning and Culture programme at the University of British Columbia. The topic of his research is: Applications of the sociocultural theory of human development in the education of children with autism.

COMMENTARY

THE COMPLEXITY OF DIALOGIC TEACHING UNDER THE SHADOW OF STANDARDIZED TESTING BY GLENDA MOSS

I was most drawn to Ash in the video. I wondered how the authors might interpret his actions. Would they think he had demonstrated non-interest, or would they have been intrigued by the way he demonstrated engagement by contributing on his own terms? He resonated with me because I taught many grade seven students with similar behaviors. I enjoyed students like Ash who were obviously very bright but modeled behaviors of non-interest or intent on doing school on their own terms. Several of my colleagues in the late 80s and 90s would label Ash's behavior on a range from off-task to defiant. Using 'assertive discipline' they would address his participation from a behavioral standpoint. It is hard to tell from a brief video clip what all the dynamics are between the teacher and Ash, and Ash and his peers.

It did seem to me like the teacher put Hayden on the spot by making an assumption that she could connect to his cultural experiences. I think that the brief interaction between the teacher, Hayden and Ash indicated that the relationship level needed for dialogue in teaching was stifled by pressure of the upcoming test. I liked that the teacher accepted Ash's participation and wondered if she could learn from Ash how to more effectively engage students on the margin.

As to the value of the video and text for professional development, I wondered to what extent the tedious examination of students' behaviors will prove to be critical to teaching development. I could see value in a group of teachers viewing the video and formulating their own interpretations and then discussing diverse views. I like that the authors' text points out that there are many complexities to the classroom. We do not know the teacher's tacit knowledge that contributes to how she works with her students. The set-up and way she guides students to an understanding of 'technique' and 'interpretation' was clear.

I appreciate the teacher's commitment to dialogue in teaching under the shadow of standardized testing. A more dialogic alternative would have put the students in small dialogue groups and let them freely interpret the poem and share their resulting ideas with the class. This would have let the students express their true thoughts and feelings about studying the poem. The teacher might then engage the students in a critical conversation about the value of standardized testing of poetry techniques, trusting they would learn the techniques in the process without making them think that she valued the techniques from her position as teacher.

Professor Glenda Moss is Chair of the Division of Teacher Education and Administration at the University of North Texas at Dallas. She worked for 13 years as a middle school teacher. Her areas of expertise include middle school teaching, portfolio assessment, multicultural education, and teacher professional development through critical, narrative action research. She is author of Crossing Boundaries and Building Learning Communities.

Notes

1 Such analysis is typically referred to as 'multimodal', since it attends to multiple modes of communication and not just verbal exchanges of information (see Kress *et al.*, 2001).

2 We are building on linguistic anthropological and sociolinguistic research that views identity as 'a relational and socio-cultural phenomenon that emerges and circulates in local discourse contexts of interaction rather than as a stable structure located primarily in the individual psyche or in fixed social categories' (Bucholtz and Hall 2005: 585–6). See also Maybin (2006), McDermott and Raley (2008), Mehan (1996), Wortham (2006).

3 For an overview of the debate on fixed versus flexible intelligence see Adey (2012). See Gould (1996) for a fascinating history of the idea of intelligence quotient and its applications.

4 As part of our research, we measured change over time in patterns of classroom interaction by systematically coding for different types of 'discourse move' (e.g. teacher question, explanation, feedback; pupil response, question, challenge). Some discourse moves were further subcategorized in order to give more detail. For example, questions were coded according to type (e.g. 'open', 'closed', 'probe', 'uptake'). For the Year 6 classroom we sampled, we noticed a significant change in classroom talk in the lessons that occurred during the SATs revision period compared to those that took place pre- and post- SATs revision. Talk in SATs revision lessons was very clearly marked by a high incidence of closed questions, while in the post-SATs revision period, the teacher used fewer closed questions and instead opted for more open questions and probes, discourse moves that are associated with dialogue. Genuinely open questions give pupils the opportunity to go 'off script', and this potential may not be welcomed by teachers who believe a more regimented approach is required for success in high-stakes tests. Similarly, probes extend individual pupil responses, challenging them to develop their thinking, but may slow down the pace of the lesson in terms of the amount of material that can be covered (and time pressure is particularly acute during the SATs revision period) and in terms of the number of pupils who can contribute to the lesson. This systematic discourse analysis suggests that standardized tests discourage the kind of teacher–pupil talk that has been shown to be productive for learning. See Snell and Lefstein (2011) for further detail.

5 Laura is off camera and thus we can't see if she raises her hand before being called upon on line 103; she does have an answer ready without any hesitation though, which indicates that she was prepared to answer and thus may well have been bidding for a turn.

6 McDermott and Tylbor (1983: 283).

7 For further detail on differentiated instruction see Black (2004).

8 When pupils are placed into different classes or 'sets' according to ability, the impact of lower teacher expectations and associated teaching practices is more keenly felt. Compelling evidence for this can be found in Ireson and colleagues' (2005) study of the effects of ability grouping on GCSE attainment. They found that students placed in sets above their assessed level of achievement for English, Mathematics and Science made more progress than students of equivalent ability who were placed in ability groups of approximately the 'right' level. For an excellent and accessible overview of the issue of grouping by ability see Baines (2012). In the US high-school setting, Martin Nystrand and colleagues (1997: Chapter 2) have shown that students placed in 'low-track classes' are far more likely than their higher achieving peers to be given narrowly focused formulaic tasks (such as fill-in-the-blank worksheets), and that this rarely helps these students to progress, because it decontextualizes learning (e.g. by focusing on individual sentence structure away from the surrounding text), fosters boredom and reinforces low self-esteem.

9 Debra Myhill's (2002) study into boys' underachievement in UK schools found that children perceived as underachievers (of either gender) are the least likely to participate positively in classroom interactions and the most likely to be engaged in off-task interactions.

10 Black (2004). See also Lefstein and Snell (2013) which describes a positive feedback loop in another Year 6 classroom in which pupils' hesitation to respond encouraged the teacher to both lower the cognitive demand of her questions and also do the bulk of the work of answering and elaborating herself.

11 Stanton Wortham (2006) demonstrates that processes of social identification are inextricably linked to learning processes. In the cases he studied, curricular themes fed into and shaped events of social identification, and social identification processes that emerged in participant examples (one particular pedagogic technique used by the teachers in his study) helped students to understand curricular themes. See also Reay (2006) and Varenne and McDermott (1998).

12 Martin Nystrand and colleagues' (1997: 49–50) observations of US high-school students reveal that those tracked into low-ability classes were often hesitant to answer their teachers' questions, and when they did respond it was more often with 'shy, cryptic guesses' than 'answers'.

13 See for example, Myhill (2002).

14 Stanton Wortham (2006) has shown that problematic school identities are constructed through interactions between teachers and pupils across the school year.

15 Alexander (2001, 2009).

16 For examples, see Wenger (1998) for a social theory of learning in which identity and belonging to a community of practice are critical components of the learning process; Sfard and Prusak (2005) on learning as closing the gap between actual and designated identities; Greeno (2011) on the idea of 'intellective identity' that is consequential for learning behaviours; and Heyd-Metzuyanim (2012) for an example of how teacher and pupil co-construction of pupil identity shaped the content and nature of teaching and learning interactions.

17 See Adey (2012). It is also worth pointing out that far from excluding low-achieving pupils, dialogic pedagogy can help all pupils to develop their thinking. For example, dialogue is at the heart of the cognitive acceleration (CA) approach to learning, developed at King's College London, which has shown significant positive effects on pupil thinking. The programme was trialled in a number of schools in which specific 'thinking lessons' were set in science classes (CASE), and in later trials, in mathematics (CAME). Benefits to learning were found not only in the target subject but across the curriculum (including in English), suggesting that the intervention stimulates children's general intelligence. For a review see Adey and Shayer (2011).

18 McDermott (1993).

Chapter 9

Discussing pupil writing in whole-class discussion

EPISODE 7: 'I THINK THERE'S MORE TO IT THAN THAT'

Mr Richards opened his Year 5 lesson by reading out loud the following story:

> Ring went the school bell. 'Yes!' went the voices of some excited screaming kids.
>
> You guessed it. It was the end of the school term. The corridors were full of shouting children. And outdoors, in the playground, Mums and Dads were standing, waiting to take their children home for five weeks.
>
> 'Home for five weeks,' I said to myself as I went through the crowd of chatting children. I held my sister's hand tightly like she was falling into a volcano of boiling hot lava below her. Finally, we got to the front of the cue to get out of the door. A teacher opened the door. And we all ran. But we froze just outside the door. The stampede ran past us. We still didn't move. Then, we turned our heads to a voice.
>
> 'What is the matter, girls? Have you not found your Mum yet?'
>
> We shook our heads. As we walked back to our classroom I managed to spit out a few words: 'Our Mum's never been late before.' Meg started sobbing.
>
> The teacher gave her a hug. 'She's probably stuck in traffic or something. Don't worry.'
>
> Meanwhile, Mum's car bonnet was stuck under a tree that had got blown down. 'I wonder if Chrystal and Meg are all right' she exclaimed.

Mr Richards informed the class that this story opening had been written the previous week by their classmate Justine in just 35 minutes. He then distributed a written copy of the story and invited the pupils to think together in groups about the story, picking out three things they like.

Before moving on to setting the scene and recounting the episode, which is extracted from later in the lesson, we invite you to also think about the story: Can you identify three things that you like about it? And, from a more teacherly perspective, what might you choose to work on with Justine in advancing her as a writer? What opportunities does it present for the teacher in working with the rest of the class?

Setting the scene

The lesson

The lesson in which our focal episode occurred took place on 12 January 2009, in the middle of a series of lessons on story writing. In a previous lesson the pupils had written stories under the standardized test conditions of limited time. In this lesson, the pupils look closely at sample stories from two pupils in the class: Justine and Carl. The lesson can be broken down into the following eight stages:

1. *'I'm going to read you a bit of a story'* (2 minutes). Mr Richards reads Justine's story out loud and instructs the class to find three things they really like about it (see above).
2. *Group work* (5 minutes). The groups look at and discuss the story.
3. *Class discussion of Justine's story* (15 minutes). Mr Richards asks the class: 'What do you notice about the story, or what do you like?' He gathers a number of responses, including vocabulary, the use of a simile ('I held my sister's hand tightly like she was falling into a volcano of boiling hot lava below her'), and metaphor. The class spend some time interpreting the simile (detailed in the episode below). Next Mr Richards projects the last paragraph of the story on the board and invites pupils to think about it in pairs and report back to the class. Pupils mention the connective 'meanwhile', the use of punctuation and the use of 'exclaimed' rather than 'said'. Mr Richards highlights the use of direct speech as a means of introducing characters.
4. *Introducing Carl's story* (3 minutes). Mr Richards reads aloud Carl's story and asks the class if they notice any differences between Carl's story and Justine's. After establishing that they use different strategies for introducing and describing their characters, Mr Richards instructs the pupils to work again in groups – this time identifying description of the characters in Carl's story.
5. *Group work* (5 minutes). The groups look at and discuss the story.
6. *Class discussion of Carl's story* (5 minutes). Pupils describe the characters and Mr Richards asks how they have inferred their impressions. Mr Richards notes that both Carl and Justine's stories have a great opening, but are incomplete. He challenges the pupils to think about how they might finish one of the stories.
7. *Pair writing* (13 minutes). Pupils pick one of the two stories and try to complete it.
8. *Conclusion* (4 minutes). A few pupils read out their versions of story continuations. Mr Richards elicits some brief feedback from the rest of the class.

The episode

In this chapter we examine a five-minute episode taken from the class discussion of Justine's story. In what follows we summarize the episode briefly. As for the preceding chapters, the companion website, www.routledge.com/cw/lefstein includes a video recording and full transcript of this episode.

The episode can be broken up into the following four stages:

1. 'I liked the vocabulary' (lines 1–41)

Mr Richards begins by asking the pupils what they noticed about the story, or what they liked about it. Roger responds, 'I liked the vocabulary' (line 9), giving 'boiling' and 'lava' as examples of words that he particularly appreciated. Mr Richards accepts that the vocabulary is good, but says, 'I think there's more to it than that' (line 39). 'Why else might we like that bit?' he asks the class (line 40).

2. 'Is it a simile' (lines 42–83)

Danny suggests that the phrase that Danny liked ('I held my sister's hand tightly like she was falling into a volcano of boiling hot lava') is a simile. Mr Richards probes this idea by questioning what is being compared to what:

```
45  Mr Richards: right ok
46               so what's it-
47               a simile is where you compare something isn't it
48  Danny:       yeah
49  Mr Richards: so wha- what's being compared
50  Danny:       erm the:
51               (3)
52               boiling hot lava
53  Mr Richards: and what's being compared to that
54  Danny:       e::r
55               (16)
56  Danny:       is i:t the::
57               (8)
58  Mr Richards: now I've heard-
59               just while Danny's working this out-
60               I've heard a few people say that this is a simile (.)
61               Carl (.)
62               Carl you were one of the people who had been
63               shouting the word simile for ages (>back there<)
64               but what's being compared
65               because she's not describing
66               the floor that they're walking along
67               they're not de- saying that the floor
68               is as hot as a volcano (2)
69               she's used that phrase to describe something else (2)
70               wha- what's she (.) trying to describe (.)
71               yeah ((to Carl))
72  Carl:        she's trying to describe how-
73               erm
74               how she's holding onto her sister's hand
75  Mr Richards: right what do you mean by that
76  Carl:        so like
77               (3)
78               ((childish voice)) I don't know (2)
79               she's holding her sisters hand so tight it's like
80               if she wouldn't let go
81               she would fall into the volcano
82  Mr Richards: okay [right
83  Carl:             [((smacks lips loudly))
```

3. 'We thought it was a metaphor' (lines 84–99)

Mr Richards asks if there is 'anything else we could say about it?' Whitney says that she and her group thought it was a metaphor, because the lava wasn't actually there (lines 85–92). Asha says that she liked the phrase because 'how she described how she was holding her sister's hand' (line 99).

4. 'Why do you think she's doing that?' (lines 100–74)

Mr Richards dramatically recounts the scene in which the narrator grabs her sister's hand (lines 100–11) and asks, 'Why? Why do you think she's doing that?' He receives a series of interpretations: Usman and Roger suggest that she is afraid of falling amidst the chaos (lines 118–22, 144–52). Megan says, 'maybe because she doesn't want to lose her sister in the crowd' (lines 125–7). Kiera speculates that maybe the sister in the story is like her sister, who wanders off (lines 135–40). And Bethan links the narrator's grip on her sister's hand to her fear that her mother may not have come (lines 155–6). Mr Richards turns to Justine, 'seeing as it was [she] who came up with this' and asks what she thinks. Justine offers her explanation, and Mr Richards summarizes the issue by complimenting her on this 'fantastic bit of description' (line 171).

Viewing the video recording

We recommend that readers now view the video recording and read the full transcript of this episode. While viewing for the first time, think about what (if anything) stands out as particularly interesting. You might like to consider the following questions:

- What is happening here? And how do you know? What (if anything) do you find interesting?
- How is this clip similar to or different from other examples of classroom interaction you've seen and/or experienced? In particular, you might want to contrast this with other strategies for giving pupils feedback on their writing.
- How do the pupils' responses to Justine's story compare with your own? Did you identify the same issues that they did? If you responded differently to them, how might the gap between your interpretations be explained? What are the main factors and conditions shaping your respective assessments of the story?
- What are the implicit criteria according to which the pupils and Mr Richards judge Justine's writing? Would you recommend changing or supplementing them?
- What is happening during the relatively long pauses in lines 55 and 57? What options were available to Danny, Mr Richards and the other pupils here? What are the advantages and disadvantages of different strategies for dealing with prolonged silence?
- Mr Richards gives very minimal feedback to pupils regarding the quality of their answers, and ultimately turns to Justine to resolve the interpretive question that has opened up. What do you think about his strategy – from the standpoint of approaches to dialogic pedagogy, and in general?
- What other strategies can you think of for getting pupils to comment on one another's writing? What are their advantages and disadvantages?

Chapter 10

Using empathy to understand character

EPISODE 8: 'TELL ME WHAT *YOU* THINK AS WILBUR'

In mid-January 2009, the three Year 5 classes began a new unit of work on the book *Charlotte's Web*. The children's enthusiasm for the lessons based on this book was evident for all to see; even pupils like Dale, a science fiction fan who was initially sceptical about the book, became enthusiastic participants in class discussion. In this chapter we present a short excerpt from Ms Cane's class in which the pupils are encouraged to empathize with the character of Wilbur as he prepares to go to the country fair. When Dale takes on the persona of the helpless pig Wilbur, he voices Wilbur's feelings of concern that he'll be killed if he doesn't win first prize at the fair. When asked who might 'save the day', Dale gives an unexpected response, but one that shows understanding and engagement with the text.

Setting the scene

The lesson

Our focal episode comes from a lesson that took place on 23 February 2009 when Ms Cane's Year 5 class was over halfway through their reading of *Charlotte's Web*. Up to this point in the book, the lovable pig Wilbur has been saved from slaughter by his friend Charlotte, a spider who has woven a series of messages into her web to convince the farmer, Mr Zuckerman, that Wilbur is special and thus cannot end up as Sunday lunch (e.g. 'Some pig', 'Terrific pig', 'Radiant pig'). The news of Mr Zuckerman's famous pig spreads, and he decides to take Wilbur to the county fair, where the pig will compete for a prize. Charlotte knows that she has her work cut out for her if she's going to help Wilbur win first prize, and is especially busy as it's time for her to lay her eggs. In this lesson, the children are encouraged to consider how Wilbur might be feeling as he prepares to go to the fair. The lesson can be broken down into the following five sections:

1. *Teacher-led reading and discussion* (20 minutes). Ms Cane reads Chapter 15 ('The Crickets') to the class, pausing to test pupils' understanding of words such as 'versatility'. Before moving on to read Chapter 16 ('Off to the Fair'). Ms Cane explains to the pupils that in the second half of the lesson they will be tasked with writing sentences about how Wilbur feels. She encourages them to think about this issue as she reads.
2. *Think–pair–share* (12 minutes). Ms Cane asks pupils: 'What do you think is in Wilbur's head as he sees that truck [which will take Wilbur to the fair] coming up to the barn? She gives pupils 30 seconds to think individually. After 30 seconds, the pupils 'pretend

that they're Wilbur' and say their thoughts out loud to their partner. Ms Cane then asks for volunteers to share their thoughts with the whole class. Five pupils volunteer. They present their feelings as Wilbur (saying 'I feel ...' etc.), and there is extended discussion as Ms Cane probes their responses.

3. *Teacher-led reading and discussion* (8 minutes). Ms Cane continues reading from the book. She pauses to ask pupils 'Why do you think Wilbur struggled when he got into the crate?'. This question prompts a three-minute exchange between Ms Cane and two pupils, Phillip and Mark. Phillip thinks that Wilbur is scared because of all the people watching him, but Mark disagrees.

4. *Brainstorm* (4 minutes). The class generate a list of words that could be used to describe how Wilbur is feeling, which Ms Cane writes onto the whiteboard.

5. *Writing task* (10 minutes). Pupils are tasked with writing a paragraph about how Wilbur is feeling. Ms Cane tells them that to gain a 'house point'[1] they must use at least one complex sentence. At the end of the lesson two pupils share their work-in-progress and receive feedback. Ms Cane tells the class that they will return to this work after lunch.

The episode

In this chapter we examine Section 2 in more detail, focusing on the opening minutes of the whole-class discussion in which pupils share their thoughts. In what follows we summarize the episode briefly. As for the preceding chapters, the accompanying website includes a video recording and full transcript of this episode.

The episode can be broken up into the following three stages:

1. 'Remember you are Wilbur' (lines 1–25)

The episode begins as Ms Cane asks pupils to volunteer to share their thoughts with the class. She reminds them that they are now Wilbur and must therefore use the first person in their responses: '*I* feel or *I* think'. She tells them playfully that it's okay if they want to begin with some sound effects to make their performance as a pig more authentic.

2. 'I'm really really really nervous' (lines 26–37)

The first two volunteers elect not to make sound effects. Wendy tells the class that she's 'pleased that Charlotte's coming along' and Calvin says he feels 'really really really nervous'. Ms Cane probes Calvin to encourage him to say more:

```
26   Calvin:    e::r I'm nervous
27              I'm really really really nervous because there-
28              there'll be lots of people watching me
29              [and (xxxx)
30   Ms Cane:   [aren't-
31              aren't you excited about people watching you
32              because you are a radiant pig after all
33   Calvin:    er (2)
34              I'm going to be nervous because there might be: (1)
35              lots and lots of people watching me
```

```
36              and I won't have anything to do
37              and my legs might shake be shaking and I'm scared
```

3. 'Probably not Charlotte … she's pregnant!' (lines 38–88)

The next pupil-pig, Dale, makes the class laugh when he begins his turn with pig-like snorts. He tells the class that he's nervous because 'I don't know what they're going to do to me'. Ms Cane probes: 'what could they possibly do to you' and elicits a series of possibilities from Dale: 'what if they like throw peanuts at me and what if I don't come first prize?'. Ms Cane then asks Dale who might save the day, but gets an unexpected response:

```
60   Ms Cane:  how sad
61             well who might save the day
62   Dale:     hmmm (.) probably:::
63             (2)
64             shsh
65             probably not Charlotte
66   Pupils:   ((laughter))
67   Ms Cane:  why not Charlotte
68             why not Charlotte
69   Dale:     she's pregnant
70   Pupils:   ((laughter))
71   Ms Cane:  okay
72             she's made her babies in the sack
73             so they're not actually (.)
74             with her anymore
75             they're in the sack
76             so you ma-
77             perhaps Wilbur
78             she has other things on her mind
79             maybe she's more worried about the babies now than you
80   Dale:     because what if like something tries to eat the
               eggs
81             o:r ma:ybe
82             someone mi:ght knock them down and think it's
               funny
83             ((Calvin turns around to face Dale))
84   Ms Cane:  so [maybe-
85   Calvin:   [unless they're (xxxx)
86   Ms Cane:  maybe              [Charlotte's got other priorities now
```

Viewing the video recording

We recommend that readers now view the video recording and read the full transcript of this episode. While viewing for the first time, think about what (if anything) stands out as particularly interesting. You might like to consider the following questions:

- What is happening here? And how do you know? What (if anything) do you find interesting?
- How is this clip similar to or different from other examples of classroom interaction you've seen and/or experienced, in particular those that have included discussion of literary characters?

- Consider Ms Cane's question on line 61 in isolation. Is this an open or a closed question? Now consider Dale's response. Does his response change the way you might categorize Ms Cane's question? If so, why? What do you make of Dale's unexpected answer? How does Ms Cane respond? How else might she have responded? What is the effect of Ms Cane's intervention on lines 71–9?
- Ms Cane encourages the pupils to get into the character of Wilbur, using sound effects to add to the drama if they wish. What are the advantages of this approach? Are there any disadvantages?
- Based on your interpretation of dialogic pedagogy (including your reading of this book), in what ways is the interaction in this episode more or less dialogic?
- What opportunities for learning are made available to pupils through this discussion?

Issues for further discussion beyond the episode

- The Year 5 Abbeyford pupils enjoyed *Charlotte's Web* and were enthusiastic about the literacy tasks associated with this text.[2] Have you had similar experiences in which pupils have been universally excited by a book? Can you extrapolate from these specific experiences to some more general principles about selecting and working with stories?
- How can we strike the right balance between creating an atmosphere of fun and excitement in a lesson and attending to learning objectives and criteria for assessment?

Notes

1 Points which contribute to the rewards system at Abbeyford Primary.
2 Nystrand and colleagues (1997: 58) found that pupils 'learn literature best in classes that encourage substantive and personal student responses to literature in both classroom interaction and writing'. We wonder whether the pupils at Abbeyford enjoyed *Charlotte's Web* at least in part because of the class discussion and activities through which it was taught. The unit on *Charlotte's Web* was planned collaboratively between all three Year 5 teachers and the researchers, and included a greater focus on the book's themes and how the children responded to these, with less focus on structural features of the writing (though this element was of course still present, as evidenced by the focus on descriptive vocabulary and complex sentences in this episode).

Part III

Where to go from here

Chapter 11

Continuing the conversation

Parting thoughts on dialogic pedagogy

How do you draw a book on dialogue to a close? As Hans-Georg Gadamer wrote, 'The ongoing dialogue permits no final conclusion. It would be a poor [dialogic philosopher] who thought he could have, or had to have, the last word.'[1] We conclude by highlighting some of the key themes that run through the chapters. But we hope that this chapter is not the last word, and that you will continue the conversation with us (details at the end of the chapter).

Grounding dialogic pedagogy in an actual school, in real classrooms

Often when we show teachers and educational researchers video recordings of practice, including the episodes in this book, we are taken aback by their reactions. 'You call that dialogic pedagogy?' they exclaim. The teacher was too dominant, they protest. Or, not enough pupils spoke. Or, pupil thinking converged on finding the right answer. You can read echoes of these responses in some of the commentaries. A good friend and respected colleague once blurted out, 'I wish that you'd do research on *good* practice.' We strongly disagree with him and the others. We have brought to you *real* practice, without apologizing for its complexities or softening its rough edges. We also think it is good practice, some of it very good, but none of it perfect. (We hope that we have shown by now that no practice will appear perfect once examined carefully.) We also believe that its imperfections are part of what makes it better than 'best practice' for teacher professional learning. And if such real practice does not fit your ideals of dialogic or good pedagogy then we recommend that you reconsider your ideals – in addition of course to imagining how the teaching in the episodes you have examined might be improved. Idealistic models of dialogic pedagogy that are not well-suited to current classroom conditions are not helpful – indeed, they may be counterproductive by causing teachers to feel inadequate about pedagogy that is otherwise perfectly fit for purpose.

Dialogic dilemmas

Dialogic pedagogy, and teaching more generally, raises dilemmas for teachers and pupils. For example, we explored, among others:

- dilemmas regarding how to challenge or disagree with pupils without overpowering their voices and closing down the discussion (Chapters 4, 5);
- the dilemma of sticking with individual pupils to probe their ideas rigorously vs encouraging and enabling the participation of many pupils (Chapters 5, 6);

- dilemmas around attracting pupils' interest by importing popular culture or other novel discourse genres vs thereby distracting them from the lesson's academic content and/ or alienating pupils less familiar with the imported genre (Chapters 6, 7);
- dilemmas of teacher positioning: taking a peripheral position can empower pupils to engage, take control of the conversation and communicate with another directly, but can also lead to disintegration of the discussion (Chapter 7); and
- dilemmas around when and how to draw reticent pupils into the classroom conversation (Chapter 8).

There are no easy solutions to these and other dilemmas. They require sensitivity to and interpretation of the situation's unique nuances, a rich repertoire of alternative courses of action, and judgement to weigh which choice is best at this particular moment. Awareness of dilemmas also primes our pedagogical planning and *in situ* thinking to consider ways of sidestepping the dilemmas or ameliorating some of the problems they raise. Of course, dilemmas in teaching cannot be entirely avoided, since they reflect our competing educational goals and the multiple institutional pressures under which we work. As Robin Alexander wrote at the end of his commentary: 'That's education. That's life' (p. 74).

The primacy of classroom culture

The emergence of dialogic pedagogy relies first and foremost upon classroom culture, which is created by teacher and pupils, together, over time. For example, teacher questioning techniques have important implications for dialogue, and 'best practice' guidance can model the use of productive 'open' questions; but a question is only open in so far as the teacher is genuinely interested in pupils' thinking, receptive to a range of possible ideas and comfortable with sharing control over the direction of the conversation with pupils. Moreover, pupils will only recognize a teacher's question as open if over time they have become accustomed to expect such questions. Where these conditions are not met, pupils are likely to approach the question as closed, re-voicing their teacher's ideas or, worse, staying silent and letting the teacher do the work. Likewise, pupils are more likely to offer their thoughts and ideas (especially those that are novel and thus 'untested') in an environment that is supportive and collaborative.

A number of the commentaries have highlighted this issue, using words such as 'culture', 'ethos' and 'atmosphere' to describe the classroom conditions that facilitate (or not) the emergence of dialogue. These words have an intangible feel. It is difficult to pinpoint the specific ingredients that come together to make up an 'ethos of collective thinking', and we see no reason to assume that every dialogic classroom culture will include the same ingredients. Nevertheless, in our detailed descriptions of the episodes and associated analyses we have tried to uncover at least some of the myriad ways teachers can foster a culture that is conducive to dialogue.

The importance of the classroom's physical environment came out in several of the episodes (for example, ordered rows versus the more egalitarian seating arrangement in Episode 2, the position of the teacher in Episodes 4 and 5, and managing the actions of overexuberant and visually dominant pupils in Episode 6). In Episode 3, we saw that classroom space can be reconfigured without physical movement. When Ms Leigh announces the *X Factor* activity and puts the spotlight on Harry, pupils' gaze moves towards the back of the room where Harry is sitting (contrary to the conventional front-of-room focus), and with this movement comes a shift in authority, from Ms Leigh to Harry.

A second recurring theme was the way pupils learn by example, modelling their own behaviour on that of their teacher. In Episode 1, Ms James' respectful disagreement with Brian inspired Deborah to similarly disagree with Julie and Ms James. In Episode 2, Ms Leigh's response to William's challenge demonstrated her openness to alternative points of view, and modelled the processes involved in interrogating a new idea. In Episode 6, Daren took Ms Alexander's lead in appealing to Hayden's out-of-school knowledge, and in doing so reaffirmed Hayden's position within the classroom community.

We have also drawn attention to more subtle interactional phenomena, including the way body language conveys meanings about the way pupils are perceived (as in Episode 1 when Ms James verbally addresses a group of pupils, but indicates through her body position who she expects to give the right answer) and perceive themselves (as was the case for Ash, Hayden, Victor and Jamie in Episode 6).

Finally, social relationships are at the heart of a supportive, collaborative culture. It is thus no surprise that this was a key concern in all of the episodes, most notably in Episodes 2, 3 and 6, where out-of-school knowledge and experience became a vehicle for constructing solidarity between teacher and pupils as well as between pupils themselves.

Classroom culture is the joint accomplishment of both teachers and pupils. This takes time: time to develop expectations, and time to habituate both teachers *and* pupils into the practices entailed. There are no short cuts; there is no quick fix.

Dialogic pedagogy involves multiple dimensions

When we think about dialogic teaching we often think about the *form* of classroom talk. And, indeed, our analysis of the episodes often began with formal features, such as the distribution of turns at talk, the use of open questions or the extent to which pupil communication went through the teacher. However, our analyses inevitably turned from there to the *content* of the talk, which is ultimately more consequential for an understanding of what pupils and teacher accomplish pedagogically. For example, Episode 3 stands out as perhaps the most dialogic with regard to interactional form: Harry takes over the teacher roles of nominating speakers; other pupils evaluate his work; and during significant stretches of interaction pupils address one another without teacher involvement. But analysis of the content of the conversation showed that most pupil contributions were a re-voicing of William's essentialist assessment of the quantity and quality of descriptive words. Indeed, Janet Maybin in her commentary argued that our analysis of the content of the talk in this episode didn't go far enough, and demonstrated how a focus on the texts themselves enriches the understanding of what is actually achieved in the discussion (see also Gemma Moss's commentary on Episode 2).

Attention to the content of the discussion needs to be balanced by analysis of social aspects, such as power relations, identity and social allegiances. So, for example, understanding the content of the debates in Episodes 4–5 would not be complete without attention to the way the football issue interacted with classroom gender relations. Similarly, we cannot adequately make sense of Hayden's responses to Ms Alexander in Episode 6 without also looking at how they combine with the actions of Ash, Daren and Ms Alexander to construct his identity. Social and cognitive aspects of interaction and dialogue are necessarily intertwined.

We have also shown that classroom talk and social relations are influenced by other pedagogical factors (for example, activities, tasks, curriculum, assessment and the use of space) and indeed by factors and forces beyond the classroom (for example, concerns with success on the SATs tests). We find it helpful to think about classroom teaching and learning as a complex, interdependent system. This system comprises discourse, topic, activity, assessment, physical organization, pupils, time, goals, curriculum, teaching aids and more. Each component of the system influences the others, so understanding and/or changing classroom talk requires attention to all the other aspects of the system.

Dialogic pedagogy vs standardized testing?

Several commentators lamented the prominence of the SATs tests in the classroom episodes, what Melanie Cooke described as 'the stranglehold ... that relentless testing has on teaching and learning'. And many seemed to agree with the Year 6 teachers that test preparation severely limits opportunities to engage in dialogic pedagogy (see Chapter 3 and also Head Teacher Jeff Barrett's commentary in Chapter 7).

The logic of this position is concisely captured by Jayne White, who argued that Episodes 4–5 'might be considered monologic from the outset' since the purpose of the discussion was to facilitate the preparation of a text according to strict, standardized assessment criteria. According to this conventional wisdom, if the criteria dominate the interaction, no space remains for pupil voices or critique.

Are test preparation and dialogic pedagogy necessarily incompatible? Must we choose between dialogue and SATs? We argue that posing the choice in such a way is counterproductive. We are unsatisfied with an approach to dialogic pedagogy that is by definition irrelevant or even inapplicable to helping teachers and pupils address one of the major challenges facing them at this time. And while we have serious reservations about the effects of the SATs and other high-stakes standardized tests on pupil learning experiences, we are aware that teachers and pupils do not have the luxury of opting out of the tests. We also reject an approach to test preparation that affords no opportunities for pupil thinking – both in principle, because we are committed to pupil thinking, and also instrumentally, we are convinced that thinking pupils will perform better on the tests.

The question 'Is it dialogic to teach pupils how to provide interpretations of poems that will satisfy test markers?' is simply not helpful to teachers and pupils who are not asked whether they want to be tested. More productive is to ask, 'How can we prepare pupils for the test while also respecting their voices, cultivating a critical stance toward accepted dogmas, developing their thinking together, fostering a caring community and empowering them to share responsibility for their learning?'

We recommend adopting an *ironic* approach to the test, which involves saying to pupils, in effect – and in deeds as well as in words – you need to learn how to play and win the standardized test game, but you do not need to treat this game as anything more than a game. So, we can both agree with the poet Pie Corbett who wrote in his commentary on Episode 6 that 'the SATs testing of a poet's "authorial intent" might be unhelpful' while at the same time teach pupils to think like a SATs tester about authorial intent – for the sake of passing the test. Similarly, we agree with Corbett that 'Poems are not sums', but argue that SATs tests are like sums. And we need to teach pupils both to calculate their sums and to understand the principles according to which the sums add up – without forgetting for a moment that poems are not like SATs or sums.

This might entail, for example, marking answers to previous years' SATs tests and comparing their assessments to those of the official markers: How can we explain the divergences between our own judgements and the official guidance? What does this exercise tell us about the test? What can we learn from the exercise about how to succeed on the test? Such a discussion offers many opportunities for pupils' voices, critique and independent thinking because it does not confer upon the test makers and assessors unwarranted authority. But neither does it ignore testing as a force with which the pupils must reckon.

Interpreting classroom interaction and working with video

Glenda Moss in her commentary characterized our analysis as a 'tedious examination of [pupil] behaviours' (p. 156). We certainly hope you haven't experienced it that way. But nevertheless, perhaps we should say a few words about what we hope to have demonstrated about interpreting classroom interaction and working with video recordings of practice.

We have presented these and other video clips of real classroom practice to educational practitioners and researchers in a diverse range of settings, and have noted remarkable consistency in the way audiences react. Observers tend to focus on the teacher (rather than the interactions between teacher and pupil), make hasty judgements about teaching quality (usually before reaching an understanding of what is happening), and think about what *they* would have done in that situation (again, prior to understanding). We argue that this is an unhelpful way of viewing classroom practice and offer an alternative.

First, we suggest that is important to suspend judgement when viewing video recordings of practice. If we rely on snap judgment rather than attention to detail, we will likely misinterpret classroom activity, falling back on faulty assumptions (for example, that those pupils who raise their hands are engaged in classroom discussion and eager to participate, see Episode 6).

Instead, we try to understand what is happening in the classroom, starting at the beginning of the video/transcript and working through it slowly. This enables us to observe how one utterance or action is linked to what came before it, and also how it sets up a limited range of possibilities for what can happen next. For example, consider the chain of events that occur around five minutes into Episode 3. Ms Leigh tells pupils: 'Come *on*, who's going to give Harry some *honest* feedback?' Her stress on 'honest' and the extended stressed vowel sound in 'on' make this sound like a rallying call, which is quite different in style and tone to her previous utterances (notice here the importance of attending to detail – Ms Leigh's 'come on' would be interpreted quite differently if stress, intonation and so on were not taken into account). When we look at what came before, however, we can better understand what motivated this move. Ms Leigh had just finished an extended question–answer sequence with Tamara, and it was evident (through pupil gaze and body position) that the rest of the class had lost interest. Having noticed this, Ms Leigh's call for 'honest feedback' shifts things up a gear and reignites interest in *X Factor*. Her stress on 'honest' also evokes the kind of 'brutally honest' feedback famously delivered by *X Factor* judge Simon Cowell, and thus constrains the range of available next moves. In response, Callum reduces his score from an original six fingers to four, and echoes the critical idea originally expounded by William, that the first version of Harry's story was better because it had more description. This in turn leads a frustrated Harry to make an appeal to the class to cut him some slack ('I didn't get up to there people'). All of these actions are linked and thus cannot be considered on their own. If we interpret teacher and pupil talk or behaviour in isolation, we will miss important information from which we can learn (for example, that pupils were re-voicing William's original answer and responding to *X Factor* cues, rather than thinking independently about the stories, to which they perhaps lacked appropriate access).

Second, we cannot understand social interaction without giving due consideration to what people are *doing* with their utterances, not just what they are saying. For example, Ms Leigh's call for 'honest feedback' served to reignite pupil interest and enthusiasm (Episode 3); in Episode 2, Harry introduced *Necropolis* to signal his close relationship with the teacher (at least in part); and Aaron called out the answers in Episode 6 in order to show that he is 'level 5' and thus 'clever' (because 'if [you] ain't clever [you] ain't clever').

Finally, we have to understand that teacher and pupil talk and actions are constrained not just by the talk and actions of others, but also by the social and institutional context. As we have already noted, the upcoming SATs tests restricted possibilities in Episode 6. Likewise, what counted as good pupil writing in Episode 3 (and what pupils could say about that writing) was driven by national assessment frameworks. Issues of participation in Episodes 2 and 6 were bound up with social relationships that extended beyond the classroom. We cannot say what *we* might have done in the teacher's place before we understand the host of contextual factors weighing upon that classroom event.

We hope that by engaging with our analyses you have become acquainted with productive ways of looking at and learning from classroom practice. You will also have acquired some useful conceptual tools with which to think about other episodes of classroom interaction and your own practice. Primary among these, of course, are the multiple dimensions of dialogic pedagogy, but we have also introduced concepts such as discourse genre, participation (including pseudo-participation and pseudo-nonparticipation) and identity. For example, we used the concept of discourse genre to explore the consequences of mixing popular culture with school knowledge in Episode 3, and to better understand why the debate format led teacher and pupils into interactional trouble in Episodes 4 and 5. In Episode 6, we introduced an approach to identity as emerging in interactive processes and developing over time, in order to explore the relationship between patterns of classroom participation, pupil identity and opportunities for learning.

We hope that you will be motivated to use these new concepts and ways of seeing in analyses that focus on your own and your colleagues' classrooms. Readers interested in taking this next step will find useful advice and guidance in the next, and final, chapter.

As we wrote at the beginning of the chapter, we hope to not have the last word on these and the other issues in the book. We would love to hear what you think. We invite you to write to us with your responses to these parting thoughts, or any other questions the book raises for you, and ideally to grant us permission to post your thoughts on the book website. Visit www.dialogicpedagogy.com to continue the conversation.

Note

1   Gadamer (1998: 581). We replaced Gadamer's 'hermeneuticist' with 'dialogic philosopher' to make the quotation more accessible to our non-philosophy audience (though this is of course not a direct translation).

Chapter 12

Do it yourself

Developing teaching through group discussion of video recordings of practice

The preceding ten chapters have explored dialogue among teachers and pupils in the classroom. We hope that you have found them interesting, and further that, if you are a teacher, engaging with the chapters has contributed to your professional development. We would also be delighted were some readers to share the book with others – not just to recommend it to friends (though that would also be nice), but to organize a study group in which the participants discuss with one another their interpretations of the episodes and implications for their own work. And, finally, our greatest ambition is that some of you will be inspired to record and discuss your *own* practice in an effort to improve it. If you're thinking of embarking upon group processes of reflection and discussion on video recordings of your own or others' practice – or already engage in such activity and are looking for further guidance – this final chapter is for you.

The chapter includes two sections: in the first we make the case for teacher professional learning through group reflection and discussion of video representations of practice; in the second we discuss practical issues you need to think about in designing a video-based professional development programme in your own context.

The promise of video in teacher professional learning

The complexities of pedagogical practice require teacher sensitivity, interpretation, repertoire and judgement. However, such capacities are difficult to learn in the abstract, away from the nitty-gritty particularities of classroom practice. The most consequential learning about practice is best done *in* practice. However, teaching is performed individually, in private, and, as such, opportunities for teachers to learn from observing and participating in one another's work are limited. Digital video technologies offer new possibilities for overcoming teacher isolation and enable new forms of teacher professional learning. Here we focus in particular on practices of joint reflection on video-recorded lessons. In making the case for such practices we will summarize briefly the research on teacher professional learning, and the potential advantages of video within teacher learning processes.

In the past two decades a consensus has emerged around crucial components of effective teacher professional development.[1] Here we consolidate and summarize the ideas into five key principles:

1. *Teacher learning should be dialogic.* The same values, processes and principles that we embrace for pupil learning apply equally well to teacher learning. Teachers learn better when their voices are heard, when they adopt a critical stance toward knowledge, when they think together, when they enjoy supportive and caring relationships and when

power is shared with them. A dialogic approach to teacher development is particularly important if we expect teachers to develop dialogic pedagogy in their classrooms. The alternative would be hypocritical and self-defeating.

2. *Teacher learning thrives in a collaborative and supportive professional community.* Community involves shared vision, shared language, shared ownership and shared problems. Teachers learn from one another through working collaboratively to address everyday tasks, such as choosing curricular materials, lesson planning, assessment design and responding to specific pupils and problems.

3. *Teacher learning should be driven by evidence from the classroom,* rich and meaningful representations of teaching and specific problems of practice. Grounding teacher learning in classroom evidence helps keep the discussion relevant, and addresses the chronic gap between professional talk and practice in teaching. *Elmore's Second Law* sums up the issue well: 'The effect of professional development on practice and performance is inverse to the square of its distance from the classroom.'[2]

4. *Teachers should be actively involved in interpreting and constructing knowledge,* rather than expected to accept and enact ideas dictated to them by others. However, external expertise is often essential for gaining critical perspective, imagining alternative possibilities and becoming acquainted with others' practices. Professional learning should be based upon a balanced, dialogic relationship between external and internal sources of expertise, and between external consultation and internal leadership.

5. *Teacher learning should be continuous and integrated into teachers' work* and the school's ongoing efforts to improve pedagogy. Some of the most important learning occurs informally, as a natural outcome of teacher interaction around the work itself.[3]

Video recordings of classroom practice can facilitate these processes in a number of ways. Among the advantages of video for teacher learning are the following:

(a) Video has the capacity to provide a relatively rich representation of practice, typically a closer approximation to participants' own experiences of that practice than afforded by other methods.

(b) As such, it can help to make teaching practice public, opening up the 'closed door' of the classroom.

(c) Video can be edited, paused, replayed and shared, thereby enabling forms of investigation that are not available to observers and participants in the heat of the moment.

(d) Video offers a common object as focus for group discussion, thereby making possible new practices of teacher collaboration.[4]

Video is commonly used in teacher professional learning as an object for critical reflection upon problems of practice. For example, Miriam Sherin and Beth van Es have organized 'video clubs', in which mathematics teachers regularly come together to view and discuss video recordings of one another's teaching. Sherin, van Es and their colleagues have shown how taking part in a video club can help teachers to learn to pay more attention to pupil thinking, both in their discussions of the video with their peers and in their classroom practice.[5] Video clubs are one of many models. Others, such as Lesson Study[6], or video-based peer feedback, situate video reflection within a broader system of collaborative inquiry and planning. In the next section we offer specific guidance on how to organize video-based processes of teacher learning.

Do it yourself: designing and conducting teacher professional learning processes with video

So you want to unleash the powers of video to advance your colleagues' and your own professional learning. The preceding account offered broad principles and potentialities. *But how to begin? Who should be in the group? Which lessons should you record? How should they be filmed and edited? Or maybe it would be wiser to use video from outside your school? How should the lessons be framed? How should the discussions be structured? Who should facilitate them? What else should you be asking?*

There is of course no one best practice answer to these questions. You need to design a process best suited to the particularities of your own setting, which means managing constraints – aligning resources, conditions and aims – and balancing the trade-offs between competing concerns and problems. In what follows we discuss some of the key design decisions you will face, draw your attention to the competing concerns you should consider and offer some principles to guide your efforts.

What are your aims?

First, you should clarify to yourself what you're hoping to get out of the process. While we agree with a head teacher with whom we worked that 'whatever makes you think about your practice is a good thing', we also suggest that you should consider what particular aspect of practice you want to think about, and in what ways. Programme design and facilitation will differ depending on your specific aims. Whether you hope, for example, to develop greater sensitivity to pupil thinking, to experiment with a new curriculum or teaching approach, to study classroom interactional dynamics or to focus on particular pupils' experience will shape how you film the classroom, select and record video clips, structure and facilitate the discussion, etc. It is important to bear this in mind as we consider these and related issues. Common goals of collaborative investigation of video include the following, all of which are aimed at different elements of teacher learning for the improvement of practice:

- developing a common language for discussing and thinking about teaching and learning in classrooms;
- sharpening participants' sensitivity and interpretation: what they notice in teaching and how they reason about it;[7]
- critical reflection on various aspects of classroom practice (content, learners, classroom interaction, teaching), and on specific programmes and policies for instructional improvement;
- giving and receiving critical, constructive feedback;
- cultivating norms of collaborative professional community.

Who should be in the group?

We recommend that the group be composed of teachers who share a common problem, topic or pupils, and who would otherwise work together, though we can envisage circumstances in which this might not be advisable (for example, because of competitive relations or distrust within the group). The group should be large enough to generate a variety of perspectives and ideas, but not so large that it loses intimacy. We have found four to eight participants to be about right. Perhaps the most important condition of any group is continuity: the group meets regularly and all participants attend each meeting. Reciprocity is also important: if filming within participants' classrooms, everyone will be expected to volunteer material to the discussion.

Original film making?

Another question to consider is whether to create original video clips – recording practice in your own and your colleagues' classrooms – or to use existing materials. Recording in your own school offers numerous advantages. First, is *relevance*: the discussion offers opportunities for direct feedback on the practice of the teacher whose practice has been recorded. Likewise, the clips are likely relevant to the other participating teachers, who may be familiar with the pupils, school culture, curriculum and classroom spaces, and likely work in similar conditions to those recorded.[8] Second, if the participating teacher and videographer participate in the discussion, then they can address participants' questions about what is happening, the background, what happened next, etc. Furthermore, by recording original clips you will have greater control over where you point the camera and how you edit the material. On the other hand, original video recording is relatively time-consuming and thus costly, and the very relevance of original clips also makes them threatening for the teachers involved. So, while we think that in the right conditions professional development processes based on video clips of participating teachers' own practice may ultimately be most rewarding, we can see good reasons for starting with materials available elsewhere. So, for example, you might want to spend the first eight sessions looking at the episodes included in this book; numerous other resources are listed in the endnotes.[9]

Which classrooms and lessons should you record?

Teachers at first will be hesitant to open their classrooms to video cameras, and for good reason: our teaching is rarely perfect, and doesn't always live up to our own and others' expectations, especially expectations raised by the current best practice culture. There are also more mundane reasons to which you should be sensitive: few of us are happy with how we look on film. So, in the first stage, you might want primarily to approach relatively confident, senior staff, and to offer the possibility of recording audio only in the first instance (two teachers participating in the Towards Dialogue project elected for audio recording only, until they became comfortable with the process). An important rule is that the teacher whose teaching is recorded owns the material, and decides what is shared with others. In terms of selecting lessons for recording, we recommend documenting consecutive lessons rather than isolated, one-off lessons. In such a way you will be able to situate each lesson within a unit of work, and to trace the development of pupil understanding over time. Likewise, video recording a lesson involving a topic taught by a number of the participating teachers, or a teaching strategy used by them, is a good strategy for making the clip directly relevant to many participants. These are just some possible strategies; lessons should be selected for filming according to the priorities and aims of the group.

How to film?

We used one camera, with a wide angle adapter lens, affixed to a tripod and placed such that we could capture both the teacher and as many pupils as possible in the same frame.[10]

Though focusing on individuals can be more visually engaging, and also allows for careful study of posture, gesture and facial expressions, it does not allow investigation of how the rest of the class responds to those individuals. Of course, you might choose to use more than one camera, in order to capture close-up shots of individuals and long shots of the class as a group, thus getting the best of both worlds. But, at the same time, more equipment, and more videographers, means greater disturbance to classroom activity, which can lead not only to less 'authentic' recordings but also to reluctance from teacher and pupils to partici-pate in future recordings. Moreover, editing together multiple tapes and sound tracks is time-consuming and expensive. Disruption can be mitigated by frequent visits, by use of less obtrusive equipment (e.g. miniature recorders), and/or by the school creating dedicated video laboratories with permanent cameras or investing in cutting-edge panoramic video cameras.[11]

Which video to use? How edited? Who decides?

Early on in the process we identified a list of issues that arose in the lessons we observed or in conversations with teachers and asked them to vote for those issues they were most interested in exploring (see Box 12.1). The issues that received the most votes then guided us in selecting episodes for analysis. You might like to try something similar, to include everyone's concerns and give the group greater ownership over the agenda. The other criteria that guided our selections were (a) that the teacher and pupils appearing would not be in any way ashamed of what we would show, and (b) that the episode offered interesting problems and/or dilemmas for the participating teachers to sink their analytic teeth into. You're going to want to strike a balance between 'regular' practice, with which everyone can identify, and extraordinary lessons, of which the video-recorded teacher will likely be proud, but may not be as helpful for investigating common problems of practice.

We edited very minimally, in most cases merely setting a beginning and end-point. This strategy preserves the integrity of the original event, saves time and requires little technical expertise. We found optimal clip durations to be four to seven minutes for a one and a half hour discussion. Sometimes we used a couple of shorter clips strung together to show development of an idea or interactional dynamics across a lesson. On one occasion we used two clips of the same activity from different classrooms (see Chapter 7), which was fascinating, but encouraged comparisons of the two teachers, which in retrospect we would have preferred to have avoided.[12] Where possible, we tried to cut the episodes at relatively natural points, when the class transitioned into a new topic or activity. Finally, as noted above, we always consulted with the video-recorded teacher, who had final say over what was included in the episode and whether or not it was made public.

How should discussions be structured and facilitated?

Our guiding principle is that we expect in our work with teachers the same dialogic princi-ples that we hope to produce in our classrooms, *vis-à-vis* interactional form, voice, stance toward knowledge, relationships and power relations (see Chapter 2). In what follows we offer some more specific considerations for the design and conduct of dialogic discussions of video-recorded classroom practice.[13]

Box 12.1 Possible issues for discussion in reflection workshops

Possible issues/topics/dilemmas for discussion in future meetings

The following list is a collection of issues – in no particular order – that have arisen from our discussions with you and lesson observations. *Which, if any, of these would you like us to focus upon in future analyses and discussions of lesson extracts? Are there any topics that you would like to add to this list?* Please circle four to eight issues you'd like us to concentrate upon in future sessions, cross out any you oppose and add any you think we should consider. Thanks!

- Teaching 'closed' content (in which there is one right answer) through 'open' discussion.
- Dealing with non-standard grammar and 'slang' in pupils' speech and/or writing (for example, 'we was' versus 'we were').
- Dealing with pupil error.
- Using criteria such as VCOP to improve pupils' writing/discuss pupils' work.
- Conditions that encourage pupils to participate actively in whole-class discussion.
- Physical arrangement of room/pupils.
- Using popular culture as a resource.
- Maintaining control/discipline when the discussion heats up.
- The relationship between pupils' oral and written work.
- Forms of teacher feedback/evaluation.
- Challenging – both teacher challenging pupils and pupils challenging teacher.
- The relationship between teacher questions and pupil responses.
- Staying with/probing one pupil versus maximizing whole class participation/interest.
- The teacher's position in class discussion/debate/drama activities.
- Sharing authority with pupils.
- The aesthetics of pupil performances on the classroom stage.
- Managing our teacher identities – for example, to what extent should we share with pupils our out-of-school persona?
- Benefits and dangers of humour.
- Working within narrow curricular objectives and assessment criteria (e.g. SATs marking sheets) – can this be an opportunity for dialogue?
- Managing pupil conflict/disagreement.
- Designing tasks that are conducive to dialogue.
- Generating pupil questions.
- Pupil strategies for getting through tasks (without necessarily learning).
- ?

Framing the episode

The video recording will necessarily be excerpted from a longer educational process (a lesson, day at school, unit of work, etc.). What we witness in the video only makes sense against a specific background regarding participants, lesson goals, tasks, how the excerpt fits into a sequence of activity, what happened immediately beforehand and afterwards, etc. Such contextualization is necessarily selective, and the selections are consequential for the discussion: the way in which a video-recorded excerpt is framed will guide participants' viewing and analysis of it. We strongly encourage you to transcribe the episode: the transcript will facilitate participants' understanding and reflection, and also offers a work-space to jot down comments.[14] Likewise, photocopies of pupil work and/or still photographs of the event can help the participants to make sense of the episode and also focus their attention on certain aspects of it.

Discourse norms

Many teachers are unaccustomed to observing and talking about practice in ways that are conducive to inquiry and instructional improvement, and there is a real danger that discussions of video will turn into scathing (unconstructive) criticism of what the teacher in the recording did wrong (or should have done differently), and/or a series of 'war stories' intended to make the discussion victim feel better about their inadequacies. In contrast, productive discourse in video-based continuing professional development (CPD) discussions will often –

(a) balance between description, interpretation, analysis and judgement, delaying judgements and suggestions until after thorough examination of what happened has been completed;

(b) be guided by a shared set of pedagogical assumptions regarding, e.g., educational goals, valuable content, learning processes, teaching practices, etc. Such assumptions can be implicitly shared, inductively derived as part of the process, and/or given to the group as an explicit framework for analysing video recordings;

(c) ground interpretations, analyses and judgements of what happened in evidence from the video, transcript and/or other records of practice;

(d) focus not only on what the teacher did but also on interactions between teacher, pupils, content and context – examining in part how teaching practice is constrained and enabled by other facets of classroom life;

(e) move between the particularities of the event discussed and general pedagogical principles; and

(f) be respectful and supportive of the teachers and pupils appearing in the video, though without 'protecting' them from constructive criticism.

Participants may find it helpful to set conversational ground rules at the outset of the process. Such ground rules are typically negotiated among group members, referred to in the actual conduct of the discussion and periodically reviewed and revised as necessary.

Facilitation

Facilitating group discussions involves balancing a wide range of tasks and concerns, for example: directing the group's attention; developing productive habits of reflection and discussion; fostering group cohesion and trust; developing common language through offering and probing concepts for phenomena observed; bridging between the particularities of the event discussed and more general principles; modelling an inquiry stance, evidence-based analysis, constructive criticism, etc.; establishing and maintaining ground rules; protecting the teacher appearing in the video; and probing and challenging the group's interpretations. Which task or concern should be given priority at any given moment depends on the group, stage in the process, available opportunities (and constraints), etc. Many models involve employing an external facilitator, from outside the specific teacher community, to organize and guide the discussions. Such an arrangement can be problematic inasmuch as (a) the facilitator takes on key leadership roles that would otherwise be occupied by members of the group, (b) the discussions become isolated from the teachers' everyday work, and (c) such an arrangement is typically not sustainable long-term (nor is it readily scaled up). As such, a key task for external facilitators is ultimately to make themselves unnecessary.

Structuring the discussion

Protocols can be used to stimulate, structure and/or otherwise support the discussion.[15] For example, here are some possible protocols, which can be adapted, combined and supplemented according to your aims, material and context:

(a) *Exploring dilemmas.* After presenting the context, watching the episode at least twice, and responding to clarification questions, ask participants to identify any dilemmas that arise and/or critical moments in which the teacher had to make a decision about how best to proceed. For each dilemma or critical moment, brainstorm possible courses of action (in addition to what the teacher did) and discuss the relative advantages and costs of each course of action. A variation on this is to stop the playback (and cut the transcript) at predetermined critical moments and discuss what is happening, what are the alternative courses of action, relative advantages of each and what participants think will happen next, and then continue the playback (and distribute the next instalment of transcript). We have used this structure to good effect with Episode 2, since it involves multiple dilemmas and a number of surprising turns (see Chapter 5).

(b) *The Tuning Protocol,* for providing respectful feedback to the video-recorded teacher. This protocol involves the following stages: an introduction in which the purpose and process are explained; presentation by the teacher of the lesson context and first viewing of the video clip; clarification questions; second viewing of the video; participants share their feedback, including both 'warm' and 'cold' reactions (presenter is silent); presenting teacher reacts to feedback (others are silent); open conversation; and debriefing about the process.[16]

(c) *Focus on content.* Preface the viewing and discussion of the episode with a discussion of the text, problem or task that the pupils address in the episode (for example, discuss the poem, 'The Owl', before viewing Episode 6 in which it is discussed by a Year 6 class). This prefatory discussion can be used to prime participants' thinking about the content, before moving on to one of the other protocols, or can be used as the basis for a comparison: How was the video-recorded classroom discussion similar to or different from the group's discussion of the same content?

(d) *Focus on pupil thinking.* Choose a few focal pupils and analyse carefully their thinking. How are they trying to answer questions and/or solve problems? What is motivating them? What, if any, are the sources of their misunderstanding? How can they best be supported?

(e) *Look, no sound.* Play the video without sound or transcript in order to tune into nonverbal communication (and focus on less vocal participants): What do we think is happening? How do we know? Compare this with the full video and transcript? What do we notice?

(f)   *Examining the episode* according to a set framework. After presenting the episode, clarifying the context and any unfamiliar details, discuss the episode in light of an established set of pedagogic principles or criteria, such as Alexander's five principles of *dialogic teaching* (see Chapter 2), Charlotte Danielson's *Framework for Teaching*, or the *South Australian Teaching for Effective Learning Framework*.[17] Care should be taken that this task not become an unreflective exercise in identifying and eradicating gaps between observed and 'best' practice, however. For example, the conversation should not only examine the episode in relation to the criteria, but also use the episode as an opportunity to clarify, critically investigate and elaborate the framework used.

What else should you be asking?

Ultimately, group discussion of video is only one component of a holistic effort to improve teaching, which requires attention to a broad range of other factors, including curriculum, timetable, assessment, teacher collaboration, teacher work conditions, management, school physical design and much more. Discussion of video will be most effective if it is integrated into other processes of teacher's work and development. For example, Borko and colleagues devised a 'professional development cycle' in which teachers collaboratively solve a math problem, design a lesson to teach that problem, video record a participant's teaching of the lesson, and then critically discuss the recorded lesson, once focusing on teaching practice and once on student understanding. Integrating the use of video into a larger process poses for participants a common problem, and provides a clear context and purpose for discussion of the video.[18] Ideally, the process should include the full cycle of teachers' work (e.g. planning, instruction, assessment) and a broad range of professional development tools and approaches. In such a process, video will constitute one of a number of sources of evidence used to investigate practice. The ultimate goal in our opinion is to create a self-sustaining process that is a recognized component of teachers' work. As a Japanese teacher said of conducting 'research lessons' within the collaborative lesson study process: 'Why do we do research lessons? I don't think there are any laws [requiring it]. But if we didn't do research lessons, we wouldn't be teachers.'[19]

Such a professional ethos, according to which teachers view their colleagues and their own professional learning as one of their core responsibilities, is unfortunately rare. It is better than best practice, and it is critical for the improvement of teaching and learning. We hope this book has both inspired you to undertake such processes, and given you some of the tools necessary in order to succeed. If you embark on such an effort, we would love to hear about it, and assist if we can. You can find us at www.dialogicpedagogy.com.

Notes

1 For reviews of teacher professional development theory and research see Darling-Hammond *et al.* (2009), Guskey and Yoon (2009), Hawley and Valli (1999) and Timperley (2007).
2 See Elmore (2004). Elmore's First Law is that students perform better on tests they can read than those they cannot.
3 The roots of this idea can be found in Lave and Wenger's (1991) situated learning theory, and Wenger's (1998) subsequent work developing the 'community of practice' concept.
4 For an excellent discussion of the affordances of video for teacher learning, see Sherin (2004). On the importance of deprivatization of teaching, see Little (1990).
5 Sherin, van Es and colleagues have documented their work in a series of publications, many of which may be found here: http://www.professional-vision.org/papers.html. See, for example, Sherin and van Es (2009) and van Es and Sherin (2009).

6 See Lewis and Tsuchida (1998) on the Japanese Lesson Study model. Lesson study is based on live lesson observation, and for good reason (see Murata 2011). Some advocate supplementing live observation with video data.

7 Goodwin (1994) calls this 'professional vision'. A productive research programme has shown how it can be developed through discussion of video (see, e.g., Sherin and van Es 2009). See also Lefstein and Snell (2011b) for exploration of the politics of teacher professional vision.

8 See Seidel *et al.* (2011) for an experimental study comparing teachers' responses to their own and others' video.

9 Here are some resources you might find helpful (there are many – this is a partial list). Specifically, for recordings of dialogic pedagogy:

   - *Talk for Learning: teaching and learning through dialogue* (DVD/CD pack), recordings of dialogic teaching in North Yorkshire, available via the local authority (see http://www.robinalexander.org.uk/index.php/dialogos/ for details).
   - The Inquiry Project: http://inquiryproject.terc.edu/
   - Chapin, O'Connor and Anderson (2011).
   - Plans are also underway to post such materials to the *Dialogic Pedagogy Journal* – watch this space: http://dpj.pitt.edu/
   - Finally, we are opening a dedicated *Better than Best Practice* web page, www.dialogicpedagogy.com, to which we hope to post further materials.

   For recordings of classroom practice in general:

   - Teachscape: http://www.teachscape.com/
   - The Trends in International Mathematics and Science Study video site (includes math and science lessons from seven different countries): http://timssvideo.com/
   - Carnegie Foundation's 'Going Public with our Teaching': http://www.goingpublicwithteaching.org/
   - The National Center for Restructuring Education, Schools, and Teaching (NCREST) 'Images of Practice': http://www.tc.edu/centers/ncrest/images.htm
   - 'Every Child a Reader and Writer': http://www.insidewritingworkshop.org/classroom/
   - Teacher's TV, now available through TES on-line: http://www.tes.co.uk/

10 Technology develops too quickly to recommend specific brands or models. Our main advice is to attend to audio quality – this is usually the biggest problem in classroom recordings.

11 The panoramic video camera records 360 degrees: the entire room with one camera. See www.kogeto.com/meet-lucy for details of one such camera, and www.teachscape.com for a comprehensive classroom observation system based on it.

12 See Lefstein and Snell (2011b) for an analysis of this workshop session.

13 This discussion is not intended to be exhaustive – note, in particular, that we have said nothing about the use of video in non-discussion group contexts such as coaching and mentoring, self-study, etc.

14 See Bezemer and Mavers (2011) on techniques for transcribing multimodal activity (on video), and Lefstein and Snell (2011b) on transcription in the context of the video-based teacher professional development workshops discussed in this book. On the transcription of discourse more generally, and some of the thorny social issues that emerge in transcription, see Roberts (1997) and Ochs (1979).

15 See McDonald (2003) on the use of protocols in teacher professional development.

16 This is an adaptation of the tuning protocol version detailed in Blythe, Allen and Powell (1999: 29). See also McDonald (2003).

17 The Danielson Framework can be found in Danielson (2007). The South Australian Framework can be found here: http://www.learningtolearn.sa.edu.au/tfel/. There are many other frameworks; these are only examples to whet your appetite.

18 Borko *et al.* (2008).

19 Lewis and Tsuchida (1998: 13).

Methodology appendix
Pedagogically oriented linguistic ethnographic micro-analysis

This book is intended primarily for education professionals, rather than researchers, and for this reason we have where possible avoided technical language, methodological issues and controversies within the research community. In this appendix we situate our methodological approach to the study of classroom practice and outline key decisions and procedures with regard to data collection, selection and analysis. Readers will find further details in the articles and reports cited in the notes.

Methodological orientation: linguistic ethnography[1]

Linguistic ethnography is the term used by a group of scholars who combine linguistic and ethnographic concepts and methods to address questions in a range of academic fields and professional contexts (education, psychology, anthropology, linguistics, health and management, among others) (Maybin and Tusting, 2011: 515). Many of these researchers have come together under the aegis of the Linguistic Ethnography Forum (www.uklef.net). Linguistic ethnographers combine linguistic methods for describing patterns of communication with ethnographic commitments to particularity, participation and holistic accounts of social practices (Rampton and UK Linguistic Ethnography Forum [UKLEF], 2004). In a sense, this synthesis constitutes a move to tie down ethnography, 'pushing ethnography towards the analysis of clearly delimitable processes, increasing the amount of reported data that is open to falsification, looking to impregnate local description with analytical frameworks drawn from outside', while simultaneously opening linguistics up, 'inviting reflexive sensitivity to the processes involved in the production of linguistic claims and to the potential importance of what gets left out' (Rampton *et al.*, 2004, p. 4). Linguistic ethnographers share a particular analytic disposition – not 'method' in the sense of a set of techniques that need to be followed, but rather a general orientation to thinking about data, which includes the following:

- *Data driven*: Language and communication data are taken as the 'principle point of analytic entry' (Rampton *et al.*, 2004: 11) into the issues researchers would like to address. For us this involves extensive immersion in classroom data, investigating interaction from multiple perspectives before homing in a particular educational issue such as dialogic pedagogy.
- *Rigorous eclecticism:* Drawing upon and combining analytic techniques from a variety of approaches to the study of language, communication and society, including the ethnography of communication (Hymes, 1972), Goffman's theories of social interaction (Goffman, 1974, 1983), interactional sociolinguistics (Gumperz, 1982), linguistic anthropology, micro-ethnography, conversation analysis and multimodal analysis.

- *Openness and systematicity:* Embracing openness and adventurousness in interpretation, yet also accountability to evidence, to procedural rigour, to conceptual frames and to competing interpretations. For us, this involves beginning with relatively free, creative (and time-consuming) interpretive brainstorming before subjecting our ideas to more disciplined, systematic investigation.
- *Attention to detail:* Aware that careful investigation of small-scale phenomena is invaluable for understanding what's going on, linguistic ethnographers work through data slowly, attending to every detail as potentially significant (the 'aesthetic of smallness and slowness' – cf. Silverman, 1999).
- *Interplay of multiple analytic lenses and procedures:* Engaging in a layered and iterative analytic process that, for us, involves zooming in on the event to investigate interactional details, and zooming out to investigate how the event fits into social structures, processes and institutions. Similarly, it involves shifting our attention between language and other modes of communication, between participants and the social, cultural and linguistic resources at their disposal.

Data collection

The study included ethnographic participant-observation in classrooms and in the school more generally from November 2008–July 2009 (see Chapter 3 for details regarding the research site and the process of its selection). Over the course of this period we attended school approximately three days a week, and video and/or audio recorded 73 literacy lessons. We also facilitated 19 professional development workshops with the seven participating teachers (all audio-recorded), conducted 15 teacher interviews, administered a classroom learning environment survey at the beginning and end of the process and collected many artefacts (e.g. lesson plans, student work, etc.). We documented each observation in detailed field notes and event logs.

Data analysis

Macro classroom discourse analysis: We used the systematic observation software, *Observer XT*, to code discourse for actor, function, and pedagogic activity in a randomly selected sub-set of 30 lessons (from three classrooms). We calculated relative durations and rates of select discourse features for each of the lessons, and contrasted the distributions of these features between teachers, over time, and between pedagogic activities. This analysis is detailed in Snell and Lefstein (2011); see Snell (2011) on the advantages and limitations of computer-assisted discourse analysis.

Meso discourse analysis: A subset of 19 episodes were selected on the basis of relatively high rates of features often associated with dialogic pedagogy, as identified in the macro analysis. The video recordings and fieldnotes for these episodes were then analysed with regard to what aspects of classroom activity did and did not change, conditions that facilitated the emergence of dialogic patterns and how the class moved between discourse genres.

Micro-analysis of classroom interaction: A dozen episodes were transcribed in detail and subjected to linguistic ethnographic micro-analysis. These episodes were selected on the basis of particularly salient phenomena that emerged in the course of the fieldwork and analysis: e.g. importing discourse genres, direct challenges to pupil and teacher positions, and radical shifts in teachers' footing in whole-class discussions. The episodes included in this book are among this subset. The precise analytic strategies differed from episode to episode, but generally included:[2]

- Detailed transcription of spoken discourse, significant non-verbal communication and main actions (e.g. moving around the room, writing on the board).
- Micro-analytic brainstorm, in which we move through the segment, moment by moment and line by line (using the recording as data and the transcript as work-space to record observations), attending to how participants build up an interactional event moment by moment, such that each utterance (or gesture) responds to what came before while simultaneously setting up expectations for what can follow (i.e. the notion of sequentiality within conversation analysis, see e.g. Heritage, 1997; and Rampton, 2006, for the use of conversation analysis as a discovery method). We asked at each moment: What is happening here? What are participants doing? Exactly what wording have they selected for their turn at talk? How else might they have formulated the turn? How does this turn connect with what the previous speaker(s) has said/done? In what ways does this turn influence what the next speaker can say? Anything else that strikes you about this turn? (Rampton, 2006).
- Multi-modal analysis – replaying and reanalysing the video recording without audio, in order to focus on non-verbal communicative resources such as seating arrangements, body postures, dress, gesture, gaze and writing, and in such a way to bring into view those pupils whose participation in the lesson was less vocal (and were thus relatively absent from the verbal transcript).
- Transcontextual analysis – examination of textual trajectories into and out of the event, attending for example to texts recruited by participants (e.g. student worksheets, preceding lessons, curricular frames), and to the entextualization of the interaction in the episode as it is distilled into teacher reports, our transcripts and so forth.
- Testing emerging interpretations against competing possibilities, on the rest of the episode and on supplementary sources of data (field notes, policy documents, other recordings, etc.).
- Using as appropriate key concepts from sociolinguistic, anthropological and pedagogical theory to interrogate the episode (e.g. discourse genre, footing, assessment for learning).
- Checking our interpretations and sharing data with the teachers involved and relevant scholars.

Analysis of teacher professional vision through (i) written responses to video clips filled out at the beginning of each reflection workshop, (ii) workshop discourse, and (iii) interviews. The written responses were coded for what teachers noticed (actor, scope and topic) and how they reasoned about it (function, stance and use of evidence). The workshop and interview data were transcribed in their entirety and select passages were analysed in detail for a case study of the politics of teacher learning (Lefstein and Snell 2011b).

Classroom learning environment surveys. We calculated average scores on the surveys (administered in all seven classrooms), tested for reliability of the scales employed, used paired t-tests to analyse change between pre and post tests, and used independent sample t-tests to explore gender differences.

For further information

Readers interested in learning more about our and related methodological approaches are encouraged to follow up on the references in the end notes, and to join the Linguistic Ethnography Form and attend the associated seminars, conferences and workshops.[3]

Notes

1 This section is adapted from Snell and Lefstein (in press).
2 Readers will see traces of these processes in the chapters themselves. For more detail of the processes, we have written two documents on the analysis of Episode 3: see Lefstein and Snell (2009) for an early account of the analytic brainstorm, and Snell and Lefstein (2012 and in press) for a retrospective look at the process of transforming the analysis of an interesting episode into a published article.
3 Sign up free of charge at www.uklef.net to receive emails about events, including a five-day summer course in Key Concepts in Ethnography, Language and Communication at King's College London, on which we both teach. Finally, an edited volume entitled *Linguistic Ethnography: Explorations in Interdisciplinarity* will be published next year (edited by Julia Snell, Sarah Shaw and Fiona Copland).

References

Adey, P. (2012). From Fixed IQ to *Multiple* Intelligences. In P. Adey and J. Dillon (Eds.) *Bad Education: Debunking Myths in Education.* Maidenhead: Open University Press, 199–214.

Adey, P. and Shayer, M. (2011). The Effects of Cognitive Acceleration. Paper presented at Socializing Intelligence Through Academic Talk and Dialogue (an AERA conference), University of Pittsburgh. Available online at <www.kcl.ac.uk/sspp/departments/education/research/crestem/CogAcc/files/TheEffectsofCognitiveAcceleration.pdf>

Alexander, R. J. (1995). *Versions of Primary Education.* London: Routledge.

Alexander, R.J. (1997). *Policy and Practice in Primary Education: Local Initiative, National Agenda*, London, Routledge.

Alexander, R. J. (2001). *Culture and Pedagogy: International Comparisons in Primary Education.* Malden, MA: Blackwell Publishers.

Alexander, R. J. (2003). *Talk for Learning: The First Year.* North Yorkshire County Council.

Alexander, R. J. (2004a). Talking to Learn. *Times Education Supplement,* 30 January 2004, 12–13.

Alexander, R. J. (2004b). *Talk for Learning: The Second Year.* North Yorkshire County Council.

Alexander, R. J. (2005). *Teaching through Dialogue: The First Year.* London: London Borough of Barking and Dagenham.

Alexander, R. J. (2008a). *Essays on Pedagogy.* London: Routledge.

Alexander, R. J. (2008b). *Towards Dialogic Teaching: Rethinking Classroom Talk* (4th ed.). Cambridge: Dialogos.

Alexander, R. J. (2009). Towards a Comparative Pedagogy. In R. Cowen and A. M. Kazamias (Eds.), *International Handbook of Comparative Education.* Dordrecht: Springer, 923–42.

Baines, E. (2012) Grouping Pupils by Ability in Schools. In P. Adey and J. Dillon (Eds.) *Bad Education: Debunking Myths in Education.* Maidenhead: Open University Press, 37–56.

Bakhtin, M. M. (1981). *The Dialogic Imagination: Four Essays* (M. Holquist, Ed.; C. Emerson and M. Holquist, Trans.). Austin: University of Texas Press.

Bakhtin, M. M. (1986). *Speech Genres and Other Late Essays* (C. Emerson and M. Holquist, Eds.; V.W. McGee, Trans.). Austin: University of Texas Press.

Bakhtin, M. M. (2004). Dialogic Origin and Dialogic Pedagogy of Grammar. *Journal of Russian & East European Psychology, 42*(6), 12–49.

Barking and Dagenham Primary English Project (2002) *Preparation for Year 6 English SATs Revision Guidance.* London: London Borough of Barking and Dagenham.

Barnes, D. and Todd, F. (1977) *Communication and Learning in Small Groups.* London: Routledge and Kegan Paul.

Barton, A. C. and Tan, E. (2009). Funds of Knowledge and Discourses and Hybrid Space. *Journal of Research in Science Teaching, 46*(1).

Bauman, Z. (2001). *Community: Seeking Safety in an Insecure World.* Cambridge: Polity Press.

Berlak, A. and Berlak, H. (1981). *Dilemmas of Schooling: Teaching and Social Change.* London: Methuen.

Bezemer, J. and D. Mavers (2011). Multimodal Transcription as Academic Practice: A Social Semiotic Perspective. *International Journal of Social Research Methodology* 14, 3.

Black, L. (2004) Differential Participation in Whole-class Discussions and the Construction of Marginalised Identities. *Journal of Educational* Enquiry 5(1), 34–54.

Blommaert, J. (2005). *Discourse: A Critical Introduction*. New York: Cambridge University Press.

Bloome, D., Puro, P. and Theodorou, E. (1989). Procedural Display and Classroom Lessons. *Curriculum Inquiry, 19*(3), 265–91.

Blythe, T., Allen, D. and Powell, B. S. (1999). *Looking Together at Student Work*. New York: Teachers College Press.

Borko, H., Jacobs, J., Eiteljorg, E. and Pittman, M. E. (2008). Video as a Tool for Fostering Productive Discussions in Mathematics Professional Development. *Teaching and Teacher Education, 24*(2), 417–36.

Briggs, C. L., and Bauman, R. (1992). Genre, Intertextuality, and Social Power. *Journal of Linguistic Anthropology, 2*(2), 131–72.

Buber, M., (1937). *I and Thou* (Smith, R. G, trans.). Edinburgh: T. & T. Clark.

Bucholtz, M., and Hall, K. (2005). Identity and Interaction: A Sociocultural Linguistic Approach. *Discourse Studies, 7*(4–5), 585–614.

Burbules, N. C. (1990). Varieties of Educational Dialogue. *Philosophy of Education 1990*, 120–31.

Burbules, N. C. (1993). *Dialogue in Teaching: Theory and Practice*. New York: Teachers College Press.

Burbules, N. C., and Bruce, B. C. (2001). Theory and Research on Teaching as Dialogue. In V. Richardson and American Educational Research Association. (Eds.), *Handbook of Research on Teaching* (4th ed., Vol. 4, pp. 1102–21). Washington, D.C.: American Educational Research Association.

Cazden, C. B. (2001). *Classroom Discourse: The Language of Teaching and Learning* (2nd ed.). Portsmouth, NH: Heinemann.

Chambers, A. (1993). *Tell Me: Children, Reading, and Talk*. Stroud: Thimble Press.

Chapin, S. H., O'Connor, M. C. and Anderson, N. C. (2011). *Classroom Discussions: Seeing Math Discourse in Action (Multimedia Professional Learning Resource, Grades K–6)*. Sausalito, CA: Math Solutions.

Cohen, D. K. (1990). A Revolution in One Classroom: The Case of Mrs. Oublier. *Educational Evaluation and Policy Analysis, 12*(3), 311–29.

Cohen, D. K. (2011). *Teaching and its Predicaments*. Cambridge, Mass.: Harvard University Press.

Danielson, C. (2007). *Enhancing Professional Practice: A Framework for Teaching* (2nd ed.). Alexandria, Va.: Association for Supervision and Curriculum Development.

Darling-Hammond, L., Wei, R. C., Richardson, N., Andree, A. and Orphanos, S. (2009). *Professional Learning in the Learning Profession: A Status Report on Professional Development in the U.S. and Abroad*. Washington, DC: National Staff Development Council.

Dewey, J. (1916). *Democracy and Education*. New York: Macmillan.

DfES (Great Britain Department for Education and Skills). (2001). *Characterisation*. London: DfES. Retrieved August 8, 2010, from www.edulink.networcs.net/sites/teachlearn/englit/Resources/Characterisation.pdf.

DfES (Great Britain Department of Education and Skills). (2003). *Speaking, Listening, Learning: Working with Children in Key Stages 1 and 2: Handbook*.

DfES (Great Britain Department of Education and Skills). (2007) Teaching Speaking and Listening (DVD) London: DfES.

Doyle, W. (1986). Classroom Organization and Management. In M. C. Wittrock (Ed.), *Handbook of Research on Teaching* (3rd ed., pp. 392–425). New York: Macmillan, p. 394.

Duff, P. A. (2004). Intertextuality and Hybrid Discourses: The Infusion of Pop Culture in Educational Discourse. *Linguistics and Education, 14*(3–4), 231–76.

Elliott, J. (2001). Making Evidence-based Practice Educational. *British Educational Research Journal, 27*(5), 555–74.

Ellsworth, E. (1989). Why Doesn't This Feel Empowering – Working Through the Repressive Myths of Critical Pedagogy. *Harvard Educational Review, 59*(3), 297–324.

Elmore, R. F. (2004). *School Reform from the Inside Out: Policy, Practice, and Performance.* Cambridge, MA: Harvard Education Press.

Fielding, M. (2004). Transformative Approaches to Student Voice: Theoretical Underpinnings, Recalcitrant Realities. *British Educational Research Journal, 30*(2), 295–311.

Freire, P. (1986). *Pedagogy of the Oppressed.* New York: Continuum.

Freire, P. (1998). *Teachers as Cultural Workers: Letters to Those Who Dare Teach.* Boulder, CO: Westview Press.

Furedi, F. (2009). *Wasted: Why Education isn't Educating.* London: Continuum.

Gadamer, H. G. (1998). *Truth and Method* (J. Weinsheimer and D. G. Marshall, Trans. 2nd ed.). New York: Continuum.

Galton, M. J., Croll, P. and Simon, B. (1980). *Inside the Primary Classroom.* London; Boston: Routledge & Kegan Paul.

Galton, M. J., Hargreaves, L., Comber, C., Wall, D. and Pell, A. (1999). *Inside the Primary Classroom: 20 Years On.* London: Routledge.

Ghouri, N. (1998). Fantastic News for Teachers. *Times Educational Supplement* 20 March, 1998.

Goffman E. (1974). *Frame Analysis: An Essay on the Organization of Experience.* New York: Harper and Row.

Goffman E. (1983) The Interaction Order. *American Sociological Review.* 48, 1–17.

Goodlad, J. I. (1984). *A Place Called School: Prospects for the Future.* New York: McGraw-HIll Book Co.

Goodwin, C. (1994). Professional Vision. *American Anthropologist, 96*(3), 606–33.

Gould, S. J. (1996). *The Mismeasure of Man* (Rev. and expanded. ed.). New York: Norton.

Greeno, J. G. (2011). A Situative Perspective on Cognition and Learning in Interaction. In T. Koschmann (Ed.), *Theories of Learning and Studies of Instructional Practice,* New York: Springer, 41–72.

Gumperz, J. (1982). *Discourse Strategies.* Cambridge: Cambridge University Press.

Guskey, T. R. and Yoon, K. S. (2009). What Works in Professional Development. *Phi Delta Kappan, 90*(7), 495–500.

Habermas, J. (1989). *The Structural Transformation of the Public Sphere: An Inquiry into a Category of Bourgeois Society.* Cambridge: Polity.

Hanks, W. F. (1996). *Language & Communicative Practices.* Boulder: Westview Press.

Hardman, F., Smith, F. and Wall, K. (2003). 'Interactive Whole Class Teaching' in the National Literacy Strategy. *Cambridge Journal of Education, 33*(2), 197.

Hare, W. (2009). Socratic Open-Mindedness. *Paideusis, 18*(1), 5–16.

Haroutunian-Gordon, S. (1989). Socrates as Teacher. In P. W. Jackson and S. Haroutunian-Gordon (Eds.), *From Socrates to Software: The Teacher as Text and the Text as Teacher* (pp. 5–23). Chicago, IL: Nsse.

Harpaz, Y. and Lefstein, A. (2000). Communities of Thinking. *Educational Leadership, 58*(3), 54–7.

Harris, R. and Lefstein, A. (2011). *Urban Classroom Culture: Realities, Dilemmas, Responses.* [London]: Centre for Language, Discourse & Communication, King's College London.

Hattie, J. and Timperley, H. (2007). The Power of Feedback. *Review of Educational Research, 77*(1), 81.

Hawley, W. and Valli, L. (1999). The Essentials of Professional Development: A New Consensus. In L. Darling-Hammond and G. Sykes (Eds.), *Teaching as the Learning Profession: Handbook of Policy and Practice* (pp. 151–80). San-Francisco: Jossey-Bass.

Heyd-Metzuyanim, E. (2012). The Co-construction of Learning Difficulties in Mathematics—Teacher–Student Interactions and their Role in the Development of a Disabled Mathematical Identity. *Educational Studies in Mathematics*, 1–28.

Heritage, J. (1997). Conversation Analysis and Institutional Talk: Analysing Data. In D. Silverman (Ed.) *Qualitative Research: Theory, Method, Practice* (pp. 116–82). London: Sage.

Heritage, J. (2005). Conversation Analysis and Institutional Talk. In K. Fitch and R. Sanders (Eds.), *Handbook of Language and Social Interaction* (pp. 103–46). Mahwah NJ: Erlbaum.

Hicks, D. (1996). *Discourse, Learning and Schooling*. Cambridge: Cambridge University Press.

Horowitz, A. (2008). *Necropolis*. London: Walker Books Ltd.

Hutchby, I. and R Woofitt. (1998). *Conversation Analysis*. Oxford: Polity.

Hymes, D. (1972). Models of the Interaction of Language and Social Life. In J. Gumperz and D. Hymes (Eds.) *Directions in Sociolinguistics: The Ethnography of Communication*. (pp. 35–71). Oxford: Blackwell.

Ireson, J., S. Hallam and C. Hurley. (2005). What are the Effects of Ability Grouping on GCSE Attainment? *British Educational Research Journal 31*(4): 443–58.

Kamberelis, G. (2001). Producing Heteroglossic Classroom (Micro)Cultures through Hybrid Discourse Practice. *Linguistics and Education, 12*(1), 85–125.

Kress, G., C. Jewitt, J. Ogborn and C. Tsatsarelis. (2001). *Multimodal Teaching and Learning: The Rhetorics of the Science Classroom*. London: Continuum.

Kwek, D. (2012). Weaving As Frontload and Backend Pedagogies: Building Repertoires of Connected Learning. In C. Day (Ed.), *Routledge International Handbook of Teacher and School Development* (pp. 335–50). Abingdon: Routledge.

Labaree, D. F. (2000). On the Nature of Teaching and Teacher Education – Difficult Practices that Look Easy. *Journal of Teacher Education, 51*(3), 228–33.

Lampert, M. (2001). *Teaching Problems and the Problems of Teaching*. New Haven: Yale University Press.

Lave, J. and Wenger, E. (1991). *Situated Learning: Legitimate Peripheral Participation*. Cambridge, England; New York: Cambridge University Press.

Lefstein, A. (2005). Thinking about the Technical and the Personal in Teaching. *Cambridge Journal of Education, 35*(3), 333–56.

Lefstein, A. (2008a). Changing Classroom Practice through the English National Literacy Strategy: A Micro-Interactional Perspective. *American Educational Research Journal, 45*(3), 701–37.

Lefstein, A. (2008b). Literacy Makeover: Educational Research and the Public Interest on Prime Time. *Teachers College Record, 110*(5), 1115–46).

Lefstein, A. (2009). Rhetorical Grammar and the Grammar of Schooling: Teaching "Powerful Verbs" in the English National Literacy Strategy. *Linguistics and Education, 20*(4), 378–400.

Lefstein, A. (2010) More Helpful as Problem than Solution: Some Implications of Situating Dialogue in Classrooms. In Littleton,K. and C. Howe (Eds.), *Educational Dialogues: Understanding and Promoting Productive Interaction*. Taylor and Francis.

Lefstein, A. and J. Snell (2009) *Linguistic Ethnography in Action: Initial, Illustrative Analysis of a Literacy Lesson*. Unpublished paper presented at Ethnography, Language & Communication Workshop, University of Glasgow, 22/5/2009.

Lefstein, A. and Snell, J. (2011a). Classroom Discourse: The Promise and Complexity of Dialogic Practice. In S. Ellis and E. McCartney (Eds.), *Applied Linguistics and Primary School Teaching*. Cambridge: Cambridge University Press, 165–85.

Lefstein, A. and Snell, J. (2011b). Professional Vision and the Politics of Teacher Learning. *Teaching and Teacher Education, 27*(3), 505–14.

Lefstein, A. and Snell, J. (2011c). Promises and Problems of Teaching with Popular Culture: A Linguistic Ethnographic Analysis of Discourse Genre Mixing. *Reading Research Quarterly 46*(1): 40–69.

Lefstein, A. and J. Snell (2013). Beyond a Unitary Conception of Pedagogic Pace: Quantitative Measurement and Ethnographic Experience. *British Educational Research Journal. 39*(1): 73–106.

Lemov, D. (2010). *Teach Like a Champion: 49 Techniques that put Students on the Path to College.* San Francisco, CA: Jossey-Bass.

Lewis, C. S. and Baynes, P. (1988). *The Lion, the Witch, and the Wardrobe.* New York: Macmillan.

Lewis, C. and Tsuchida, I. (1998). A Lesson is Like a Swiftly Flowing River. *American Educator, 22*(4), 12–17.

Little, J. W. (1990). The Persistence of Privacy – Autonomy and Initiative in Teachers' Professional Relations. *Teachers College Record, 91*(4), 509–36.

Littleton, K. and Howe, C. (2010). *Educational Dialogues: Understanding and Promoting Productive Interaction.* London: Routledge.

Lortie, D. C. (1975). *Schoolteacher: A Sociological Study.* Chicago: University of Chicago Press.

Loughran, J. (2010). *What Expert Teachers Do: Enhancing Professional Knowledge for Classroom Practice.* London: Routledge.

Luxton, R. and Last, G. (1998). Under-achievement and Pedagogy. *Teaching Mathematics and its Applications, 17*(1), 1-11.

McDermott, R. P. (1993). The Acquisition of a Child by a Learning Disability. In S. Chaiklin and J. Lave (Eds.) *Understanding Practice: Perspectives on Activity and Context.* Cambridge: Cambridge University Press.

McDermott, R. and Raley, J. (2008). The Tell-tale Body: The Constitution of Disability in Schools. In W. Ayers , T. Quinn and D. Stoval (Eds.), *Handbook of Social Justice in Education* (pp. 431–45). Mahwah, NJ: Lawrence Erlbaum.

McDermott, R., and H. Tylbor. (1983). On the Necessity of Collusion in Conversation. *Text* 3(3), 277–97.

McDonald, J. P. (2003). *The Power of Protocols: An Educator's Guide to Better Practice.* New York: Teachers College Press.

Marsh, J. (2008). Popular Culture in the Language Arts Classroom. In J. Flood , S. B. Heath and D. Lapp (Eds.), *Handbook of Research on Teaching Literacy Through the Communicative and Visual Arts* (Vol. 2, pp. 529–36). New York: Lawrence Erlbaum Associates.

Marsh, J., G. Brooks, J. Hughes, L. Ritchie, S. Roberts, and K. Wright (2005). *Digital Beginnings: Young Children's Use of Popular Culture, Media and New Technologies.* Sheffield: University of Sheffield. [Accessed 30 October 2012 at <www.digitalbeginnings.shef.ac.uk/DigitalBeginningsReportColor.pdf>]

Matusov, E. (2009). *Journey into Dialogic Pedagogy.* Hauppauge, NY: Nova Science Publishers.

Maybin, J. (2006). *Children's Voices: Talk, Knowledge, and Identity.* Basingstoke: Palgrave Macmillan.

Maybin, J. and K. Tusting (2011). Linguistic Ethnography. In J. Simpson (Ed.). *Routledge Handbook of Applied Linguistics.* London: Routledge, 515–28.

Mehan, H. (1979). *Learning Lessons: Social Organization in the Classroom.* Cambridge, MA: Harvard University Press.

Mehan, H. (1996). The Construction of an LD Student: A Case Study in the Politics of Representation. In M. Silverstein and G. Urban (Eds.), *Natural Histories of Discourse* (pp. 253–76). Chicago: University of Chicago Press.

Mercer, N. (2000). *Words and Minds: How We Use Language to Think Together.* London: Routledge.

Mercer, N. and Littleton, K. (2007). *Dialogue and the Development of Children's Thinking: A Sociocultural Approach.* London: Routledge.

Michaels, S. and O'Connor, C. (2013) Conceptualising Talk Moves as Tools: Professional Development Approaches for Academically Productive Discussion. In Resnick, L. , Asterhan, C. and Clarke, S. (Eds.) *Socialising Intelligence*, Washington DC, AERA.

Michaels, S., O'Connor, C. and Resnick, L. B. (2008). Deliberative Discourse Idealized and Realized: Accountable Talk in the Classroom and in Civic Life. *Studies in Philosophy and Education, 27*(4), 283–97.

Michaels, S., Shouse, A. W., Schweingruber, H. A., and National Research Council (U.S.). Board on Science Education. (2008). *Ready, Set, Science!: Putting Research to Work in K-8 Science Classrooms.* Washington, DC: National Academies Press.

Moll, L. C., Amanti, C., Neff, D. and Gonzalez, N. (1992). Funds of Knowledge for Teaching: Using a Qualitative Approach to Connect Homes and Classrooms. *Theory into Practice,* 132–41.

Moss, G. (2007). *Literacy and Gender: Researching Texts, Contexts, and Readers.* New York: Routledge.

Murata, A. (2011). Introduction: Conceptual Overview of Lesson Study. In L. C. Hart , A. S. Alston and A. Murata (Eds.), *Lesson Study Research and Practice in Mathematics Education* (pp. 1–12). Dordrecht: Springer.

Myhill, D. (2002). Bad Boys and Good Girls? Patterns of Interaction and Response in Whole Class Teaching. *British Educational Research Journal 28*(3), 339–52.

Myhill, D., Jones, S. M. and Hopper, R. (2006). *Talking, Listening, Learning: Effective Talk in the Primary Classroom.* Maidenhead, England: Open University Press.

Nassaji, H. and Wells, G. (2000). What's the Use of 'Triadic Dialogue'?: An Investigation of Teacher-student Interaction. *Applied Linguistics, 21*(3), 376–406.

Nix, G. (2000). *The Fall.* New York: Scholastic.

Nystrand, M., Gamoran, A., Kachur, R. and Prendergast, C. (1997). *Opening Dialogue: Understanding the Dynamics of Language and Learning in the English Classroom.* New York: Teachers College Press.

Nystrand, M., Wu, L. L., Gamoran, A., Zeiser, S. and Long, D. A. (2003). Questions in Time: Investigating the Structure and Dynamics of Unfolding Classroom Discourse. *Discourse Processes, 35*(2), 135–98.

Ochs, E. (1979). Transcription as Theory. In E. Ochs and B. Schiefflin (Eds.), *Developmental Pragmatics* (pp. 43–72). New York: Academic Press.

Ochs, K. (2006). Cross-national Policy Borrowing and Educational Innovation: Improving Achievement in the London Borough of Barking and Dagenham. *Oxford Review of Education, 32*(5), 599–618.

O'Connor, M. C. and Michaels, S. (1993). Aligning Academic Task and Participation Status Through Revoicing: Analysis of a Classroom Discourse Strategy. *Anthropology & Education Quarterly, 24*(4), 318–35.

Office for Standards in Education (Ofsted). (2010). *Learning From the Best: Examples of Best Practice from Providers of Apprenticeships in Underperforming Vocational Areas.* Manchester: Ofsted.

Office for Standards in Education (Ofsted). (2011). *School Governance: Learning From the Best.* Manchester: Ofsted.

Plato, Hamilton, W. and Emlyn-Jones, C. J. (2004). *Gorgias* (Rev. ed.). New York, NY: Penguin Books.

Plochmann, G. K. and Robinson, F. E. (1988). *A Friendly Companion to Plato's Gorgias.* Carbondale: Southern Illinois University Press.

Qualifications and Curriculum Authority (Great Britain). (2004). *Introducing the Grammar of Talk.* London: QCA.

Qualifications and Curriculum Authority (QCA). (2005). *Opening Up Talk* (DVD). London: QCA.

Rampton, B. (2006). *Language in Late Modernity: Interaction in an Urban School.* Cambridge: Cambridge University Press.

Rampton, B., and UK Linguistic Ethnography Forum. (2004). *UK Linguistic Ethnography – A Discussion Paper.* Retrieved February 15, 2012, from http://www.ling-ethnog.org.uk/documents/papers/ramptonetal2004.pdf.

Reay, D. (2006). 'I'm Not Seen as One of the Clever Children': Consulting Primary School Pupils about the Social Conditions of Learning. *Educational review 58*(2), 171–81.

Reich, R. (1998). Confusion about the Socratic Method: Socratic Paradoxes and Contemporary Invocations of Socrates. *Philosophy of Education 1998*.

Reichard, G.A. (1934). *Spider Woman: A Story of Navajo Weavers and Chanters.* Albuquerque: University of New Mexico Press.

Resnick, L. B., Michaels, S. and O'Connor, C. (2010). How (Well Structured) Talk Builds the Mind. In R. Sternberg and D. Preiss (Eds.), *From Genes to Context: New Discoveries about Learning from Educational Research and their Applications.* New York: Springer.

Resnick, L.B., Asterhan, C.A. and Clarke, S.N. (in press) *Socializing Intelligence through Academic Talk and Dialogue.* Washington, DC: American Educational Research Association.

Roberts, C. (1997). Transcribing Talk: Issues of Representation. *TESOL Quarterly*, 167–72.

Roth, W. M., Lawless, D. V. and Masciotra, D. (2001). Spielraum and Teaching. *Curriculum Inquiry, 31*(2), 183–207.

Row, M. B. (1974). Wait Time and Rewards as Instructional Variables, their Influence on Language, Logic, and Fate Control: Part One Wait Time. *Journal of Research in Science Teaching, 11*(2), 81–94.

Schiller, F. (2009). *On the Aesthetic Education of Man in a Series of Letters.* Cambridge: Charles River Editors.

Schön D. (1983) *The Reflective Practitioner.* New York: Basic Books.

Seidel, T., Stürmer, K., Blomberg, G., Kobarg, M. and Schwindt, K. (2011). Teacher Learning from Analysis of Videotaped Classroom Situations: Does it Make a Difference Whether Teachers Observe their own Teaching or That of Others? *Teaching and Teacher Education, 27*(2), 259–67.

Sfard, A. (2008). *Thinking as Communicating: Human Development, the Growth of Discourses, and Mathematizing.* New York: Cambridge University Press.

Sfard, A. and Prusak, A. (2005). Telling Identities: In Search of an Analytic Tool for Investigating Learning as a Culturally Shaped Activity. *Educational researcher, 34*(4), 14–22

Sherin, M. G. (2004). New Perspectives on the Role of Video in Teacher Education. In J. Brophy (Ed.) *Using Video in Teacher Education* (pp.1–27). New York: Elsevier Science.

Sherin, M. G. and van Es, E. A. (2009). Effects of Video Club Participation on Teachers' Professional Vision. *Journal of Teacher Education, 60*(1), 20–37.

Shor, I. (1996). *When Students Have Power: Negotiating Authority in a Critical Pedagogy.* Chicago: University of Chicago Press.

Shor, I. and Freire, P. (1987). *A Pedagogy for Liberation: Dialogues on Transforming Education.* South Hadley, MA: Bergin & Garvey Publishers.

Sichel, B. A. (1998). Your Socrates, My Socrates, Everyone has a Socrates. *Philosophy of Education 1998*.

Silverman, D. (1999). Warriors or Collaborators: Reworking Methodological Controversies in the Study of Institutional Interaction. In S. Sarangi and C. Roberts (Eds.), *Talk, Work and Institutional Order* (pp. 401–25). Berlin: Mouton de Gruyter.

Sinclair, J. M. and Coulthard, M. (1975). *Towards an Analysis of Discourse: The English Used by Teachers and Pupils.* London: Oxford University Press.

Slavin, R. E. (2002). Evidence-based Education Policies: Transforming Educational Practice and Research. *Educational Researcher, 31*(7), 15–21.

Smith, F., Hardman, F., Wall, K. and Mroz, M. (2004). Interactive Whole Class Teaching in the National Literacy and Numeracy Strategies. *British Educational Research Journal, 30*(3), 395–411.

Snell, J. (2011). Interrogating Video Data: Systematic Quantitative Analysis Versus Micro-ethnographic Analysis. *International Journal of Social Research Methodology, 14*(3), 253–8.

Snell, J. and A. Lefstein (2011) Computer-assisted Systematic Observation of Classroom Discourse and Interaction: Technical Report on the Systematic Discourse Analysis Component of the Towards Dialogue Study. *Working papers in Urban Language & Literacies, #77*. London: King's College London. <http://www.kcl.ac.uk/depsta/education/wpull.html>.

Snell, J. and A. Lefstein (2012) Interpretive and Representational Dilemmas in a Linguistic Ethnographic Analysis: Moving from "Interesting Data" to Publishable Research Article. *Working Papers in Urban Language & Literacies, #90*. London: King's College London. <http://www.kcl.ac.uk/depsta/education/wpull.html>.

Snell, J. and A. Lefstein (in press) Moving from "Interesting Data" to Publishable Research Article – Some Interpretive and Representational Dilemmas in a Linguistic Ethnographic Analysis. In P. Smeyers, D. Bridges, N. Burbules and M. Griffiths (Eds.) *International Handbook of Interpretation in Educational Research Methods*. Dordrecht: Springer.

Steiner, G. (2003). *Lessons of the Masters*. Cambridge: Harvard University Press.

Teo, P. (2008). Outside In/Inside Out: Bridging the Gap in Literacy Education in Singapore Classrooms. *Language and Education, 22*(6), 411–31.

Timperley, H. (2007). *Teacher Professional Learning and Development: Best Evidence Synthesis Iteration (BES)*: Ministry of Education.

Tymms, P. and Merrell, C. (2010). Standards and Quality in English Primary Schools Over Time: The National Evidence. In R. Alexander (Ed.), *The Cambridge Primary Review Research Surveys* (pp. 435–60). Abingdon: Routledge.

van Es, E. A. and Sherin, M. G. (2009). The Influence of Video Clubs on Teachers' Thinking and Practice. *Journal of Mathematics Teacher Education*, 1–22.

Varenne, H. and McDermott, R. (1998). *Successful Failure: The School America Builds*. Boulder, CO: Westview Press.

Vygotsky, L. S. (1978). *Mind in Society: The Development of Higher Psychological Processes*. Cambridge: Harvard University Press.

Wegerif, R. (2007). *Dialogic Education and Technology: Expanding the Space of Learning*. New York: Springer.

Wegerif, R. (2013) *Dialogic: Education for the Internet Age*. London: Routledge

Wells, C. G. (1999). *Dialogic Inquiry: Towards a Sociocultural Practice and Theory of Education*. Cambridge: Cambridge University Press.

Wenger, E. (1998). *Communities of Practice: Learning, Meaning, and Identity*. Cambridge: Cambridge University Press.

Wertsch, J. V. (1979). From Social Interaction to Higher Psychological Processes: A Clarification and Application of Vygotsky's Theory. *Human Development, 22*(1), 1–22.

Wertsch, J. V. (1985). *Vygotsky and the Social Formation of Mind*. Cambridge, MA: Harvard University Press.

Wertsch, J. V. (1991). *Voices of the Mind: A Sociocultural Approach to Mediated Action*. London: Harvester Wheatsheaf.

Wertsch, J. V. and Stone, A. (1985). The Concept of Internalization in Vygotsky's Account of the Genesis of Higher Mental Functions. In J. V. Wertsch and Center for Psychosocial Studies. (Eds.), *Culture, Communication, and Cognition: Vygotskian Perspectives*. Cambridge: Cambridge University Press.

Westfahl, G. (2005). *The Greenwood Encyclopedia of Science Fiction and Fantasy: Themes, Works, and Wonders*. Westport, CT: Greenwood Press.

White, E.B. and DiCamillo, K. (1952). *Charlotte's Web*. New York: Harper Collins.

White, E.J. (in press). Circles, Borders and Chronotope: Education at the Boundary? *Knowledge Cultures*.

Wortham, S. (2006). *Learning Identity: The Joint Emergence of Social Identification and Academic Learning*. New York: Cambridge University Press.

Index